PHOTOVOICE RESEARCH IN EDUCATION AND BEYOND

Photovoice is a form of participatory action research, which has been gaining use and momentum since its inception in the mid-1990s. Within the enactment of this methodology, research participants are invited to document aspects of their lives through photography and then provide written or oral accounts of the images they create. Designed to situate participants as experts on their lives and their experiences, photovoice is a powerful and visceral approach to policy change efforts.

In this book, the photovoice methodology is conceptualized as being comprised of eight steps: identification, invitation, education, documentation, narration, ideation, presentation, and confirmation. Each of the steps is explained and expanded upon, and insights are drawn from the extant photovoice literature and the author's personal experience. In addition, attention is given to the history of photography and inquiry, theoretical underpinnings and aims of the methodology, ethical considerations, methods and procedures, approaches to data analysis, and photovoice exhibitions. Finally, the author has attended to some aspects of photovoice that have historically been left unattended, such as: building a conceptual framework for a photovoice study, viewing the photovoice exhibition as a site of inquiry, and thinking through the ways in which ever-evolving photography technologies can and should impact decision-making throughout the photovoice process.

While many texts exist that touch on and/or address photovoice, this is the first book solely dedicated to the entirety of the photovoice methodology—from theory to exhibition. Built as a practical guide, readers will find a wealth of information, resources, and advice within this book. Educators, students, and academic researchers will find this an accessible and compassionate text, one that will be a trusted companion while on the photovoice project journey.

Amanda O. Latz is Associate Professor of Adult, Higher, and Community Education in the Department of Education at Ball State University, USA.

Thalia M. Mulvihill, Ph.D, Professor of Social Foundations of Education and Higher Education, and Virginia B. Ball Center for Creative Inquiry Fellow at Ball State University, teaches qualitative research methods courses focusing on arts-based educational research and life writing.

PHOTOVOICE RESEARCH IN EDUCATION AND BEYOND

A Practical Guide from Theory to Exhibition

Amanda O. Latz with Thalia M. Mulvihill

Routledge
Taylor & Francis Group
NEW YORK AND LONDON

First published 2017
by Routledge
711 Third Avenue, New York, NY 10017

and by Routledge
2 Park Square, Milton Park, Abingdon, Oxon OX14 4RN

Routledge is an imprint of the Taylor & Francis Group, an informa business

© 2017 Taylor & Francis

The right of Amanda O. Latz to be identified as author of this work has been asserted by her in accordance with sections 77 and 78 of the Copyright, Designs and Patents Act 1988.

All rights reserved. No part of this book may be reprinted or reproduced or utilized in any form or by any electronic, mechanical, or other means, now known or hereafter invented, including photocopying and recording, or in any information storage or retrieval system, without permission in writing from the publishers.

Trademark notice: Product or corporate names may be trademarks or registered trademarks, and are used only for identification and explanation without intent to infringe.

Library of Congress Cataloging in Publication Data
A catalog record for this book has been requested

ISBN: 978-1-138-85147-4 (hbk)
ISBN: 978-1-138-85148-1 (pbk)
ISBN: 978-1-315-72408-9 (ebk)

Typeset in Bembo
by Keystroke, Neville Lodge, Tettenhall, Wolverhampton

This book is dedicated to all the individuals who have been generous enough to participate in the photovoice studies of which I have been a part. Thank you. This book is for all of you.

CONTENTS

Preface   *ix*
Acknowledgments   *xi*

1 Photography and Inquiry   1

2 Theoretical Underpinnings and Aims of Photovoice   25

3 Photovoice Methods and Procedures   58

4 (Participatory) Data Analysis   91

5 Photovoice Ethics and Working with Review Boards   104

6 Photovoice Exhibitions (Amanda O. Latz and Thalia M. Mulvihill)   119

7 The Pros, Cons, and Future of Photovoice   152

Appendices   *161*
Index   *178*

PREFACE

This book is about photovoice, a qualitative research methodology. Specifically, this book is about conducting photovoice research. Photovoice is a form of participatory action research, and it can also be considered arts-based research. The methodology is most closely associated with the work of Caroline C. Wang and Mary Ann Burris, who coined the term in the mid-1990s. This book is constructed as a practical "how-to" guide for those just beginning to use the methodology as well as those who have been using it for some time.

The main themes and objectives of this book include the following:

- Situate photovoice within the long history of the use of photography within inquiry.
- Emphasize that photovoice is an action research methodology, which is often participatory in nature.
- Differentiate photovoice from research methods that include photography such as photo elicitation.
- Provide an overview of how to conduct photovoice research.
- Give practical examples from photovoice research projects.
- Guide researchers through some of the more tenuous aspects of the photovoice methodology, such as navigating institutional review, creating consent and media release forms, and orienting participants to photography ethics and "ground rules."
- Meet the pragmatic needs of aspirant photovoice researchers.
- Complement existing texts related to qualitative research methodologies.

While a handful of books exist that either showcase photovoice projects (e.g. Kaplan, 2013) or explicate how photovoice can be used with specific populations

(Delgado, 2015), no book exists that is solely dedicated to the photovoice methodology. Since the completion of my doctoral dissertation, which was a photovoice project, I have received many requests for information regarding the particulars of the methodology. This suggests a need for a practical "how-to" book written by someone with experience using the photovoice processes. This text is the guidepost needed for those—both inside and outside of the academy—endeavoring to use photovoice.

More and more researchers are engaging in photovoice research as seen in the recent proliferation of journal articles wherein the authors have used the methodology. PhotoVoice (2017), a UK-based non-profit organization, does provide some free online resources, as well as a manual (PhotoVoice, 2014). However, the UK- and USA-based definitions of photovoice differ. Within the aforementioned manual, PhotoVoice stated: "PhotoVoice [UK] works more towards income-generating opportunities within the photographic and media industry and establishing partnership projects with other international and community organisations, and Photovoice (USA) remains more grounded in academic and policy research" (p. 10). Other photovoice manuals do exist (e.g. John Humphrey Centre for Peace and Human Rights, n.d.; Palibroda, Krieg, Murdock, & Havelock, 2009; Photovoice Hamilton Youth Project, n.d.), but a detailed, robust, and comprehensive work is needed as a complement to the extant guideposts. This book was written from my perspective as a USA-based university researcher who is situated within academic research spheres. The primary audience is also the university-based researcher, but as mentioned before, the book is appealing to a broad audience because of its accessibility.

References

Delgado, M. (2015). *Urban youth and photovoice: Visual ethnography in action*. New York: Oxford University Press.

John Humphrey Centre for Peace and Human Rights. (n.d.). *Photovoice: Social change through photography*. Retrieved from https://scribd.com/document/133435755/Photovoice-Manual-May-2010

Kaplan, E. B. (2013). *"We live in the shadow": Inner-city kids tell their stories through photographs*. Philadelphia, PA: Temple University Press.

Palibroda, B., Kreig, B., Murdock, L., & Havelock, J. (2009). *A practical guide to photovoice: Sharing pictures, telling stories and changing communities*. Retrieved from http://pwhce.ca/photovoice/pdf/Photovoice_Manual.pdf

PhotoVoice. (2014). *The PhotoVoice manual: A guide to designing and running participatory photography projects*. Retrieved from https://photovoice.org/wp-content/uploads/2014/09/PV_Manual.pdf

PhotoVoice. (2017). *Reframing the world*. Retrieved from https://photovoice.org/

Photovoice Hamilton Youth Project. (n.d.). *A guide to developing a photovoice project in your community*. Hamilton, Ontario, Canada: Community Centre for Media Arts.

ACKNOWLEDGMENTS

I offer my sincerest gratitude to the following individuals who have offered their help and support during the writing process: Dr. Thalia Mulvihill, Dr. Renae Mayes, Dan Royer, Ashleigh Bingham, Jessika Griffin, and Dr. Serena Salloum. Many thanks also go to the amazing scholars with whom I have had the tremendous pleasure of working and writing during the past few years: Drs. Katie Branch, Carrie Kortegast, Bridget Turner Kelly, Chris Linder, and Kristin McCann. I hope our good work on participant-generated visual methods continues to reverberate. Big thanks and many hugs go to the students who were a part of the photovoice projects in EDCC 641 (*Community Colleges and Diversity*): Adam Brunner, Kevin Caputo, Debbie Greisel, Nichole Oltz, Robin Phelps-Ward, Abby Vannatta, Cedric Wilson (Spring 2014), Amy Baize-Ward, Vashon Broadnax, Jamie Burton, Kathy Herbert, Erica Hoffman, Patty Lyczkowski, Fernando Martinez, LeAnne Myers, and Katie Pratt (Spring 2016).

Thanks and love are offered to my mom and dad, who put up with my need to write during trips home around the holidays. Thank you for all your love and support and questions and emojis. I am also grateful for, and thankful to, my two favorite canines and pals, Scooter and Wink, who have spent countless days staring at me writing while wishing I would take them for a walk or give them a belly rub or a rawhide. And my biggest thanks goes to my amazing partner, Annette Payne, who lovingly told me a thousand times to "go write." I write this with a gigantic smile on my face. All my love.

1
PHOTOGRAPHY AND INQUIRY

A Vignette

We were sitting in a dark, smoky bar. I knew I would need to shower before bed. It was 2010, and the county had not yet banned smoking in bars and restaurants. One of my colleagues, another doctoral student, and I were sitting, sipping on a couple Belgian ales. She and I would routinely have intense conversations about our classes, things we were reading, and the research we aimed to carry out. My dissertation topic was the focus that evening. We disagreed. I was certain I should be studying community college faculty and how they typically teach classes that house significant levels of diversity in terms of everything, but specifically students' college readiness, cognitive abilities, and interests. This topic stemmed from my own experiences—and struggles—as an adjunct faculty member within the community college setting. But like I said, she disagreed.

She had good reason. Every time I talked about teaching at the community college, I talked about my students—how smart they were, how hard they worked, how many struggles they were battling, and winning. I marveled at them. Wanting to come into solidarity with them, I always yearned to understand them better. They were always on my mind; I was always thinking of ways to support—and challenge—them. They told me their stories in person and in their papers. My curiosity never waivered. And while my students told me their stories, I wanted their stories to be known to a broader audience. That only I knew their stories was not enough. I wanted everyone to know these stories. If more people understood these students, I felt certain the stigma surrounding the community college could be—at least in some small way—dismantled. I wanted that to happen.

Regardless, I was still stuck. What in the world was I going to do for this dissertation? Moving from my comprehensive exams to my dissertation proposal was excruciating. I did not want to write a dissertation proposal because I did not have any idea what I wanted to study. Actually, I thought I did. But I slowly realized that while I was passionate about faculty and teaching at the community college, I was most passionate about students—my students. I stalled my process, taking extra classes and writing creative nonfiction. I slowly came around to my eventual study. Over time, I realized that a dissertation—my "magnum opus," as one of my participants referred to it—was as good a container as any to hold some of my students' stories.

When you are embarking on a dissertation—or any study, for that matter—having a clear, focused, and discernable topic—with all the other requisites, of course, like research questions and a problem and purpose statement—is one thing. Settling into a methodology is another thing entirely. And it is also important to note that methodology is just of one many elements of a study's overarching conceptual framework, which also includes but is not limited to epistemologies, theoretical perspectives, and other notables regarding researcher positionality. There are methods as well. How will you actually collect data? What are the logistical steps involved? There are also analytical approaches to consider. Carrying out research is a necessarily complex endeavor.

So I had a topic—community college students' educational lives. But, what was I going to do methodologically? Ideas came together in my mind like three-dimensional puzzle pieces moving toward one another in a space where gravity had no bearing. Pieces came into focus as they crossed the line of vision of my mind's eye. While taking courses in pursuit of my doctoral degree, I attended a number of conferences where I was exposed to a broad swath of methodologies and methods. It was at a conference when I first heard the term *photovoice* uttered. Paraphrasing and simplifying, the researcher explained how she was interested in better understanding youth perceptions of literacy within the context of the home environment. For example, how does the presence of books within the home environment impact the child's perceptions of reading as a normative behavior? Elementary-aged children were recruited as participants and then given disposable cameras to document their home environment. Then, alongside the researcher, the children engaged in storytelling about the photographs they created. In essence, the researcher facilitated a focus group wherein the children discussed their photographs. The photographs themselves were not data per se, but they served as data antecedents, or elicitation devices, meant to spur on storytelling, which served as data to be interpreted by the researcher. The photographs, however, were to be interpreted by the children. Only the children knew, really, why they took the photographs they took. Intriguing. It was at this conference presentation where I first heard the term photovoice. What was this photovoice? Where did it come from?

★ ★ ★

Photovoice in Brief

In the early 1990s, Caroline C. Wang and Mary Ann Burris (1994) coined the term *photo novella*, a research methodology that later came to be known as photovoice. The importance of Wang and Burris's seminal work cannot be overstated, as it is difficult to locate any subsequent piece of writing about photovoice that does not reference these two scholars. Wang and Burris implemented photo novella as one part of a four-part needs assessment related to women's health in rural China, which evolved into an empowerment education project. The women participants were asked to document intangibles such as "worry" and "love" with cameras. Soon it was realized that the photographs alone were insufficient to understand the women's sentiments. The explanations—or narrations of the photographs—were paramount. Because of the importance of both the photograph (photo) and the story behind the photograph (novella), a new term was born. In time, however, photovoice supplanted photo novella as the term of choice for this particular research approach. Wang and Burris noted that the process "provides participants the opportunity to spin tales about their everyday lives" (p. 179). And while the tales spun by photovoice participants are certainly valuable and even critical, the notion that photovoice makes space for participants' voices—the vehicles of those stories—was the impetus for the change in terms.

Photovoice is a form of participatory action research, which is often community-based and "contrasts sharply with the conventional model of pure research, in which [participants] ... are treated as passive subjects" (Whyte, Greenwod, & Lazes, 1991, p. 20). In most cases, photovoice participants are actively interwoven into the research process, and that involvement can take many forms—from helping to build photography prompts to analyzing the data. Photovoice necessarily positions participants both as participants and co-researchers. Choice on the part of the participants is always involved, however. According to Argyris and Schön (1991), participatory action research "aims at creating an environment in which participants give and get valid information, make free and informed choices (including the choice to participate), and generate internal commitment to the results of their inquiry" (p. 86). It should be noted that participatory action research is applied research (Whyte, Greenwod, & Lazes, 1991), and as such, participants are often quite keen to see the fruits of their efforts affect change. While the creation of new knowledge is certainly a possible outcome of the photovoice methodology, it is not always the primary aim.

According to Sutton-Brown (2014) "[photovoice] oscillates between private and public worlds in its attempt to publicize and politicize personal struggle via photography, narratives, critical dialogue, and social action" (p. 70). Historically, photovoice has been used to highlight the experiences and perspectives of those who have been marginalized, those with voices not ordinarily heard by those in positions of power. For example, the rural Chinese village women who participated in Wang and Burris's (1994) needs assessment were marginalized within their community. Photovoice brings the marginalized to the center, as the "photographs 'listen into speech' [participants'] voices that ordinarily would not be heard, and broadcast[s] them into the halls of decision-making power" (Wang & Burris, 1994, p. 182). It is through this process that positive changes can be influenced and implemented.

Photovoice is not without its detractors, however. Even though "[p]eople . . . experience their own lives as parades of visual encounters" (Brunsden & Goatcher, 2007, p. 44) and life narration has become increasingly visual considering the proliferation of myriad image-based social media sites, Prosser (1996) noted that "[m]any commentators on research methodology perceive image-making as being inappropriate to research" (p. 26), citing its subjective nature and assuming researcher as photographer. Prosser explained that "[t]here is a general belief that images are unacceptable as a way of objectively 'knowing' because they distort that which they claim to illuminate" (p. 26). While this could be the case, photovoice disrupts this vein of thinking because the photograph is meant to symbolize a participants' response to a prompt. Higgins (2014), however, asserted that photovoice is the most frequently used approach among social scientists who use participatory visual methods. And the use of photovoice shows no signs of slowing down. I recently conducted a search for articles with the word *photovoice* in the title of the manuscript using Google Scholar and found 1,060 results.

Photovoice in Eight Steps

Procedurally, photovoice can be distilled down to eight steps: identification, invitation, education, documentation, narration, ideation, presentation, and confirmation. First, photovoice researchers must identify the place, people, and purpose of the study. What is the research site? Who will be involved? What is the purpose of this project? These three questions, among potential others, require consideration during the identification step. Next, individuals are invited to participate in the project. After participation is confirmed, participants must be informed about how the project will unfold and what their participation might entail. This step, which I have termed education, also includes talking with participants about their consent to participate and how the photographs they take might be used. Once participants are fully on board with and oriented to the project, they are asked to respond to questions or prompts related to the purpose of the project through photography. In some, but not all cases, cameras are provided to participants. This is the documentation phase. Once the photography is complete, it is time for the narration stage. During either individual interviews or focus groups, participants are asked to narrate the contents of their photographs. These narrations give meaning and context to the participant-produced images. This phase sometimes unfolds as a writing exercise. Next, ideation occurs. This step may or may not involve the participants directly. In short, the researchers—sometimes in concert with the participants—generate thematic strands within the narrations, selecting from a plethora of analytic approaches that have been established within the qualitative research literature. These thematic strands are then converted into the findings of the work, complete with practical implications. Furthermore, the findings are typically situated against what is already known about the project's topic. Consider the following research question as an example: How do elementary school students describe the presence of science, technology, engineering, art, and mathematics (STEAM) in their everyday lives? During the ideation phase, researchers ought to consider existing research on this topic to provide context and highlight resultant new knowledge. It should be noted, however, that photovoice "envisions a self-defined space that would diverge from depictions by outsiders superimposed on a culturally charged background" (Wang & Burris, 1994, p. 180). How often are children asked about how STEAM "works" in their lives? Not often. Therefore, the findings of such a project would have great potential to diverge from what is already known. As such, photovoice is a methodology that has rich potential for generating new knowledge vis-à-vis counter stories, stories that diverge from dominant narratives. The next step is presentation, which typically takes the form of an exhibition. Here I use the term exhibition very broadly. An exhibition could take the form of a poster, brochure, website, digital story, or museum installation. And this is not an exhaustive list. It is during this phase, typically, when participants have the opportunity to interface with individuals within the community who wield power—policy makers and others who have the capacity to make decisions—and can affect change. Last is confirmation. This step has several components. By confirmation, I am insinuating that photovoice researchers should endeavor to understand how those who interfaced with the exhibition received the presentation phase. Was the message clear? What were the perceptions? Have policy changes been made? In addition, the researchers should try to find ways to sustain the project's energy and broaden the reach of the participants' voices. This is photovoice in brief.

Historical Sketch

Before delving further into the ins and outs of the photovoice methodology, it is important to sketch out the history of the relationship between photography and research. This chapter is focused on the ways in which photography has been used within inquiry over time. Since the advent of the camera and the still image, photography and inquiry have been intertwined. But the relationship between photography and inquiry presents itself in different and highly nuanced ways based upon discipline. For example, the historical trajectory of the use of photography and inquiry within the field of journalism looks rather different than the historical trajectory of the use of photography and inquiry within the field of psychology.

As will become evident throughout this book, photovoice has utility within a number of disciplines, and the methodology has no specific disciplinary home. Viewed another way, however, it could be argued that photovoice has a plethora of disciplinary homes. The flexibility and broad potential use of the approach is one of the methodology's many strengths. And in many ways, photovoice provides a methodological space ripe for transdisciplinary research teams to ask and answer research questions. For example, if photovoice were to be employed in response to the following research question, a transdisciplinary approach may be apt: In what ways do middle school students describe their school environment? While education is certainly the most obvious discipline within which this question might have been generated, it should be noted that education has foundations within a number of other parent disciplines such as psychology, sociology, philosophy, history, and anthropology. Imagine the vastly different ways in which a research team comprised of diverse individuals—a psychologist, sociologist, and so on—would understand the response(s) to the abovementioned research question.

Understanding the history of photography and the ways in which it has been integrated into everyday life and what have become the disciplines (e.g. sociology, anthropology, journalism, psychology, history, biology) are critical to understanding the historical and philosophical underpinnings of the photovoice methodology. Collier (1967), an anthropologist, said the following:

> In 1837 Louis Daguerre perfected the first efficient light sensitive plate, the mirror with a memory. The daguerreotype introduced photography to the world . . . Now it was not only perspective and principles of light that were recorded for study, but the human image, a precise memory of exactly how a particular person looked, that could be examined again and again by any number of observers, now or years later. The camera image because of this facility ushered in a new phase of human understanding that continues to expand our social thinking.
>
> *p. 3*

Collier's words still resonate today, nearly 50 years later. The advent of the camera has changed the ways we think about, act within, and see the world.

For a more comprehensive treatment of photography's conception and origin—including camera obscura—see Gernsheim (1982) and Batchen (1997). At the same time, it should be noted that "photography has neither a singular identity or a unified history" (Batchen, 1997, p. 176).

Human Orientations to Photographs and Photography

Consider the following questions for a few moments. What is your orientation to photographs and photography? Do you have photographs on your wall, on your desk, inside your wallet, tucked away safely? A shoebox filled with old photographs? What about photo albums? Digital spaces filled with photographs? Do you take photographs? Often? Of what? Why? How? Are your photographs online? What about social media? Share aspects of your life with photographs and photography? Has this changed over time?

What do you think? Photographs and photography are—in many cases—important aspects of society, culture, and personal life. We cherish them; we give them meaning. In the early days of photography, individuals marveled at the capacity to capture an image (Heisley & Levy, 1991). Imagine what that would have been like! At this point in my own life, I rarely go anywhere without my cell phone close by. And my cell phone includes an incredibly powerful camera and storage capacity. Therefore, I can take photographs—and videos—at almost any time. This ability is profoundly different than any other time in modern history. Over time, photographs were used to report, document, and illustrate. They were evidentiary and archival. They were a means of detailing and recording social, cultural, familial, and personal history. In more recent times, but not universally, photographs are seen as art (Heisley & Levy, 1991). Consider, for a moment, the works of well-known photographers such as Ansel Adams, Annie Leibovitz, Sally Mann, and Gregory Crewdson. While I certainly believe their photographic work is art, this categorization is assailable. But let us further consider the work of a photographer such as James Mollison, whose photography can be thought of as contemporary socially engaged fine art. In the introduction of the book, *Where Children Sleep*, Mollison (2010) wrote:

> I hope the pictures and the stories in this book speak to children. Yes, so that lucky children (like I was) may better appreciate what they have. But more than that, I hope this book will help children think about inequality, within and between societies around the world, and perhaps start to figure out how, in their own lives, they may respond.
>
> *p. 5*

We must wonder about the point at which fine art photography becomes socially engaged and to what end? Mollison's work provides a salient example. Perhaps it depends on the audience. I imagine that children will not think much of Mollison's photographic prowess, but they will certainly remember the awe—and perhaps empathy—they felt when learning about other children's bedrooms throughout the world.

In that same vein and as a thought experiment, think of childhood. Consider your own childhood and the memories associated with that part of the life course. Have photographs played a part in the stories you tell yourself and others about your journey through life? The importance of photography is instilled at an early age. The prevalence of school and family photographs and yearly holiday photographs is unmistakable. According to Bloustien and Baker (2003) "[t]he photograph . . . is a powerful tool in the representation of identity . . . photography has established a pervasive presence in children's lives" (p. 69). This presence is now exacerbated vis-à-vis digital photography and social media. Photographs help us understand, interrogate, and build identity. Social media has become the new home for baby books, a once strictly analogue phenomenon. Social media has also become the new shoebox, a place where physical items were stored in an attempt to crystalize memories, house precious objects, and store one's beloved tchotchkes. Some of these physical items remain important to individuals, of course, but the rise of online life narration has limited the need for the no-longer-inimitable baby book or shoebox. In fact, "[t]he gradual takeover of analogue by digital technologies marks a new chapter in the mediation of cultural memory" (Van Dijck, 2005, p. 312). And this new chapter is made manifest in large part by the Internet.

The Memex

In 1945, Vannavar Bush wrote an essay that appeared in *The Atlantic*. Within this piece, Bush argued that scientists collaborated and shared extensively in the name of war (e.g. World War II), yet Bush wondered about how to keep this momentum moving in a post-war era. He argued that specialization led to massive amounts of information, which was (and still is) increasingly hard to grasp. He noted that:

> [t]he summation of human experience is being expanded at a prodigious rate, and the means we use for threading through the consequent maze to the momentarily important item is the same as was used in the days of square-rigged ships.
>
> *Bush, 1945, para. 8*

In other words, within the masses of ever-expanding knowledge, most of which is very specific, it becomes hard to locate and then identify that which is consequential. Bush proposed a machine called the "memex," one that could house information—books, communications, photographs—and act like an extension of our minds. He likened the form of the memex to a desk, where one would normally work and complete tasks. At this desk, one could pull up relevant information easily, as documents, photographs, and the like would be housed as tiny information bits, ready for expansion appropriate for the human eye. The memex could also receive and store new information from the individual. While we could think of the memex as the shoebox—or a solution to the shoebox "problem" (Van Dijck, 2005)—it is more like a cross between a smartphone and a workstation. I am reminded of the Internet of things. Has the Internet of things (e.g. Fitbit) surpassed the vision of the memex? In many ways, Bush predicted the Internet, but specifically an Internet with Web 2.0 affordances. Much of what he wrote reminds me of a combination of smartphones (storage of photographs, videos, text messages), social media (sociability and moment sharing), Wikipedia (information repository), and the Internet of things (object-Internet connection). The accuracy of Bush's work—published in 1945—is mind-boggling.

We can and should place Bush's (1945) work into conversation with Nicholas Carr's (2008) essay featured in *The Atlantic* entitled "Is Google Making Us Stupid" because the Internet gives us little incentive to commit tedious things to memory. In a sense, the Internet has become a place were we can "outsource" aspects of our memories. This was, largely, the vision for the memex. Where do frogs go in the winter? Google it. How do batteries work? Google it. When did Alaska become a state? Google it. Who invented Kool-Aid? Google it. But it is not simply this kind of information or these kinds of facts that we have come to outsource from our minds to the Internet; many of us have also done the same—in large part—with memories of our families and friends, places we have seen, and myriad personal experiences. Van Dijck (2005) said "[s]ince the 1960s, the 'shoebox' containing a variety of private documents (photos, letters, diaries, home videos, voice recordings, etc), has expanded into a giant suitcase or attic" (p. 312). This explosion of personal data, or information, has created a need for a new kind of storage space. And we could argue that a version of the memex actually exists today—currently meeting the needs of this shoebox expansion. The Internet is the new shoebox.

Memory

Is the Internet a digital memory machine—a place where personal, cultural, and social memories are stored, sorted, and curated? Perhaps. Since the advent of the Internet, memory has experienced digitization, multimediatization, and Googlization (Van Dijck, 2005). According to Kuhn (2007), "[photographs provide] occasions for performances of memory" (p. 284). Moreover, Kuhn argued that the photographic medium, its form, is critical to memory work and the performance of memory. In what ways do we interact and remember differently with printed photographs versus digital photographs? All photographs are temporal, but physical, printed photographs have several layers of temporality based on their objecthood. Here is an example from my own shoebox, which is filled with photographs, concert tickets, greeting cards, and sundry other small items. When I leaf through the photographs, I receive and interpret a number of messages related to when the photograph was taken and when it was printed. When I look at an image, I can guess when it was taken based on any number of factors—what I look like, how others look, clues within the context of the photograph such as home decorum, food being served (e.g. birthday cake), and cars in the background. One the other hand, there are clues about when the photograph was printed based on its objecthood. For example, the month and year might be stamped onto the back of the print. The size, quality, texture, and smell of the print also yields clues related to temporality. All of these factors interface within the ways in which we carry out memory work and raise questions about our collective and cultural memories. When photographs are made, stored, retrieved, and interacted with in a digital format, some of the temporal features fade. And the interaction becomes less embodied—smell and touch are much less salient in this case. So, what does this mean?

Digitization

How do people interact with digital photographs? And how has digital photography changed us? According to de Castella (2012), digital photography has changed "us" (certainly a contested pronoun, but in this case is likely referring to the British considering the outlet) in the following ways: public behavior has changed (e.g. taking a photograph of a meal at a restaurant before eating it); more photographs are being taken; more people are good at photography; citizens can be journalists (e.g. sharing newsworthy images via social media before traditional journalists); and nearly everyone is an archivist.

The ways in which public behavior has changed has given rise to the term "phubbing," which is a blend of the words phone and snubbing. This phenomenon has been the focus of several recent studies (e.g. Roberts & David, 2016). Phubbing occurs when someone snubs another person in favor of her of his cell phone. The merger of cell phones and cameras has exacerbated the digitization of photography. It seems reasonable, then, that the digitization of photography has been an underpinning for the growth of phubbing, especially taking into account the example above. Moreover, when we interact with our phones, much of the content with which we interact is visual, including digital photographs. If we think about the objecthood of digital photographs, the device we use to interact with those photographs certainly plays a role. For me, that device is my smartphone. With a smartphone you can easily take, modify, share, curate, and store photographs. While my phone frames and contributes to the objecthood of my photographs, so too do the various apps I use to take, modify, share, curate, and store photographs. For example, when I post a photograph on Instagram, the image will be square because of the design of the platform. This is not the case with other platforms where photographs can be shared such as Twitter and Facebook. In addition, I am more likely to add a filter to an Instagram post because the app environment prompts me to do so. As such, the objecthood of my digital photographs changes based on the platform I am using. Similarly,

> the experience of looking at an historical image on a computer screen is profoundly different in the understandings it might generate from the experience of, say, looking at the same image as an albumen print pasted in an album or a modern copy print in a file.
>
> *Edwards, 2002, p. 68*

In other words, what the photograph *is* is as important as what the photograph is *of*.

Because digital photography is rather simple and accessible, especially with the ubiquity of smartphones, it makes sense that more photographs are being taken than ever before. It also follows that nearly everyone is an archivist. Upon reflection, I take photographs with my phone nearly every day. This is quite an archive—one that I have not consciously built. However, if I scroll through the photographs in my phone, which are conveniently grouped by date by default, I can build a thorough archive of the events of my personal past. With practice comes improvement. With the number of photographs being taken, it should come as no surprise that those who would not consider themselves photographers are actually quite skilled in the craft. Finally, because of the ways in which the coverage of newsworthy events has morphed into a swarm-like phenomenon, digital photography has allowed non-journalists to fill the role of citizen journalists. When "news" happens, social media networks are likely to populate with content from major news outlets as well as content and footage—both photographs and video—of the events as they are unfolding. The profound ways in which digital photography has changed "us" cannot be overstated.

Crowdsourcing

As I was writing this chapter, I paused for a moment to wonder about how I could gain some additional insights on how individuals orient themselves to photographs and photography. So I turned to the Internet for a miniature crowdsourcing endeavor. I created a simple Survey Monkey "survey" with a link to an open-ended response textbox. I posed the same questions from the first paragraph of this section. Then I sent out the link to my social networks—Facebook and Twitter—and asked folks to share. After a few days, I received a handful of responses, which were beautiful and inspiring and essentially human. So much of what individuals wrote to me really resonated with all the reading I had been doing in preparation for writing this chapter. That photographs—having them, making them, viewing them, talking about them—are an integral part of life was clear as I read and reviewed all the responses. This excerpt was particularly striking and poignant:

> Photos are everything. I document my life with photos and videos from my phone everywhere I go. In my office I have photos almost everywhere . . . the front of my file cabinet is covered in photos from various times of my life. My photos are on my social media sites as well because that's how I can express my self [sic], share my story with the world. I keep old photos at home in a box (although I should buy a photo album); I love to go back to look at the pictures. I can burst out into laughter just from one picture a few months ago or even years ago because it takes me back to that moment

and allows me the opportunity to reflect and engage with a past, memorable experience.

 A line-by-line analysis of the paragraph above illustrates the profound impact and imbeddedness of photographs and photography within human life in some contexts. The phrase "photos are everything" lays bare the absolute criticality of photographs within some individuals' lives. There is also a profound totality of this statement, which comes with the word "everything." This sentiment is reminiscent of the book *Photography Changes Everything*, edited by Marvin Heiferman (2012), wherein each chapter title begins with the phrase "Photography Changes." The second line is emblematic of the ubiquity of the camera—with video recording capability—and the propensity to document life happenings in an ongoing way. The next line describes how physical photographs, objects, are present within this individual's workspaces. Oftentimes interaction with a photograph is not about reliving an event or reinvoking a specific experience. Rather, individuals place decorative items within their spaces, such as photographs, and gaze at these images with the hopes of triggering a specific sensation or emotion (Van Dijck, 2005). When I gaze around my own work and living spaces, I can empathize. My spaces are filled with personal photographs that evoke feelings and emotions I desire to have when in those spaces—love, creativity, calm, warmth, and belonging. Turning back to the excerpt, personal identity development and expression are inferred within the next line (Bloustien & Baker, 2003), as this person shares how she or he is publicly expressive with personal photographs through social media sites—which are like (public) digitized, online shoeboxes. Note, however, that "old" photographs are relegated to a box—likely because they remain in a physical, rather than a digital, form. Within the last sentence, we receive a glimpse into potential of the human-photograph relationship. While this individual said that a photograph can allow her or him to engage with a past experience, that she or he noted bursting with laughter gives credence to the notion that images actually allow us to relive feelings and emotions connected to past experiences rather than reliving past experiences.

 The paragraph I analyzed above is certainly not an anomaly. Here are some additional comments from the crowdsourcing venture:

> In my home, I have frames in every room with photos of friends, family, my travels, and special life moments. I'm not one to remember the very specific details of long-ago stories, but when I browse my photos from a certain time, I find myself reliving those moments. All my friends say I'm quite the nostalgic. Most of my photographs are taken when I travel and are of places and things, although some of my favorite shots are usually of smiling faces.

> I started off with a Kodak camera back in 2004 and took lots of pictures in college. I would get a few printed here and there and would literally tape them on my wall. Nowadays I mostly use my phone. I do get them printed

from time to time or they get shared with social media, but I also like having these moments captured in time that I can look back at. I realize that I make meaning out of moments that others may not get so having something just for me is really special.

I seem to want to document everything that happens . . . I question my need to document so much though as I see an ever increasing need for so many to take all these selfies. I wonder what is that saying about us as a society? I love capturing the emotions of people!

With camera obscura dating back to 300BC, we as humans have always had a fascination with preservation. Documenting moments, ideas, thoughts, experiences, emotions have always been a part of human culture. Since we live in a digital age where everything can be uploaded to Facebook, Instagram, Tumblr, Flickr, almost instantly, it is important to me that I spend the extra time and money on printed photos. Printed photos are tangible, have a physical substance, and have more meaning. One of my favorite things growing up was going through countless shoeboxes and bins of pictures my parents took of me and my siblings. Every birthday, holiday, family vacation, baby book, scrap book, photo album all were reminiscent of memories I will forever hold near and dear to my heart . . . Most of the photos I have today are of my daughter. I am a little bias [sic], but she is pretty adorable! Each day, we sit down on our couch together and look through them. She points out each picture that has me or her Daddy in it. She finds the ones with her "Jidu" (Lebanese for Grandpa), her aunties and pictures of puppies I have all collected for her. It is our nightly ritual. This ritual I would not be able to have if it were not for photography.

The ease with which I can snap a quick photo has changed how I think about photography. It is no longer this special skill, or something necessary to document important events in my life. I use it more as a tool, like writing down a note or sending an email. It is another way to collect, store, and transmit information. I really value that I can find my friend's photos on [F]acebook or [I]nstagram, and sometimes I will go back and remember just like with my mom's photo albums, I still have pictures around; I don't think that has changed much compared to what my parents do. We have wedding photos, family photos, and pictures of our pets around the apartment and at work.

Photography is a very important part of my life. I think of it as visual history. Photographs have been telling my story since high school . . . I have them in albums, scrapbooks, and photo boxes, plus dozens all over my home on walls and on shelves. Photographs are also a large part of the decor in my work office.

Within these excerpts, what themes do you notice? Are these statements you could imagine yourself saying? What resonates with you most? Because acts of photography and photographs themselves are so integrated into many human cultures, it would make sense, then, that photography is also integrated into the disciplines. Before looking specifically at a handful of the social sciences to better understand the relationship between photography and inquiry over time, we will take a look at photojournalism first because it highlights a number of pertinent moments within United States and English history and the ways in which photography and photographs have both been impacted by, and impacted the course of, modern events and social movements.

Photography + Journalism = Photojournalism

Photography's "history has no unity. It is a flickering across a field of institutional spaces. It is this field we must study, not photography as such" (Tagg, 1988, p. 63). That in mind, let us begin with an exploration of the ways in which photography has interfaced with journalism over time. In 1989, *Time* magazine released a special collector's edition focused on "150 Years of Photojournalism." The creators of this edition used a chronological approach to address the ways in which photography has been used to document "newsworthy" events throughout recent human history. Some of the most recognizable and sensational images within the field of photojournalism are featured in this edition, which includes a series of short written pieces from Richard Lacayo, a prominent writer with *Time* since 1984. This edition was later converted into a book entitled *Eyewitness: 150 Years of Photojournalism* (Lacayo & Russell, 1990).

Lacayo (1989b, Fall) began with an overview of the "Early Days" of photography: 1839 to 1880. Noting the prominence of modernism and the rise of industrialization within the Western world during this period of time, Lacayo brilliantly described the camera as being seen as a "trap for facts" (p. 12), and he noted that William Henry Fox Talbot, a prominent photography pioneer, called photography the "pencil of nature" (p. 12). During this time, photographic technology did not afford the ability to take photographs of events in action. However, the technology of the time did afford the opportunity to document the aftermath of those events. Think war. Photography and war have always been close cousins. Photographers followed the aftermath of war, movement of colonial powers, and industrial progress. Sontag (2003) noted that "[e]ver since cameras were invented in 1839, photography has kept company with death" (p. 24).

Next, Lacayo (1989a, Fall) chronicled 1880 to 1920, or what he called "Conscience." This was an era of booming industrialism. It was also an era of urging for social and workplace responsibility. During this time, photographs became increasingly potent. Enter the muckrakers. Continuing with his use of the phrase "trap for facts," Lacayo noted that the camera "could be pointed at misery. The trap for facts could be a trumpet of justice too" (p. 22). The saliency of the images of the time affected readers; it also brought them in. Within this short piece, Lacayo references Jacob Riis and Lewis Hines, notable activist-photojournalists of the time.

Lacayo (1989a, Fall) discussed the differences in approaches between Jacob Riis and Lewis Hine. Hine approached photography with a certain gentleness, which characterized his approach to unearthing the social and workplace ills of the time. His work acknowledged the dignity and personhood of working individuals. The images he took were piercing yet kind somehow. He documented myriad working individuals—among other individuals—in a variety of settings, and had a knack for making photographs that demanded attention. This is apparent in several of his complied works (e.g. Hine, 1932/1977, 1977). And Hine's work still resonates in recent times, as is evident in *Lewis Hine 55* (Panzer, 2002), a small square of a book wherein 55 of his works are featured with elaborate captions. Riis was more straightforward, brash. He was a New York City newspaper reporter who saw the connection between photography and the public's collective conscience. As a Danish immigrant who came to the United States in 1870, poor and homeless, Riis was once a part of the "other half." His muckraking experiences resulted in a book titled *How the Other Half Lives* (Riis, 1890/2010), which I will discuss more in later parts of this chapter.

After World War I, photography expanded greatly. Lacayo (1989c, Fall) termed the time period 1920 to 1950 the "Golden Years." With the advent of the Leica, which replaced glass plates with 35mm film, photography—and photographers by extension—became faster, more mobilized. Photographs could be taken at almost any light at this point. This era gave way to the Farm Security Administration's—created by Roy Stryker who was inspired by Robert and Helen Lynd of the famous Middletown studies (Harper, 2012)—documentary photography of American life in the 1930s. Many of these images, created by photographers such as Margaret Bourke-White, Dorothea Lange, Walker Evans, Carl Mydans, and Aurthur Roshstein, were published in *Fortune* magazine. But *Fortune* was not enough. Then *Fortune* owner Henry R. Luce wanted to launch a magazine dedicated to photography stories. He purchased *Life* magazine in 1936 and dedicated it to photojournalism. As photojournalism matured during this time, its practitioners flirted with flamboyance. Lacayo (1989c, Fall) noted that "[t]he sensibilities they [photojournalists] had forged in peacetime brought a powerful dimension to the record of atrocity: a sense of intimacy with the intersections where individuals could create and suffer history" (p. 32). Sontag (2003) said "[p]hotojournalism came into its own in the early 1940s—wartime" (p. 34), and she argued that we often revel in the pain of others through the consumption of photographs of carnal, violent scenes. And while the notion that photography could create an objective image of the world remained, the eye behind the lens became important during this time. Personal vision and its intersections with the photographic were gaining attention.

By the 1950s, according to Lacayo (1989d, Fall), "[p]hotojournalism could even claim a theoretical foundation, as in Henri Cartier-Bresson's idea of the photographer as instant organizer of reality" (p. 56). There was a new awareness of the photographer as the arbiter of how the world was seen. The three decades between 1950 and 1980 were referred to as "New Challenges." There were tensions within the field, however, which was, ironically, "at war with itself" (p. 56). War coverage turned to coverage of suburban life. Coverage of war never ceased, however, and the battle for Civil Rights became a major interest of photographers within the United States. High-speed color film became normative. But photojournalists jockeyed for prominence with television news coverage, and television coverage was becoming more and more accessible over time.

Within Lacayo's (1989e, Fall) final essay, wherein he addressed 1980 to the present, he said "the dominion of the camera is total—the trap for facts has snared the world" (p. 66). This powerful statement was accurate at the time, and it is ringing truer each and every day. With the conversion of many traditional, print-based news outlets to online platforms, journalism has never been more visual.

Photography + Sociology = Visual Sociology

So, who used photography in social science research first? It appears as though it was the sociologists, followed by the anthropologists. But even though I am separating the combination of photography and research by discipline with section headings in this part of the chapter, the disciplines are not as discrete and tidy as we might assume. Recall Jacob Riis, the muckraking photojournalist. His photojournalistic work is quite difficult to discern from sociology. Heisley and Levy (1991) noted that "[f]rom about 1896 to 1916, the *American Journal of Sociology* routinely included photographs that dramatized the need for social reform" (p. 257). Sounds much like the work of Riis and Lewis Hines. Enter the books *Street Life in London* (Thomson & Smith, 1878/2014) and *How the Other Half Lives* (Riis, 1890/2010). Both of these books remain difficult to sort into one disciplinary home or another, as they each have roots within photojournalism. Perhaps like photovoice, they transcend disciplinary boundaries to open up spaces for transdisciplinary looks at social life. As Harper (2012) argued, visual sociology and visual anthropology ought to be brought closer together. But for the purposes of clarity, they will be presented separately in what follows.

According to Stasz (1979), visual sociology can be traced back to early documentary photographers within the United States such as Jacob Riis and Lewis Hine as well as photographers associated with the Farm Security Administration like Dorethea Lange. In addition, visual sociology also finds its roots within anthropology, beginning with the pioneering work of Gregory Bateson and Margaret Mead and their text, *Balinese Character* (1942). Stasz (1979) also noted that between 1896 and 1916, the *American Journal of Sociology* published 31 articles that included 244 images. However, this aspect of visual sociology's history went largely unnoticed. The early 1970s saw a resurgence of the visual. And Stasz (1979) said "the intervening years suffered the loss of a valuable research tool" (p. 131), and she offered a series of factors that may have inhibited the use and dissemination of visuals within sociological work. Those inhibitors included: shortages of physical materials after World War I, gatekeepers concerned with scientific rigor, the fact that contributors of visual work were more likely to be female and have a non-university affiliation, and photographic technology was cumbersome and crude.

Both sociology and photography were born in "the period between 1835 and 1850" (Cheatwood & Stasz, 1979, p. 261). During the two decades following this period, both experienced tremendous growth and sophistication. One of tenuous points in the history of visual sociology is that "[b]oth photography and sociology are troubled with self-definition" (Cheatwood & Stasz, 1979, p. 261).

Are photographs objects of art or objects of science? This question calls to mind the notion of what *counts* as data or as documentation. This is a question those grappling with the infusion of photography into the art/science of sociology ask(ed) themselves. And this is a question we still face today within the field of educational research. Another question is whether or not the subjective is correct. For example, can a photograph that has been manipulated in some fashion (e.g. cropping, filtration) be considered an acceptable form of documentation? I would certainly say yes, but with the understanding that an image is never a value-free, objective representation of reality. Cheatwood and Stasz (1979) said "what the sociologist or photographer sees as real comes from unstated assumptions about the nature of social life derived from his or her general culture and the culture of the discipline involved" (p. 265). We must bear this in mind when enacting the visual within research processes.

Thinking about this within the context of photovoice, it becomes clear that photovoice researchers must interrogate their orientation to both photographs and the theoretical underpinnings that foreground the photovoice methodology as well as the analytical approach(es) applied to the data. For example, is it most appropriate to ask participants to all use disposable cameras during the documentation phase? This way, they cannot see their images as they are taking them. Moreover, there is no way to manipulate those images prior to development. When they arrive to the narration phase, the images are a surprise, and the reception of those images can influence the tone and tenor of the narration. On the other hand, what if participants take photographs with their own devices and make the choice to carefully vet and manicure the images before putting them forward to the researcher(s) and other participants for joint viewing during the narration phase? Will there be apprehensions because of a perception of differentiated photographic and editorial talent? Cheatwood and Stasz (1979) noted that "technical criterion can lead us away from contemplating the meanings and implications of what we have before us" (p. 266).

Harper (1998) described visual sociology as a "two-headed beast" (p. 24)—one head dedicated to the empiricists' and one head dedicated to the symbolists' versions of the utility and place of photography within inquiry. Empiricists see visuals just as they are—documentations of reality. The symbolists see visuals as having primary and secondary meanings (and perhaps tertiary meanings, as well)—artifacts ripe for interpretation. Regarding his text *Visual Sociology*, Harper (2012) noted that

> [t]he book is based on the premise that the world that is seen, photographed, drawn or otherwise represented visually is different than the world that is represented through words and numbers. As a result, visual sociology leads to new understandings and insights because it connects to different realities than do conventional empirical research methods.
>
> *p. 4*

He also contended that seeing as a social construction is at the core of visual sociology; seeing is bound up in the seer.

Becker (1995) noted that "[p]eople who want to use photographic materials for social science purposes—to do what is sometimes now called visual sociology—often get confused" (p. 5). While this statement is humorous, it is also true. Oftentimes, photo-elicitation studies are misnamed photovoice studies. And disciplinary genres are often blurred depending on how a photograph is used. Becker illustrated, through examples, how any photograph within any of the following genres—photojournalism, documentary photography, and visual sociology—could be placed within another genre if the context changes. In essence, it is not about the photograph itself. Rather, what matters is the context in which the photograph is situated. Reader/viewers who consume photographs created by photojournalists do not expect to have to decipher the contents of the image. On the other hand, documentary photography is meant to spur on social change or affect those who view the images created for this purpose. Finally, images created by visual sociologists are meant to address questions raised within the discipline. The very same image could exist in all three categories; it depends on context.

Television, video, and the Internet have also caused boundary blurring. Let us consider what some call the first reality television series, *An American Family* (Raymond & Raymond, 2011). According to McCarthy (1973), "*An American Family* was hailed as a great breakthrough in the use of the camera in the service of knowledge" (para. 2). And the knowledge generated through that series most certainly addressed a plethora of sociological questions. McCarthy went on to argue that the television documentary was an extension of documentary photography, and suggested that *An American Family* and *A Family of Man* (Steichen, 1955/2006) portray the same content—just in different forms. McCarthy asked whether or not television is the best form for this content. Because tensions arose between the creators and the Loud family within *An American Family*, she (1973) wrote "[c]ontent was questioning form" (para. 16). We should ask ourselves similar questions when considering photographic objecthood in the use of images throughout the course of a photovoice project.

Photography + Anthropology = Visual Anthropology

Anthropology and photography, entwined, have quite a deep history (Edwards, 1992; Strong & Wilder, 2009). Collier (1979) noted that one of the benefits of "photography is not only that it can gather valuable research tangibles, but that the detail of the visual evidence it provides can preserve a constantly 'present' context for subsequent analysis" (p. 272). This is important within photovoice. The images produced within the process serve the generation of data at, potentially, multiple points. For example, reacting to and narrating the contents of the images through the narration phase is one way the presentation of context is important. During the presentation phase, these preserved contexts may also affect those who see and consume the work, giving way to emotions, conversations, reactions, and additional data generation in some cases.

Within Collier's (1979) work, we can clearly see the positivistic orientations to visual anthropology that were—and to a large degree still are—long-held within the discipline. He contended that visual anthropologists must aspire toward "reading the photographic evidence with accuracy" (p. 273). How can we be sure about what is accurate? Accurate to whom? Within photovoice, we, as researchers, must aim to ascertain what is accurate to our participants. Then we aspire toward interpreting those collective accuracies vis-à-vis whichever analytical approach(es) we bring to the project and through our specific positionalities as researcher-human-instruments.

Collier (1979) credited Bateson and Mead's (1942) *Balinese Character* as the first use of visual anthropology. They wrote: "we are attempting a new method of stating the intangible relationships among different types of culturally standardized behavior by placing side by side mutually relevant photographs" (p. xii). The book is dense—both textually and photographically. It represents a significant pivot point in the use of photography within anthropological inquiry. From that point onward, the use of photography as a method has been used in the field extensively (Collier, 1957; Collier, 1967; Collier & Collier, 1986). Ethnographers have integrated photography into their repertoire of data gathering while in the field. However, Becker (2012) argued that the book was not revolutionary. He explained: "*Balinese Character* remains a strong argument for a visual ethnography. It is artful science; a vision of what the discipline could become. Why then, did it fail to revolutionize anthropology and, perhaps, social science in general?" (p. 14, italics in original). Harper outlined four reasons:

- No single book can have that significant an effect.
- The work done by Mead and Bateson was massive and deep. The bar was set too high for others to follow.
- At the time of publication, critics said the work was not scientific enough.
- Contemporary critics say the work is too scientific.

This photographic approach to fieldwork, which is sometimes termed photoethnography, incorporates the photograph as both an object of analysis and a means of eliciting visceral responses in consumers of the completed work. Concomitantly, the postmodern era has allowed questions of voice, authority, and authenticity to emerge within the field of anthropology (Ruby, 1991), thus problematizing the photoethnographic approach. Photovoice places participants behind camera lenses and asks them to assign meaning to their own images, thereby addressing and dismantling the traditional researcher-centered approach to photography as a research method.

Caldarola (1988) argued that "text [within an ethnography] continues to function as the medium of valid reference in anthropology, while photographs are used to illustrate conclusions explicated in the lexical mode and to assist in the communication of ethnographic authority and realism" (p. 434). Photographs, argued Caldarola, are often seen as objective documents within ethnographic work, which makes them immune to the tensions imbedded in the task of representing elements of culture through writing. However, representation via photography can encompass some of these same representational tensions. When making photographs, the photographer makes a series of decisions, regardless of whether or not he or she is consciously aware of those decisions. While leading photovoice projects, I have found that participants often incorporate symbolism, staging, and metaphors within their photography. Participants select the perspective(s) taken. But without the lexical complement—the photo-elicitation interview data—this may not be immediately apparent. The symbiosis of image and word within the photovoice process is critical in comprehensively conveying meaning.

Photography + Psychology = Auto-Photography

While many sociologists and anthropologists would acknowledge that visuals—in addition to discourse—are critical in understanding how cultures operate, some psychologists are also acknowledging the importance of the visual in understanding how individuals construct identity and subjectivity and experience the culture(s) to which they belong (Reavey, 2011). The existence of measures such as the Rorschach Test (Rorschach, 1945) and the Thematic Apperception Test (Murray, 1943) suggest that human-visual stimuli interactions matter in the understanding of personality and cognition. These projective tests are administered by asking individuals to interpret ambiguous visual stimuli. The responses are then interpreted, resulting in insights about the individual—personality, motivations, and attitudes that may be outside of consciousness. The Rorschach Test, or the inkblot test, includes a series of symmetrical, yet ambiguous, inkblots as the projective stimuli. And the Thematic Apperception Test, or the TAT, includes scenes of people, ambiguous enough to invite a host of interpretations, or story lines. In both examples, individuals are prompted to explain what they see and/or generate a story about the stimuli, respectively. The projective stimuli are standardized, pre-made, and necessarily decontextualized. What might be learned about individuals and concomitant social and cultural contexts if the individuals being tested generated those projective stimuli? This question challenges the dominant framework through which psychologists have traditionally viewed projective tests.

Even though "[p]sychology has been slower to recognize the benefits of visual data than other social science disciplines" (Brunsden & Goatcher, 2007, p. 46), inroads are being made (Han & Oliffe, 2016). A methodology similar to photovoice, but used mainly within the field of psychology, has been termed auto-photography, or photo-communication (Combs & Ziller, 1977; Dinklage & Ziller, 1989; Johnsen, May, & Cloke, 2008; Noland, 2006; Ziller & Rorer, 1985). Used largely to measure self-concept, auto-photography asks participants to take photos in response to prompts. Photographs are then used to guide discussions during interviews—or counseling sessions. In Combs and Ziller's (1977) study, counseling clients were asked to take 12 photos that described who they were. The authors asserted that through photography, "the client can become a more active participant in the process of self-disclosure. The task is open ended and encourages creativity in defining one's self-concept nonverbally" (p. 452). In regards to the photographs themselves, "there is a 'rich revealingness' about . . . self-presentation" (p. 455), and the drawbacks of verbal-only exchanges are avoided. Photovoice also offers rich revealingness, as Stinson's (2010) work most certainly illustrated. However, photovoice has quite ambitious goals that encapsulate and extend beyond participants by moving into larger social spheres, which makes it unique among other methods that include photography as will become clear later in this book.

Summary

Historically, photographs used within research projects have been taken from the perspective of the researcher, the inquirer, or the observer. However, photovoice researchers, who center the participants' life worlds, place cameras in the hands of participants, which shifts the essential nature of the research itself, making it more authentic to the experiences and perspectives of the participants. Within this chapter, I put forward eight steps that comprise the photovoice methodology. In addition, I outlined the history of the marriage between inquiry and photography. I also highlighted the ways in which human beings orient themselves to photographs and photography. Photography is becoming increasingly ubiquitous as technology pushes the boundaries of photographic activity. The following chapter is focused on the theoretical underpinnings and aims of photovoice.

References

Argyris, C., & Schön, D. A. (1991). Participatory action research and action science compared: A commentary. In W. F. Whyte (Ed.), *Participatory action research* (pp. 85–96). Newbury Park, CA: Sage.
Batchen, G. (1997). *Burning with desire: The conception of photography*. Cambridge, MA: The MIT Press.
Bateson, G., & Mead, M. (1942). *Balinese character: A photographic analysis*. New York: New York Academy of Sciences.
Becker, H. (1995). Visual sociology, documentary photography, and photojournalism: It's (almost) all a matter of context. *Visual Sociology*, *10*(1–2), 5–14.
Bloustien, G., & Baker, S. (2003). On not talking to strangers: Researching the micro worlds of girls through visual auto-ethnographic practices. *Social Analysis*, *47*(3), 64–79.
Brunsden, V., & Goatcher, J. (2007). Reconfiguring photovoice for psychological research. *The Irish Journal of Psychology*, *28*, 43–52. doi: 10.1080/03033910.2007.10446247
Bush, V. (1945, July). As we may think. *The Atlantic*. Retrieved from http://theatlantic.com/magazine/archive/1945/07/as-we-may-think/303881/
Caldarola, V. J. (1988). Imaging process as ethnographic inquiry. *Visual Anthropology*, *1*, 433–451. doi: 10.1080/08949468.1988.9966499
Carr, N. (2008, July/August). Is Google making us stupid? *The Atlantic*. Retrieved from http://theatlantic.com/magazine/archive/2008/07/is-google-making-us-stupid/306868/
Cheatwood, D., & Stasz, C. (1979). Visual sociology. In J. Wagner (Ed.), *Images of information: Still photography in the social sciences* (pp. 261–269). Beverly Hills, CA: Sage.
Collier, Jr. J. (1957). Photography in anthropology: A report on two experiments. *American Anthropologist*, *59*, 843–859.
Collier, Jr. J. (1967). *Visual anthropology: Photography as research method*. New York: Holt, Rinehart and Winston.
Collier, Jr. J. (1979). Visual anthropology. In J. Wagner (Ed.), *Images of information: Still photography in the social sciences* (pp. 271–281). Beverly Hills, CA: Sage.
Collier, Jr. J., & Collier, M. (1986). *Visual anthropology: Photography as a research method*. Albuquerque, NM: University of New Mexico Press.
Combs, J. M., & Ziller, R. C. (1977). Photographic self-concept of counselees. *Journal of Counseling Psychology*, *24*, 452–455.
de Castella, T. (2012, February 28). Five ways the digital camera changed us. *BBC News Magazine*. Retrieved from http://bbc.com/news/magazine-16483509
Dinklage, R. I., & Ziller, R. C. (1989). Explicating cognitive conflict through photo communication: The meaning of war and peace in Germany and the United States. *The Journal of Conflict Resolution*, *33*, 309–317.
Edwards, E. (Ed.). (1992). *Anthropology & photography: 1860–1920*. New Haven, CT: Yale University Press.
Edwards, E. (2002). Material beings: Objecthood and ethnographic photographs. *Visual Studies*, *17*, 67–75.
Gernsheim, H. (1982). *The origins of photography*. New York: Thames and Hudson.
Han, C. S., & Oliffe, J. L. (2016). Photovoice in mental illness research: A review and recommendations. *Health*, *20*, 110–126. doi: 10.1177/1363459314567790
Harper, D. (1998). An argument for visual sociology. In J. Prosser (Ed.), *Image-based research: A sourcebook for qualitative researchers* (pp. 24–41). London: Falmer.
Harper, D. (2012). *Visual sociology*. New York: Routledge.

Heiferman, M. (Ed.). (2012). *Photography changes everything*. New York: Aperature Foundation.

Heisley, D. D., & Levy, S. J. (1991). Autodriving: A photoelicitation technique. *Journal of Consumer Research, 18*, 257–272.

Higgins, M. (2014). Rebraiding photovoice: Methodological métissage at the cultural interface. *The Australian Journal of Indigenous Education, 43*, 208–217. doi: 10.1017.jie.2014.18

Hine, L. W. (1977). *America & Lewis Hine: Photographs 1904–1940*. Millerton, NY: Aperature.

Hine, L. W. (1977). *Men at work: Photographic studies of modern men and machines*. New York: Dover Publications. (Original work published in 1932.)

Johnsen, S., May, J., & Cloke, P. (2008). Imag(in)ing 'homeless places': Using auto-photography to (re)examine the geographies of homelessness. *Area, 40*, 194–207.

Kuhn, A. (2007). Photography and cultural memory: A methodological exploration. *Visual Studies, 22*, 283–292. doi: 10.1080/14725860701657175

Lacayo, R. (1989a, Fall). Conscience: 1880–1920. *Time: 150 Years of Photojournalism*, 22–30.

Lacayo, R. (1989b, Fall). Early days: 1839–1880. *Time: 150 Years of Photojournalism*, 12–18.

Lacayo, R. (1989c, Fall). Golden years: 1920–1950. *Time: 150 Years of Photojournalism*, 52–55.

Lacayo, R. (1989d, Fall). New challenges: 1950–1980. *Time: 150 Years of Photojournalism*, 56–64.

Lacayo, R. (1989e, Fall). Today and tomorrow: 1980–. *Time: 150 Years of Photojournalism*, 66–75.

Lacayo, R., & Russell, G. (1990). *Eyewitness: 150 years of photojournalism*. Des Moines, IA: Oxmoor House.

McCarthy, A. (1973, July). 'An American Family' and 'The Family of Man.' *The Atlantic*. Retrieved from http://theatlantic.com/magazine/archive/1973/07/an-american-family-the-family-of-man/394577/

Mollison, J. (2010). *Where children sleep*. London: Chris Boot.

Murray, H. A. (1943). *Thematic apperception test*. Cambridge, MA: Harvard University Press.

Noland, C. M. (2006). Auto-photography as research practice: Identity and self-esteem research. *Journal of Research Practice, 2*(1), 1–19. Retrieved from http://jrp.icaap.org/index.php/jrp/article/view/19/65

Panzer, M. (2002). *Lewis Hine 55*. New York: Phaidon Press.

Prosser, J. (1996). What constitutes an image-based qualitative methodology? *Visual Sociology, 11*(2), 25–34.

Raymond, A., & Raymond, S. (Producers) (2011). *An American family: Anniversary edition* (motion picture). USA: PBS.

Reavey, P. (Ed.). (2011). *Visual methods in psychology: Using and interpreting images in qualitative research*. New York: Psychology Press.

Riis, J. (2010). *How the other half lives*. USA: Readaclassic.com. (Original work published in 1890.)

Roberts, J. A., & David, M. E. (2016). My life has become a major distraction from my cell phone: Partner phubbing and relationship satisfaction among romantic partners. *Computers in Human Bahavior, 54*, 134–141.

Rorschach, H. (1945). *Rorschach test*. Bern, Switzerland: Hans Huber Publishers.

Ruby, J. (1991). Speaking for, speaking against, speaking with, or speaking alongside—An anthropological and documentary dilemma. *Visual Anthropology Review, 7,* 50–67.

Sontag, S. (2003). *Regarding the pain of others.* New York: Farrar, Straus and Giroux.

Stasz, C. (1979). The early history of visual sociology. In J. Wagner (Ed.), *Images of information: Still photography in the social sciences* (pp. 119–136). Beverly Hills, CA: Sage.

Steichen, E. (2006). *The family of man.* New York: The Museum of Modern Art. (Original work published in 1955.)

Stinson, D. L. (2010). This ain't something you can pray away: Grandparents raising grandchildren, a photovoice project. *Journal of Health Care for the Poor and Underserved, 21,* 1–25.

Strong, M., & Wilder, L. (Eds.). (2009). *Viewpoints: Visual anthropologists at work.* Austin, TX: University of Texas Press.

Sutton-Brown, C. A. (2014). Photovoice: A methodological guide. *Photography & Culture, 7,* 169–186. doi: 10.2752/175145214X13999922103165

Tagg, J. (1988). *The burden of representation: Essays on photographies and histories.* Amherst, MA: University of Massachusetts Press.

Thomson, J., & Smith, A. (2014). *Street life in London.* Lexington, KY: Omo Press. (Original work published in 1878.)

Van Dijck, J. (2005). From shoebox to performative agent: The computer as personal memory machine. *New Media Society, 7,* 311–332. doi: 10.1177/1461444805050765

Wang, C., & Burris, M. A. (1994). Empowerment through photo novella: Portraits of participation. *Health Education Quarterly, 21,* 171–186.

Whyte, W. F., Greenwood, D. J., & Lazes, P. (1991). Participatory action research: Through practice to science in social research. In W. F. Whyte (Ed.), *Participatory action research* (pp. 19–55). Newbury Park, CA: Sage.

Ziller, R. C., & Rorer, B. A. (1985). Shyness-environment interaction: A view from the shy side through auto-photography. *Journal of Personality, 53,* 626–639.

2
THEORETICAL UNDERPINNINGS AND AIMS OF PHOTOVOICE

A Vignette

I was first introduced to bell hooks in undergraduate school. A required text in one of my communications courses—a course focused on communication in popular culture, I think—was *Outlaw Culture: Resisting Representation* (hooks, 1994/2006). I thought, who is this author? Everything in that book resonated with me. She blew my mind. Reading her work was like looking into the brain of someone who thought like I was desperately trying to think, but she was able to place words around those thoughts in a way I never could. Later, while taking courses in pursuit of my doctoral degree, I read another book by hooks. This time it was *Ain't I a Woman: Black Women and Feminism* (hooks, 1981). Wow. I was enamored by this text and could not fathom that hooks wrote it as such a young scholar. Unbelievable. I wrote a book review of the text in the fall of 2007. The book review—not the book specifically—was a required assignment for one of the classes I was taking on the history of adult education. Reading that book was transformative for me. Through the reading, I was able to grasp a fuller understanding of the importance of philosophy and theory and how our ways of seeing the world are shaped by our philosophies and theories related to how we think things work. Whether or not we are aware of or have names for these theories, nearly everything we do can be traced back to how we believe the world works—as well as our position in that world. An abbreviated excerpt of the review is below.

> bell hooks offered a powerful critical and historical analysis of the social status and state of being of Black women in her book, *Ain't I a Woman: Black Women and Feminism* (1981). She chronicled the lives of Black women

as a collective within the US from the inception of slavery until the women's liberation movement of the 1970s. With a focus on providing a critical analysis of the sexist nature of the Black liberation movement and the racist nature of the women's movement, hooks asserted that Black liberation was/is reserved for Black men and women's liberation was/is reserved for White women. Therefore, Black women, through both the Black and women's liberation movements, have been intentionally ousted and therefore marginalized and unable to benefit from either. This left Black women in what hooks described as a double bind, unable to participate fully in either movement.

hooks delivered a critical and informed perspective of both Black women and feminism in the United States. I was completely enthralled from start to finish . . . hooks was able to unpeel layers upon layers of social and cultural attitudes, structures, and institutions that have systematically and consistently oppressed Black women over time. She cites writing, lectures, popular media, and draws upon personal experience to assert claims. Thorough and convincing evidence and arguments are brought forward that nail down her assertions into truth.

This text is valuable. First, it provides an unequivocal example of a philosophical (and/or theoretical) perspective. Her stance is both critical and feminist. She provides a new way of thinking about feminism, which could translate into a deeper and more meaningful understanding of the lived experiences of Black women (along with the experience of Black men, White women, and White men). As a self-identified White woman, my eyes have been opened. I see the mistakes and wrong routes made and taken by the White women feminists who have come before me who now have a current and real manifestation in my experiences as a White woman working along side of women of many racial/ethnic identities.

This book has had a profound effect on me because I am more wide-awake in my day to day. hooks awakened me to the true nature of endemic racism, sexism, and classism. I have thought in this way before, but to have the words articulated in front of me with clear examples I perked up in an already perked up state. Her work will continue to live in me throughout my life as an educator, a woman, and a human being. I feel that after reading this book, I am more able to contribute to the work of feminism in a selfless way so that I can stop myself from recreating same scenes with different casts. I have been a hooks fan and advocate for a while, but not until reading this seminal work have I felt so compelled to read more.

Her work is a contribution to a social movement . . . Her writing offers the reader both a lens and a panoramic view . . . The reader can use this new lens (philosophy) to view other topics most relevant in his or her own life. This is what philosophers do. Without lenses, the world would be hard to see.

So, why would I include this here? For many neophyte researchers, theoretical underpinnings can seem ethereal, adjunct, and sometimes simply confusing. I know this because I used to be a neophyte researcher—and in some ways, I still am. Yet I include this book review here because there are few things more powerful than genuinely connecting theory to practice—and intimately understanding that connection. Photovoice exists in the world today because so many individuals and groups of individuals engaged in countless cycles of theorizing, acting, reflecting, refining, and repeating. Photovoice is the child of many mothers, and its praxis is built upon a strong theoretical foundation. Understanding the keystones of this foundation is a critical component of engaging the methodology effectively.

★ ★ ★

Methodological Umbrellas

The photovoice method is underpinned by three theoretical strands: (a) feminism; (b) Paulo Freire's notion of critical consciousness; and (c) participatory documentary photography. Within this chapter, I outline each of these three strands, pointing to the ways in which an understanding of these theoretical perspectives breathes life and meaning into the actionable methods and techniques embedded within the methodology. But first, we must understand the methodological umbrellas under which photovoice can be conceptualized.

Participatory Action Research

Although its originations are debatable (Lykes & Hershberg, 2012), action research is often traced back to the work of Kurt Lewin (Bradbury, Mirvis, Neilsen, & Pasmore, 2008), a social psychologist whose early work with the methodology was focused on community action programs in the United States in the 1940s (Lewin, 1946). Action research is a broad-spanning phrase that includes many specific variations such as participatory action research, critical action research, classroom action research, action science, soft systems approaches, and industrial action research (Kemmis & McTaggart, 2005). Stringer (2014) explained that "[a]ction research is a systematic approach to investigation that enables people to find effective solutions to problems they confront in their everyday lives" (p. 1). I cannot emphasize enough how this approach to research is a complete departure from what is typically seen as research within the academy. For Stringer, engagement in action research requires a new way to view the social world. This new perspective "rejects the mindless application of standardized practices across all settings and contexts and instead advocates the use of contextually relevant procedures formulated by inquiring and resourceful practitioners" (Stringer, p. 3).

Photovoice is a form of participatory action research (Bogdan & Biklen, 2007; Kemmis & McTaggart, 2005; Whyte, 1991). In participatory action research,

> some of the people in the organization or community under study participate actively with the professional researcher throughout the research process from the initial design to the final presentation of results and discussion of their action implications. PAR thus contrasts sharply with the conventional model of pure research, in which members of organizations and communities are treated as passive subjects, with some of them participating only to the extent of authorizing the project, being its subjects, and receiving the results.
> *Whyte, Greenwood, & Lazes, 1991, p. 20*

According to Kemmis and McTaggart (2005), participatory action research has three attributes that distinguish it from conventional research: (a) shared ownership of research; (b) community-oriented understanding of social problems; and (c) propensity for community action (p. 560).

Tandon (1981) noted that two forces have contributed to the growth of participatory research: (a) researchers who have found classical research processes to be oppressive and therefore problematic; and (b) the increasing exploitation and oppression of a large majority of people around the world. Tandon also articulated the following characteristics of participatory research: (a) collapses producing and using knowledge; (b) occurs in the participants' context(s); (c) recognizes that participation levels are varied; (d) relinquishes (some) control to the participants; (e) reduces the limitations of classical research; (f) emphasizes the collective; and (g) nurtures learning among everyone involved. The dominant research framework, which still presides now as it did in 1981, suggests that research can only be done, and knowledge can only be produced, by the "haves" of society, not the "have nots." Tandon noted that " participatory research is an attempt to provide an alternative to the dominant research paradigm" (p. 22). Participatory research can serve as a democratizing agent in the production of knowledge. While the advent of the Internet has served as a means of democratizing the access to and consumption of knowledge—to some extent—participatory research serves this end as well.

Maguire (1987) stated that participatory research is a way for researchers to openly express solidarity with groups that have been marginalized. The key here is that researchers are working with research participants rather than on research participants. As researchers, we can have the best-laid plans, but if those plans are not copasetic with those with whom we are working, the plans are subject to change. For Maguire, participatory research is comprised of the following: "investigation, education, and action" (p. 35). It is an educational process for all involved, and there is a clear link between research and action.

Those who engage in participatory research assume "ordinary people, provided with tools and opportunities, are capable of critical reflection and analysis" (Maguire, 1987, p. 47). Moreover, shared power is a cornerstone of the approach.

Maguire (1987) outlined a five-phased approach to participatory research: (a) gathering, organizing, and analyzing information related to the project/area of research; (b) taking stock of problems; (c) linking perceptions of problems to the larger social world; (d) gathering, organizing, and analyzing information related to the larger social world; and (e) deciding on and carrying out action. Maguire's steps can be mapped onto the eight steps in the photovoice process I will outline in detail later in this book.

There are certainly limitations and numerous difficulties in doing—and completing—this work. Maguire (1987) suggested the following: participant passivity and apathy, demands on the researcher, externally defined and mandated projects, power hoarding, lack of organizational entity, lack of resources, and lack of time.

But how do we, as researchers, actually know if we are doing participatory action research—and doing it well? Allen and Hutchinson (2009) provided exemplary work related to critically examining their own use of participatory action research vis-à-vis a photovoice study that culminated in the creation of a documentary film centered on what it is like to live with end stage renal disease (ESRD). The researchers questioned to what extent their work aligned with the tenets of participatory action research. As their study unfolded, it was apparent that getting all 11 participants together for photo elicited discussion would be difficult because of each individual's dialysis schedule. The logistics of a photovoice project are oftentimes complex. However, a whole group meeting was eventually scheduled. Participants were given disposable cameras and asked to take photographs related to the challenges of living with ESRD and the potential solutions to those challenges. To facilitate the conversations, the researchers showed the photographs with a document camera. This was useful for two reasons: (a) some of the images were underexposed, which is common when using disposable cameras, as the flash must be made operational; and (b) participants were also encouraged to bring photographs from their personal collections if those photographs were deemed appropriate. Conversational ground rules were set, which were grounded in respect, and the researchers reported that the use of photovoice as a form of participatory action research was more powerful than they originally expected.

In fact, the photovoice process generated enough momentum for the group to advocate for the creation of a documentary film, to be used as a means of exhibiting the work, the experiences of these *patient-collaborators*, as Allen and Hutchinson (2009) referred to the study's participants. When considering the use of film as exhibition—or as an extension of data collection—it is important to note that "[d]oing good research is not the same as making a good film" (Allen & Hutchinson, p. 124). The authors explained that "the social action [they] thought most appropriate to pursue in light of our patient-collaborators' interest in raising public awareness about their illness" (p. 125).

Even though Allen and Hutchinson (2009) facilitated a study that I would deem a success in terms of adherence to the guiding principles of participatory action research, the authors critically interrogated their process and procedures with regards to whether the work used or abused participatory action research. Based on Allen and Hutchinson's thoughtful reflection on their own work, I generated a list of questions all photovoice researchers can ask themselves and collaborators about their use of the methodology—while using it—as it relates to adherence to participatory action research principles:

- Who is making the decisions about the project? Why?
- Who is being heard? Why?
- To what degree are the participants participating? Why?
- Are our requests of participants practical? Why, or why not?
- Is consensus possible or desirable? Why, or why not?
- If we were to view participatory action research as existing on a continuum, where would our project be? Why?
- Is our current work sustainable? Why, or why not?

Allen and Hutchinson (2009) pointed out that "academics conducting PAR studies can find themselves awkwardly situated between meeting the demands of the institution . . . and fulfilling the promise of social action for the community and/or users with whom they have worked" (p. 126). While this situation might be awkward for some, it is perhaps the most optimal orientation to research practice when attempting to create positive change for the community and additional knowledge from which interested others might benefit. When doing participatory action research, researchers can certainly find themselves pulled in different directions. However, these directions need not be at odds with one another. There are many ways in which those in the academy can attend to their own professional realities while doing positive work within communities. Examples are threaded throughout this text.

Feminist Participatory Action Research

In 1987, Maguire wrote that "feminist and participatory research are parallel but as yet unconnected approaches, largely ignorant of each other" (p. 95). Gatenby and Humphries (2000) agreed, noting that "PAR has traditionally been conducted as if the social world were place of gender-neutrality or gender-equality" (p. 90). Maguire (1987) wondered if "participatory research and feminist research can join forces to eliminate androcentrism from research while constructing a truly emancipatory approach to knowledge creation for both women and men" (Maguire, p. 104). In addition, Maguire put forward nine items feminist participatory researchers would "include or consider" (p. 129) when "planning, implementing, and evaluating feminist participatory research" (p. 132): (a) a critical stance on the positivist and androcentric nature of much social science research; (b) a centralized focus on gender, but with an inclusion of the intersections between gender, class, race, and culture; (c) an inclusive version of feminism, which is attentive to many forms of oppression and domination; (d) a focus on gender during all phases of the work; (e) a focus on how men and women benefit from the work; (f) attention to language use; (g) attention to the composition of a diverse research team; (h) a focus on gender within the project evaluation; and (i) the use of a gendered lens when conducting meta-analyses on participatory research projects. To a large degree, photovoice is the result of such a joined force Maguire wrote about in 1987, and the phrase used to describe this approach to inquiry is feminist participatory action research. Lather (1991) said

> to do feminist research is to put the social construction of gender at the center of one's inquiry . . . The overt ideological goal of feminist research in the human sciences is to correct both the *invisibility* and *distortion* of female experience in ways relevant to ending women's unequal social position.
>
> *p. 71, italics in original*

In many ways, feminist participatory action research is attentive to Lather's description.

Reid and Frisby (2008) laid out a series of dimensions of feminist participatory action research, which highlights areas of overlap between action research, participatory action research, and feminist research:

1. Centering gender and women's diverse experiences while challenging patriarchy;
2. Accounting for intersectionality;
3. Honoring voice and difference;
4. Exploring new forms of representation;
5. Reflexivity;
6. Honoring many forms of action.

pp. 97–102

Reid and Frisby do not put forward these dimensions definitively. Rather, they suggest that those who engage in feminist participatory action research work use this list as a way to assess practice before, during, and after the enactment of research processes thereby encouraging a more reflexive approach.

Arts-Based Research

Is arts-based research an oxymoron? To many, the answer is yes. Here it is not. Positioning science and art as oppositional entities or as a binary is unwise. Even though the common perception of research is that it descends from science, research done well necessarily involves artistry. Certain aesthetic decisions are made during research processes, regardless of methodology. Yet these decisions are overlooked and undervalued. How should research notes be organized? What is the best way to convey the results? How can attention be drawn to select, specific parts of the research report? Would certain chunks of data be best presented within a table or as a figure? To be sure, "borders between art and science are malleable and porous . . . [and] artistry in action is ubiquitous" (Barone & Eisner, 2012, p. 7). Throughout their book, Barone and Eisner dedicate large portions of text to the definition of arts-based research, but when viewed through the lens of the photovoice methodology, this one seems most relevant: "[arts-based research] is an evocative and emotionally drenched expression that makes it possible to know how others feel" (p. 9). Here is an example. Photovoice participants are afforded the opportunity to both create images and words to express their realities and feelings. In a recent study in which I was involved, our community college student-participants expressed both their apprehension and their hopefulness about their ability to handle what the future brings them. One poignant image depicted a coming thunderstorm, in a photograph that was taken from inside a home and through a screen door. The participant noted that she was questioning whether or not she could handle the storms that may be ahead. When our research team presented this digitized image-text amalgam to a team of community college administrators, there were visceral reactions—furrowed brows, paralanguage (e.g. "huh"), and stares across the room. If we had simply said to the research team "students are both apprehensive and hopeful about being able to handle what the future holds," I contend the reactions would have been different. By using a form of art—photography—photovoice participants are more equipped to convey the contours of their feelings than if they were relegated to discursive forms of expression alone.

When sharing the contents of our minds with others, we are confronted with the duality of constraint and possibility regarding the form(s) we use to share. The notion that nondiscursive means (e.g. music, images, theater) can be used within research practice, however, is not widely accepted within the academy (Barone & Eisner, 2012). When only certain forms are acceptable within the dominant research community, there are "enormous ramifications for understanding human behavior and social interaction" (Barone & Eisner, 2012, p. 2). While experimental research has yielded copious amounts of new knowledge to what is presently known about human behavior and social interaction, one methodological approach cannot produce results that address the entirety of any given behavior or interaction. Similarly, arts-based research is not a methodological approach that can address entireties either. Rather, it is a "heuristic through which we deepen and make more complex our understanding of some aspect of the world" (Barone & Eisner, 2012, p. 3). Not only is arts-based research important because it can help us see more of the whole, it is also important because it signals the value of methodological pluralism.

Barone and Eisner (2012) delineated a list of ten concepts upon which arts-based research is built:

1. Humans have invented a variety of forms of representation to describe and understand the world in as many ways as it can be represented.
2. Each form of representation imposes its own constraints and provides its own affordances.
3. The purpose of arts based research is to raise significant questions and engender conversations rather than to proffer final meanings.
4. Arts based research can capture meaning that measurement cannot.
5. As the methodology for the conduct of research within the social sciences expands, a greater array of aptitudes will encounter forms that are most suited to them.
6. For arts based research to advance, those who prepare researchers will need to diversify the development of skill among those who are being taught.
7. Arts based research is not only for arts educators or professional artists.
8. In arts based research, generalizing from an n of 1 is an acceptable practice.
9. The aim of arts based research is not to replace traditional research methods; it is to diversify the pantry of methods that researchers can use to address the problems they care about.
10. Utilizing the expressive properties of a medium is one of the primary ways in which arts based research contributes to human understanding.

pp. 164–171

Because "[t]here is no single definition or conceptions of what art is, nor of what its effect upon the world should be . . . neither is there one single artistic method for research" (Rolling, 2013, p 10). As such, Rolling delineated several models of art making. The model that most closely resembles the documentation phase of the photovoice methodology is termed the critical-theoretic art-making model (Pearse, 1983, pp. 161–162), which defines art as critical reflection meant to make visible unjust social situations and disrupt the status quo. Photovoice participants have cited critical reflection as being an important part of their photography processes (Latz, 2012), and notions of disrupting the status quo through showcasing unjust social situations are emblematic of the Freirian (Freire 1970/2003, 1974/2007) principles that undergird the photovoice methodology.

The ever-growing and expanding methodologies and methods that exist under the umbrella of qualitative research have given rise to all manners of boundary crossing. Photovoice is an example. And within the photovoice methodology, both participants and researchers are encouraged to engage in data generation and presentation. Those data have aesthetic qualities and are artistic in nature.

A/r/tography

The practice of a/r/tography within education research highlights the identities of the individual engaged in inquiry as a simultaneous artist/researcher/teacher, hence the use of the forward slash. It is a form of arts-based research (Leavy, 2015). Springgay, Irwin, and Kind (2005) argued that arts-based research ought to become its own paradigm, one that is not beholden to the same value criteria as qualitative research, under which it is typically categorized. This proposed reconceptualization is illustrated through six renderings of a/r/tography, "an approach to research that is attentive to the sensual, tactile, and unsaid aspects of artist/researcher/teachers' lives" (p. 899): contiguity (roles of artist/researcher/teacher are contiguous as are the forms of art and writing), living inquiry (inquiry and life are synonymous), metaphor and metonymy (simultaneous absence and realization of something; allows for contextual ambiguity of meaning), openings (inquiry involves making openings, disrupting patterns), reverberations (allows the art making/researching/teaching to resonate, to sink in deeply), and excess (appeals to the senses rather than the intellect). A/r/tography is an arts-based research methodology wherein researchers inquire about educational ideas, acts, and approaches through artistic and aesthetic avenues; it is attentive to the co-location of art making, researching, and teaching, which are all seen as embodied acts and a way of being in the world. Springgay et al. noted that to engage in a/r/tography is to make "art and words that are not separate or illustrative of each other but instead, are interconnected and woven through each other to create additional meanings" (p. 899). Within the context of these six renderings, the authors suggested that to do a/r/tography is to live deeply and to make meaning vis-à-vis all possible affordances—thinking, feeling, seeing, sensing, touching, smelling, emoting, and so on.

A Three-Legged Theoretical Base

Photovoice was developed from three main sources: (a) feminism; (b) Frierian education for critical consciousness; and (c) participatory documentary photography (Wang & Burris, 1997).

Feminism(s)

Maguire (1987) defined feminism as (a) the belief that all women face oppression or exploitation to some degree; (b) commitment to comprehend how oppression works; and (c) commitment to work against oppression. So the question remains, how do we *do* feminism? For Maguire, one answer—and the most viable in her own experience—is feminist participatory research. This in mind, I assert that photovoice, which falls under the umbrella of participatory action research, is one way to *do* feminism.

Naples and Gurr (2014) reminded us that "[t]he burgeoning women's movements of the 1960s and 1970s brought with them challenges to traditional forms of social science" (p. 14). In large part, this is why we have photovoice today. While early action researchers had concerns about social inequities and sought to address and redress them, "they failed to include women as independent actors in their local projects or problematize gender oppression or heterosexism" (Lykes & Hershberg, 2012, p. 333). Feminist approaches to participatory action research address this failure. Wang and Burris (1997) noted that "feminist theory and practice has shed light on the male bias that has influenced participatory research" (p. 370). Through their seminal photovoice work with Chinese village women, Wang and Burris highlighted their feminist approach: "[a]s [Freirian] empowerment education has challenged traditional approaches to schooling, so have feminist critiques of positivist research methods and the construction of knowledge pushed new aims and methods of inquiry" (1994, p. 175). While Freire's work has been subjected to feminist criticism (hooks, 1994; Maguire, 1987), photovoice blends Freirian and feminist approaches to make space for participants to be authors of and authorities on their own lived experiences. Wang and Burris (1994) explained: "[g]rounded in an ideology of accountability, feminist scholars have contended that knowledge or practice that exploits or oppresses is unjustifiable. They have argued for an inclusive form of knowledge construction" (p. 174). Photovoice responds to this call.

Brisolara (2014) explained that the term *feminist theory* is broad and cuts across disciplines. Moreover, "there is no one, unifying feminist theory; neither does there exist a consensus on how diverse feminist theoretical contributions should be categorized" (p. 4). And Maguire (1987) noted that feminist research "consists of no single set of agree upon research guidelines or methods" (p. 91). Despite this, there are common themes among most iterations of feminist theory such as the importance of gender equity and working against oppression. Photovoice researchers would be well served to elucidate their particular application or version of feminist theory within any particular photovoice project.

Brisolara (2014) outlined the major feminist social research theories, which include: feminist empiricism; standpoint theories; critical theories, poststructural theories, and postmodern theories; global and postcolonial theories; Black feminist, Chicana, Indigenous, and race-based feminist theories; and sex, sexuality, queer, and lesbian theories. According to Brisolara, feminist standpoint theory posits that "where we are socially situated (i.e. where we stand) matters and has important implications for social and political power and the creation of knowledge" (p. 6). The application of this version of feminist theory to photovoice is has both theoretical and literal importance. Theoretically, photovoice places the standpoints of participants at the center of the work. Because photovoice is a form of participatory action research, participants typically have high levels of input throughout all aspects of the project. As such, their versions of the world are centered, honored, and brought forward. Where participants stand in the world is made clear and valued. Bringing forward individuals' social positions within the world creates the understandings essential for the beginnings and permutations of critical consciousness—an espoused outcome of the methodology. Let us consider this literally, physically as well. In asking participants to make photographic images, when those images are viewed, the images are what the participants' saw from their physical vantage point within the world. These images, these vantage points, these stances within the world, would not be seen—literally seen— otherwise. Feminist standpoint theory, therefore, undergirds and imprints the photovoice methodology both theoretically and physically.

Feminist standpoint theory was created "in the context of third world and postcolonial feminist challenges to the so-called dual systems of patriarchy and capitalism" (Naples & Gurr, 2014, p. 25). It represents a large bucket of theories including Black feminist thought (Collins, 2000/2009), differential oppositional consciousness (Sandoval, 2000), and feminist historical materialism (Hartsock, 1983). Its most basic premise is the criticality of centering women's experience within inquiry. Scholars who utilize feminist standpoint theory employ a wide array of methods and aim to carry out analyses of the intersections of a broad range of individual identity markers that impact persons' social agency such as race, ethnicity, and sexual orientation.

There are a variety of strands of feminist standpoint epistemology. For some scholars, standpoint refers to the actual lived experiences of particular marginalized persons in the social world. For others, it is relational. One standpoint cannot exist in the absence of a relationship to another. And for others still, it is a way to view a total community, not a position or relationship tied to particular individuals or specific groups of people. Despite the variation, it should be noted that "[f]eminist standpoint theorists typically resist focusing their analyses on individual actors removed from their social context" (Naples & Gurr, 2014, p. 32).

When considering theoretical underpinnings, we must also consider total conceptual frameworks used to approach inquiry. How do feminist theories shape, inform, and/or stem from specific epistemologies (nature of knowledge), ontologies (nature of being), and methodologies (nature of inquiry)? Even when left unannounced, researcher applications of epistemology are implicit within the products of research (e.g. papers, presentations). From a binary or paradigmatic view of social science research, quantitative and qualitative approaches are informed by vastly different epistemologies. Consider, for example, what constitutes new knowledge formation. Might the systematic inquiry of the career of a third grade teacher, by that third grade teacher, generate new knowledge? Why, or why not? Might the systematic inquiry of the test scores of thousands of third grade students, by an educational researcher, data generate new knowledge? Why, or why not? Which inquiry *counts* more? What about the generalizability of each? *Who* should do research? Whose research *counts*? Is knowledge uncovered or built? The answers to these questions hinge upon epistemologies. Various iterations of feminist theory can pose challenges to characteristics of dominant epistemologies. For example, that a positivist epistemology embodies characteristics such as objectivity, totality, certainty, androcentrism, and even misogyny may be identified, highlighted, and called into question through a feminist lens.

Just as feminist theory can imbue epistemology, it can also imbue ontology. Furthermore, and as a brief aside, it is unwise to even attempt to view epistemologies, ontologies, and methodologies as operating separately within the conceptual framework applied to any inquiry; there are necessary connections and synergies throughout the total framework, or the "superstructure for the work" (Ravitch & Riggin, 2017, p. 9). With regards to ontology, let us consider modernism. Those harboring a modernist ontology would argue that an objective reality exists. Moreover, someone with a modernist ontology would see all things as having elemental parts, which can be taken apart and examined discretely. Social scientists who ascribe to a modernist ontology view the social world in a similar fashion to those who study the natural world (e.g. geologists, biologists). Feminists critiques of this ontology may include the notions that objectivity is not possible, situatedness (social, cultural, temporal, physical) of the researcher and the research matters, and the whole is just as if not more important than the parts.

While no methodology or method is atheoretical, no methodology or method is inherently feminist (Brisolara, 2014)—photovoice included. It is one thing to acknowledge that photovoice has feminist underpinnings, and it is entirely another to embody actions aligned with feminism when carrying out a photovoice project. Brisolara noted that "feminist methodologies pay close attention to the ethical, policy, and political consequences of the practice of inquiry" (p. 20). So while photovoice researchers ought to be diligent in thinking through the consequences of photovoice projects (i.e. enact a feminist approach in methodology and methods), this does not mean all photovoice projects upend patriarchy, center the perspectives of the marginalized, promote equity, or influence policy in some positive way. To be sure, all methodological approaches have the potential to do more harm than good. Inequities, stereotypes, stigmas, and marginalization can all be amplified and reconstituted through photovoice work. Photovoice researchers must endeavor to be consistently cognizant of the potential consequences of the work throughout each phase of the methodology and execution of the various methods contained therein. One way to do this is to engage in acts of reflexivity throughout the process. Brisolara noted that reflexivity "combines an invitation to become aware of one's perspective and potential blind sides, as well as to thoughtfully document one's developing perspective" (p. 34). Keeping a researcher's journal, making analytic memos and concept maps, and/or having ongoing dialogue with a critical friend throughout the research process can foster reflexivity (Pillow, 2003).

Weiler (1988) outlined three major tenets of feminist epistemology and methodology, which can be a useful model when considering photovoice: (a) research must be situated within an acknowledged male-dominated society at the onset; (b) emphasis must be placed on the actual lived experiences and everyday lives of women; and (c) a politicized commitment to changing the existing social order must be in place. Taking each of these tenets one by one can highlight the specific ways in which feminism underscores the photovoice approach. In addition, their utility within the methodology's enactment is also important to consider. Caroline C. Wang and Mary Ann Burris carried out the first photovoice study (Wang & Burris, 1994; Wang, Burris, & Ping, 1996). They worked with village women in rural southwestern China, a marginalized group within their society. These women were asked to document—through photography—specific aspects of their daily lives and unique perspectives. Space was made within the larger project, of which photovoice was only one part, for these women to share their images, narrations of those images, thoughts, and experiences germane to the study. Therefore, the first and second tenets above were embodied and honored. The initial exhibition that flowed from this project was a major event, attracting over 3,000 common people and a number of interested local and national journalists at the first opening exhibition in Chengjiang County (Wang, Burris, & Ping, 1996). The media can impact public opinion as well as policy. Having such an audience at this exhibition was a major catalyst for change. The subsequent events and other forms of dissemination that transpire toward the end of the process are significant in influencing policy, which is an example of the third tenet above.

Though photovoice has been used with both men and women, the tenets of feminist espistemology and methodology still underpin its use. Women are marginalized in patriarchal societies and cultures. Most societies and cultures are patriarchal. But women are not the only marginalized subgroup within any given society or culture. Photovoice researchers do well to draw from an empathic stance related to project participants. Working with, and alongside, marginalized groups is typical within photovoice projects. According to Wang, Burris, and Ping (1996), feminist scholars "have argued for a form of knowledge construction that includes those who are the subjects of research" (p. 1392), and this is certainly the case within and throughout the photovoice process. When carrying out photovoice projects, it is important to provide those who engage with or consume the work contextualized information about the social and cultural realities and nested systems within which the participants live. For example, Bronfenbrenner's (1976) work, which draws heavily on Kurt Lewin's ideas, could be helpful in explaining nested systems. What is the texture of participants' social and cultural positions, what is the best way to bring the marginality of these positions to light, and how can participants be engaged in dialogue about this? Additionally, how can all this be done in a way that pushes against deficit models or perspectives? All these questions, among others, should be addressed throughout the process in an effort to embody feminist theory and embodied action. Finally, within feminist research endeavors, the methods are oftentimes a major part of the findings. In other words, the journey may be an important part of the destination within photovoice work, and the process is sometimes more telling than the product.

Feminist researchers are concerned with the lived and day-to-day experiences of women just as photovoice researchers are concerned with the lived and day-to-day experiences of project participants. The dignity, personhood, wholeness, and humanity of participants are paramount; humanness is not reducible to a number or a statistic. While this stance may seem to be oppositional and perhaps adversarial to quantitative approaches to inquiry, in many ways, photovoice can be leveraged in tandem with relevant quantitative data (e.g. survey data, census data) to bring fullness, story, emotion, and humanness to the lived realities of project participants. For example, think of a photovoice project wherein the following research question is addressed: How do secondary students describe their ideal study spaces? What kinds of quantitative data might help situate the total study's context? The potential importance of this contextual data cannot be overstated.

Photovoice is a form of participatory action research, and because photovoice researchers and participants are interested in reaching policy makers with the findings of their projects, an inherent desire to affect change is evident. Connecting the findings with those who have the power and position to participate in the policy making and changing process is critical. This process can be difficult, as the appropriate person (or persons) is not always apparent. Educational entity policies are often nested within broader reaching policies. For example, within an institution of higher education, a departmental-level policy cannot typically supersede a university policy. Again, Bronfenbrenner's (1976) ecological theory is an excellent model to consider when strategizing about spurring on change and knowing where energies should be focused. When thinking about policy change, locus of power must be considered, thereby making the process a politicized one. In their discussion of photovoice, Wang, Burris, and Ping (1996) noted that the union of feminist theory and policy yields political commitment.

Freirian Education for Critical Consciousness

Just as Freire used images as catalysts for dialogue during cultural circles (Freire, 1974/2007), photovoice uses images to engage groups of participants in discussions about their photographs and lives. Freire's drawings represented community realities, and photovoice images are community realities. Photovoice takes "[Freire's] concept one step further so that the images of the community are made by the people themselves" (Wang & Burris, 1997, p. 370). This approach allows participants to identify community issues, critically consider contributing factors, and move toward implementation of solutions, while raising critical consciousness among participants and creating social change (Carlson, Engebretson, & Chamberlain, 2006).

Freire (1970/2003) recognized three levels of consciousness that influenced how individuals interpret their realities and how those interpretations influence behavior. The levels are magical, naïve, and critical. At the lowest, or magical, level of consciousness, individuals view themselves as inherently inferior while silently existing and unknowingly reifying the status quo. At the naïve level, individuals view their social structures as corrupt yet livable. While they recognize injustice, they do not attempt to understand or analyze it. Rather, they exhibit lateral violence through blaming peers for their social situations. At the critical level of consciousness, individuals realize that their actions can either maintain or disrupt their social realities (Carlson et al., 2006; Freire, 1970/2003, 1974/2007). Freire (1974/2007) explained: "[c]ritical consciousness is integrated with reality; naïve consciousness superimposes itself onto reality; and fanatical [i.e. magical] consciousness, whose pathological naïveté leads to the irrational, adapts to reality" (p. 39). Freire used a particular process to move individuals toward critical consciousness:

> On entering a new community, he would take time for informal conversation with the inhabitants. He would listen specifically for emotionally charged connections to people's daily lives. These emotionally charged themes would be translated into drawings, which he would use to stimulate collective introspection and discussion. The influence of culture on the individual and the influence of the individual on culture were always the emphases of the discussions and the cocreated knowledge. The goal was to engage the people to participate in their own learning, a combination of action and reflection that he called praxis.
>
> *Carlson et al., 2006, pp. 837–838*

A similar approach is used vis-à-vis the photovoice method.

Participatory Documentary Photography

Documentary Photography and the Participatory Turn

Following on the heels of the poignant and arresting black and white photographs that were generated for publicity through sponsorships from United States government agencies, the Farm Security Administration under the leadership of Roy Stryker and the Works Progress Administration, new kinds of publications where images overshadowed text came about and affected society's consciousness. *You Have Seen Their Faces* (Caldwell & Bourke-White, 1937/1995) and *Let Us Now Praise Famous Men* (Agree & Evans, 1939/2001) provided raw and searing images of the lives of poor rural Southerners and sharecroppers in the rural South, respectively. These books held the gravity of their predecessor's similar work such as Riis's (1890/2010) *How the Other Half Lives*. Other examples followed, such as Banish's *City Families* (1976), documenting families in their homes in Chicago and London. One of the most well-known contemporary examples of documentary photography is *Humans of New York* (Stanton, 2013, 2015, 2017), a project that began as a blog in 2010 and has since resulted in two books. Yet all the aforementioned examples lack the participatory dimension that holds such prominence within photovoice. Worth and Adair's (1972) work was pivotal in asking questions about who is best suited to serve in the role of documentarian in the pursuit of conveying aspects of a particular culture. They wrote: "[o]ur object in the summer of 1966 was to determine whether we could teach people with a culture different than ours to make motion pictures depicting their culture and themselves as *they* saw fit" (p. 11, italics in original).

Jo Spence, Wendy Ewald, and Jim Hubbard

Documentary photography has been used to raise awareness about individuals and societies. Typically, photographers are outsiders in relation to the subjects and settings they photograph. Photovoice assumes that those within the group or culture being documented have more expertise and insight than outsiders. In her collaborations with children, the work of Wendy Ewald (e.g. 1985, 1996, 2000, 2001, 2002; Ewald, Hyde, & Lord, 2012) serves as an example of the expansion of documentary photography to include the images created by the subjects of documentaries. Spence (1995) explained:

> Community photographers are encouraging people to photograph each other, friends and family, then their social environment. This provides immediate feedback for discussion, provides aids for storytelling and reading, and makes it possible to look at the world differently. People can discover how to relate to themselves and to others more positively when armed with images of themselves—images which counteract stereotypes usually seen in the mass media.
>
> *p. 35*

Harper (2012) argued that Wendy Ewald's (1985) work, *Portraits and Dreams*, was the major watershed moment for those considering placing cameras in the hands of participants. Ewald and others such as Jim Hubbard (1994, 1996) have provided creative and innovative models of participatory documentary photography, which undergird the photovoice method.

Born into Brothels

What if children—born and raised in Indian brothels—could tell their stories through photography? Participatory documentary photography hit the big screen in 2005 with the release of a documentary that answered that question. *Born into Brothels: Calcutta's Red Light Kids* (Briski & Kauffman, 2004) tells the story of the children of Calcutta's red light district and their interactions with Zana Briski, a photographer who taught the children how to use cameras and take photographs.

This award-winning documentary caught the attention of many, and amplified the use of photovoice among community organization and academic researchers alike (e.g. Kaplan, 2013).

Aims of Photovoice

While this book is mainly targeted toward researchers operating within academic contexts, engagement in participatory action research must not be simply about advancing what is known about a particular thing by contributing the findings and implications of those findings to traditional outlets for such knowledge like academic conferences, journal articles, and books. That type of work is certainly critical, and there are ways in which photovoice research can and does make those kinds of contributions. However, we must bring the work into the practical realm; we must act. Participatory *action* research is not called participatory action research for nothing. Action is paramount. But we ought not act alone.

Reaching policy makers is a vital aim of this research approach. This is, in fact, where a lot of the action takes place. And reaching policy makers is one of many ways subsequent and sustainable action can happen through photovoice. As will be noted in the next chapter, sometimes it is appropriate to identify and even contact key policy makers as an initial step when embarking on a photovoice project. But connecting with policy makers can occur at any point during the project's life, and sometimes making multiple contacts during a project makes sense as well.

In a study I was engaged in recently, a group of students/co-researchers and I met with an institutional agent from the research site where we were engaging first year community college students in a study about their needs. This individual was an ardent supporter of the work and understood the ways in which the findings could be impactful to a broad audience, which could certainly include interested individuals far beyond the project's site. At the same time, she knew our work could shed light on how these students could be better served. And she wanted to know how. During this meeting, she articulated exactly what she needed—a one-page bulleted list of findings and implications. She wanted answers to the following questions: What did we find, and what should they do about it (they being her and her colleagues)? While this individual and her colleagues are not the official architects of every policy impacting the ways in which they work with students, they are certainly enacting at least some of those policies on a daily basis. Understanding what was found during the study was important to her as both an institutional policy maker and actor at the site as well as a policy actor when it comes to policies impacting the institution that are external to the institution (e.g. state law, federal regulations, mandates from accrediting bodies).

What Are We Trying to Do?

Photovoice researchers typically have three primary aims: (a) encourage participants to document elements of their lives within their own terms; (b) raise levels of critical consciousness within participants through critical dialogue; and (c) reach policy makers with project findings to catalyze positive change, which will address the needs and/or issues identified by the participants (Wang & Burris, 1997). While these are the espoused goals, Catalani and Minkler (2010), for example, reviewed a total of 37 articles germane to health and public health to better understand the application of the photovoice methodology. One of the most salient elements of this piece is their photovoice impact model (p. 446), which suggests that training plus research/documentation and discussion results in three outcomes: (a) action and advocacy to affect policy change; (b) increased understandings of community needs and assets; and (c) individual empowerment. It is heartening to see that the espoused aims were met—with some variation—within the articles reviewed. The purpose of this section is to flesh out these aims and explain how to achieve them. This is important as "the early [photovoice] literature left several questions unanswered . . . [and] did not provide a model or tools for how to evaluate photovoice processes and outcomes" (Catalani & Minkler, 2010, p. 447).

Life Documentation and Narration

By placing cameras in the hands of participants, photovoice enables individuals of various social statuses to document the most salient aspects of their lives. This approach decentralizes the role of the researcher and honors the authenticity of participants' vantage points. As authors of their own experiences, photovoice positions participants as active instead of "passive subjects of other people's intentions and images" (Wang & Burris, 1997, p. 371). While I take issue with the notion of "giving voice," it is a common idiom within the feminist literature, and I believe it is an important aim of the photovoice methodology. But I suggest the use of the phrase "making space" because, typically, those of us in a position to carry out or facilitate a photovoice project have considerable power and privilege. Perhaps I prefer to make space for a voice rather than give one—I do not see that kind of "giving" as something I can do. I should note that "making space" is not an original term. I first encountered the phrase when interacting with Sheared and Sissel's (2001) work. Becker (2007) noted that "[n]o matter what the makers of representations do, if the users don't do their part, the story doesn't get told, or doesn't get told as the story the makers intended" (p. 286). This resonates so much as I consider the role of the photovoice researchers in making space for the life narrations of the participants to come through loud and clear. We must keep in mind that "[h]umans communicated with pictures long before they developed the kind of non-pictographic language that are you currently reading" (McKim, 1980, p. 129). We must also realize that visual life narration has become a normative and habitual online practice as was explained within Chapter 1.

Building Critical Consciousness

The photovoice methodology draws heavily from Freire's notion of empowerment education, which "involves people in group efforts to identify their problems, to critically assess social and historical roots of problems, to envision a healthier society, and to develop strategies to overcome obstacles in achieving their goals" (Wallerstein & Berstein, 1995, p. 380). Communal engagement in empowerment education often results in the development of critical consciousness, a belief in one's ability to affect his or her personal and societal worlds. Moreover, "Freire's central premise is that education is not neutral and takes place in the context of peoples' lives" (Wallerstein & Berstein, p. 381). Education can influence people to become passive objects, or active subjects, in their societies and their lives. Freire's approach champions the latter through group dialogue where all voices are honored as co-participants in the process. The goal is to create new knowledge germane to the local social realities and built steps for action from that knowledge. The three-step process Freire used is directly crosswalked into the photovoice process—listening, dialoguing, and acting.

Stage two in Freire's educational process, dialoguing, is catalyzed by discussions of *codes*—objects that represent community realities. These codes can take the form of photographs. Within photovoice, however, these codes are generated by those engaged in the dialogue—the participants. This is a departure from Freire's approach, a departure that is attentive to the full complement of the theoretical underpinnings of the methodology.

Thomas et al. (2014) explained that "[w]hile much work has been done to develop programs to foster critical consciousness and civic engagement, valid and reliable measures of critical consciousness development are needed" (p. 486), That need is being met. Critical consciousness can be thought of as an element of self-identity and a critical way of seeing oneself in the world, having an awareness and understanding of power relations and social structures that oppress and privilege. It can also be thought of as sociopolitical development and civic engagement. The purpose of Thomas et al.'s work was to develop a scale for assessing critical consciousness, which they termed the Critical Consciousness Inventory (CCI). The instrument showed promise and "may be useful in helping to assess changes in critical consciousness development . . . in youth" (p. 493). While assessments of levels of critical consciousness can certainly be made through the analysis of qualitative data (i.e. interview data), such an instrument could be seen as a useful tool within photovoice researchers' toolkits. Using the CCI as a pre- and post-test could be an interesting way—hopefully one of many—to understand whether or not engagement in the photovoice process contributed to a rise in levels of critical consciousness among participants.

Measuring or gauging another person's, or even our own, level of critical consciousness is elusive. This is largely because "Freire did not provide a clear and parsimonious conception" (Diemer, McWhirter, Ozer, & Rapa, 2015, p. 812) of critical consciousness. While we might *know it when we see it*, translating that understanding into a piece of scholarship is another story. Developing a precise definition of critical consciousness is difficult, as there is no consensus within the extant literature. Moreover, it is hard to detangle critical consciousness from other related concepts within the psychometric testing lexicon. Nonetheless, since the emergence of the CCI (Thomas et al., 2014) several additional measures have been developed such as the Measure of Adolescent Critical Consciousness (McWhirter & McWhirter, 2016), the Contemporary Critical Consciousness Measure (Shin, Ezeofor, Smith, Welch, & Goodrich, 2016), and the Critical Consciousness Scale (Diemer, Rapa, Park, & Perry, 2014). Again, these measures may have efficacy for photovoice researchers seeking to find way to assess whether of not this particular aim of the method is met.

Building Reflective Consciousness

Are there other forms of consciousness that could be nurtured by photovoice? Thomas et al. (2014) explained that "critical consciousness includes the importance of developing the ability for reflection" (p. 487). Concerted reflection is an activity many photovoice participants experience throughout the process. Holtby, Klein, Cook, and Travers (2015) said "photovoice ... gave [participants] space to reflect" (p. 330) during the course of their study. One of the goals of Wilson and Flicker (2015) was thoughtful reflection among participants. Han and Oliffe (2016) suggested that photovoice may have therapeutic qualities. Strack, Lovelace, Davis Jordan, and Holmes (2010) used the phrase "photovention," which they used to describe individual-focused photovoice projects. Here, the intended change is within the participant; they note three areas: knowledge, attitude, and behavior. There may be some connection between what these various authors are alluding to and what I have termed photovoice for reflective consciousness (Latz, 2012). We must harken back to the original research questions driving the inquiry—or at least the topic/goals/outcomes to best understand and construct the specifics of how we imagine the process affecting the participants.

It should be noted that not all photovoice participants benefit from the process in the same way. According to Wang, Yi, Toa, and Carovano (1998) participant benefits are based on participants' levels of power (p. 82). They noted the following as potential advantages for all: contribute to change, improve status, exchange information, and gain credibility. These are the potential advantages for participants with the most power: learn from others, do valued work, innovate, and recognize others. Finally, here are the potential advantages for participants with the least power: represent self and community, build self-esteem and status, show appreciation, build relationships, and increase access to power. When photovoice projects are assessed, considerations should be made relative to how much power each participant has upon entering the project.

Psychological Empowerment

Mamary, McCright, and Roe's (2007) two-tiered qualitative study involved in-depth interviewing (tier one) and photovoice (tier two) to understand the perceptions of general health and specific HIV risk among non-gay identified African American men who have sex with other men. One of the participants in the study said that the "project made me take stock of my life and, to not make big changes but I live a pretty different life" (Mamary et al., 2007, p. 367). This was similar to what I found among the photovoice participants with whom I have worked. Participation requires participants to pause and consider their lives in some way. This can lead to growth, critical reflection, and in some cases, critical consciousness—depending on the purpose and topic of the study. Mamary et al. (2007) used the term psychological empowerment, which "includes beliefs that goals can be achieved, awareness about resources and factors that hinder or enhance one's efforts to achieve those goals, and efforts to fulfill the goals" (Zimmerman, 1995, p. 582), to describe the change experienced by their participants.

Reaching Policy Makers

Lastly, photovoice aims to garner the attention of policy makers. The power of the visual image allows the photovoice technique to gain the attention of policy makers in a way that words cannot. Reaching policy makers typically occurs through exhibitions where participants showcase their photographs. Photovoice projects have resulted in policy changes as the following extract illustrates:

> A few weeks after the hanging of the first exhibit at the teen center, an assistant to the state comptroller came to the teen center for a meeting. He paused at a 12-year-old photovoice participant's photograph of a crumbling classroom ceiling at a local middle school with a caption that read: 'My middle school is a bad school. The ceiling is falling apart and it is not good.' ... The comptroller wrote down the name of the school and promised to look into the matter.
>
> Strack, Magill, & McDonagh, 2004, p. 53

Building a Conceptual Framework for Photovoice Projects

When building a conceptual framework for a photovoice study, it is important to remember that "the researcher's theories of being (ontology) and knowing (epistemology) influence who she is, the positions she assumes, the methodologies she engages during the research process, and the advocacy or actions she mobilizes" (Lykes & Hershberg, 2012, p. 351). Moreover, a researcher's ontological and epistemological frames, which are often the outcome of life experiences and disciplinary training (e.g. geology, psychology, history), influence the kinds of research questions asked. A study's guiding research questions both shape and are shaped by the researcher's conceptual framework for any given study. According to Ravitch and Riggan (2017), "a defining characteristic of conceptual frameworks is that they *evolve*" (p. 13, italics in original).

In addition,

> [a] conceptual framework allows you to make reasoned, defensible choices about how you might explore research topics or themes heretofore underexplored, explore existing research questions in new contexts, and/or reexamine established topics or questions using different theoretical, epistemological, and methodological frames and approaches.
>
> *p. 17*

So, how might a conceptual framework for photovoice project look? Figure 2.1 showcases a potential conceptual model for a photovoice project. It should be noted that this is merely a possibility; conceptual models for specific projects will certainly contain variations of this configuration and additional nuance. Moreover, this model and all its discrete components are constantly affected by all the people involved in the process—along with the context(s) within which the process is taking place. At the top of the model we see the interplay of the extant literature on the topic at hand/researcher's personal experiences/research "problem," research questions, and theoretical frameworks. Here I place the word *problem* in quotation marks because while this word is often a part of the research lexicon—specifically among thesis and dissertation committee members (e.g. "What is the problem your study is meant to address?")—not all research endeavors to solve a problem. Nonetheless, these three elements, which inform one another, provide the impetuses for and clues about the ontologies, epistemologies, and methodologies employed. Methods, analytical approaches, and data generated flow from the methodology. The methodological literature informs the employment of methods and the analytical steps taken. The methods, data, and analytical approach all have influence on the shape of the findings. Because the photovoice methodology borrows concepts and techniques from both participatory action research and arts based research, these also affect the generation of the findings and the manner in which the findings are placed on display during/in an exhibition. The data generation or collection process, the exhibition(s), and the actions that take place after the exhibition(s) are typically where the aims of the photovoice methodology are met. It should also be noted that the interplay of the extant literature on the topic at hand/researcher's personal experiences/research "problem," research questions, and theoretical frameworks

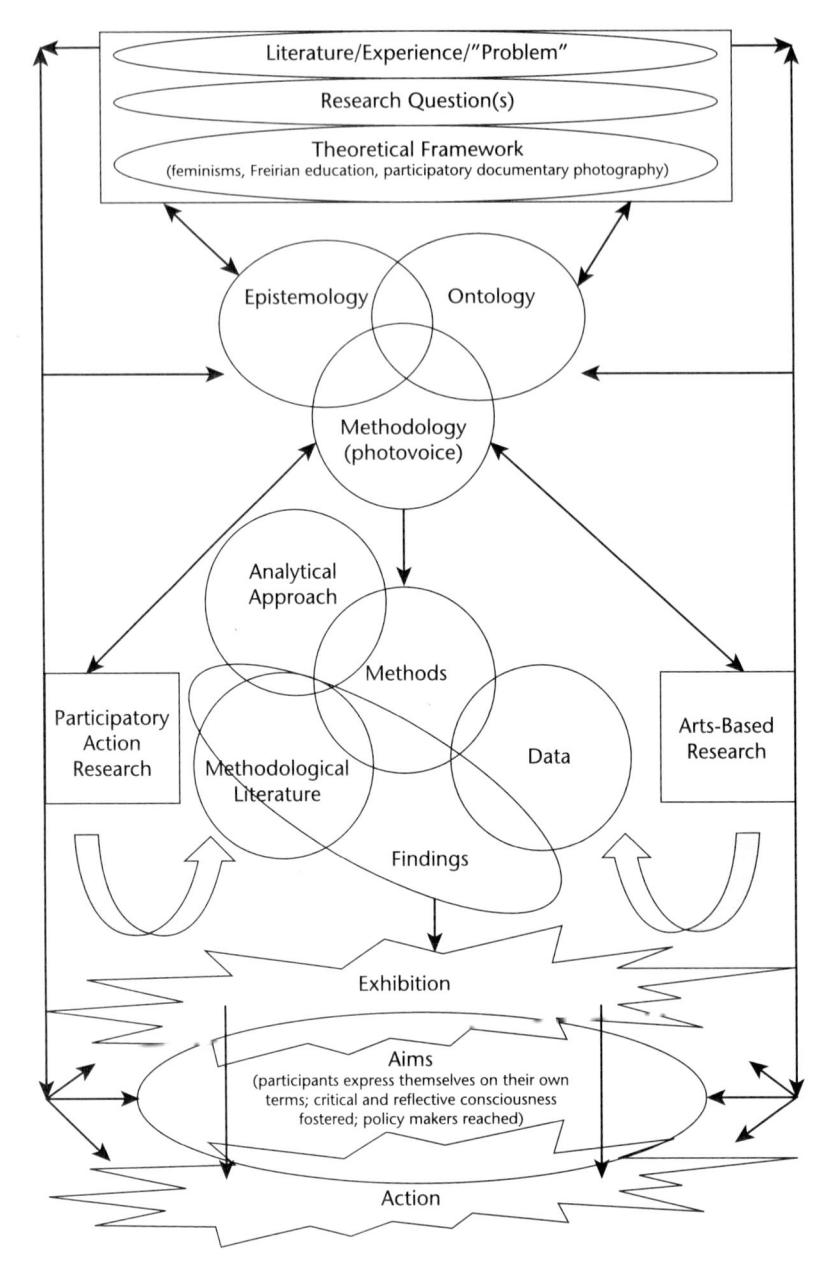

FIGURE 2.1 This illustration is an emergent conceptual model of a photovoice project.

affects the totality of the work at each stage of the process. For example, the exhibition could be framed in such a way that it addresses or answers the original research questions that prompted the study in the first place.

Ravitch and Riggan (2017) described an empirical study's conceptual framework as being both a "guide and ballast" (p. 194) for the work. In other words, it assists researchers in knowing where to go and remembering from where they came. It helps us, as researchers, to explain what we did and why. In addition, Hesse-Biber and Piatelli (2012) said

> [m]ethods are simply research techniques, tools that get at the research problem, whereas epistemology shapes our research questions and theories we hold about the social world. Methodology can be thought of as a bridge between epistemology and method, shaping *how* we approach and conduct research.
>
> p. 176, italics in original

Qualitative research is notoriously messy, and Figure 2.1 is an oversimplified distillation of a complex, dynamic, emergent process. Stringer (2014) noted that:

> [a]s experience will show, action research is not a neat, orderly activity that allows participants to proceed step-by-step to the end of the process. People will find themselves working backward through the routines, repeating processes, revising procedures, rethinking interpretations, leapfrogging steps or stages, and sometimes making radical changes in direction.
>
> pp. 9–10

As such, when in the midst of a photovoice project you can sometimes forget how you got started in the first place, so referring back to this, or a similar, schematic is helpful in refocusing and recentering the work. Having an illustration of the conceptual framework can also be helpful when describing the study. This level of detail and depth will likely be too much for policy makers, but it will be advantageous when communicating your work in academic settings such as conference presentations, manuscripts for scholarly journals, or doctoral dissertation defenses.

Theoretical Tinkering

Higgins (2016) argued that photovoice has become unintelligible. We must consider the ways in which the theoretical underpinnings of photovoice have evolved, shape shifted, and been appropriated since the advent of photo novella in the early 1990s (Wang & Burris, 1994). He noted that critically and temporally examining the original theoretical foundation of the methodology "is a differential tracking of their [the theories'] growth in order to put to work that which photovoice is (not) theoretically framed by: praxis and feminist standpoint theories which exceed that which was originally mapped onto photovoice" (p. 681). This kind of thinking about the methodology generates a space ripe for reconsidering concepts crucial to photovoice such as "empowerment and voice" (p. 681). Moreover, photovoice researchers ought to consider *which* feminist theory (or theories) undergird their approach to the methodology. That theory should be clearly communicated and be embodied throughout the enactment of the process.

Black Feminist Photovoice

Salazar Pèrez, Ruiz Guerrero, and Mora's (2016) work is an excellent example of what Higgins (2016) referred to in urging photovoice researchers to name the specific feminist theory underpinning their approach to the methodology.

This was a college classroom-based project, photovoice as pedagogy. These authors named their approach Black feminist photovoice, drawing upon the work of scholars such as bell hooks (1995) and Patricia Hill Collins (2000/2009), which "explicitly politicizes the field [in this case, the field of early childhood education] by encouraging critical reflection of power dynamics present in the lived experiences of the marginalized" (Salazar Pèrez, Ruiz Guerrero, & Mora, 2016, p. 42). This approach also brings intersectionality to the forefront—laying bare the ways in which power works within the interplay of various identity constructs (e.g. gender, race, ethnicity, nationality, class, language, ability, sexual orientation, religion).

Related to the foundational theoretical frames upon which photovoice was built, contemporary photovoice researchers' work is "grounded in, but moving beyond" (Salazar Pèrez et al., 2016, p. 42) those original frames, calling to mind Higgins's (2016) work.

Students in the course explored the following forms of power: structural (systemic oppressions), disciplinary (oppression from dominant group), hegemonic (oppression comes from one's state of mind), and interpersonal (oppression within daily interactions, stemming from intersectional identities). Students took photographs of abstract images, wrote narrations, and presented their work in groups.

Critical Race Theory

The aim of Kessi and Cornell's (2016) paper was to "discuss the experiences of black [sic] students at [University of Cape Town], to voice their views on transformation, and to build a framework for resisting and altering the negative discourses associated with the transformation discourse" (p. 2). The transformation discourse, in this context, refers to the shifting racial landscape within many South African universities—from a majority White population to a majority Black population. In total, 24 Black students participated in this study. Three findings were gleaned from the work: out of focus: racial identity and belonging; daily experiences of segregation, othering, and inequality; and the Whiteness of UCT: cultural and symbolic exclusion. While these researchers did not employ critical race theory (CRT) (Crenshaw, Gotanda, Peller, & Thomas, 1995) within their analysis, I think the use of CRT could add another level of sophistication to their discussion of the findings. While some researchers have employed CRT within their work (e.g. Allen, 2010), this theoretical application—as well as similar theoretical applications (e.g. LatCrit) (Solarzano & Delgado Bernal, 2001)—has been underused.

Is Photovoice Queer?

Ingrey (2013) suggested that photovoice has the possibility of being a queer—specifically a genderqueer—methodology, especially in light of her use of the approach to understand how secondary students understand and explicate gender and gendered spaces. Ingrey's inquiry was focused on school washrooms; this particular paper zeroed in on one aspect of a larger study. She drew inspiration from school mapping, a/r/tography, and photovoice's propensity to excavate subjugated knowledge. She also drew heavily on Foucault's work. Specifically, she viewed the washroom as a space wherein students engaged in various levels of gendered acts of self-regulation and complicity with power structures; students negotiated the panopticon, a mechanism of disciplinary power (Foucault, 1975/1995). Ingrey (2013) also saw the washroom as a version of the closet, where students must constantly navigate gender and sexual identities within the school space.

While I would not categorize Ingrey's (2013) work as a photovoice study—at least not what was put forward in this paper, she brings up an important question about the theoretical framing that can inform photovoice studies. This work could be thought of as a photo-elicitation study wherein participant-generated photographs were used. Only two participants' data were presented, and no mention of an exhibition was made. Moreover, participants took photographs within washroom spaces. This certainly raises ethical concerns about privacy, and the act of photography within a washroom space could place participants at risk. The reliance on Foucault's work is apt, however, as notions of subjugated knowledge excavation and using photography to understand the influence of the panopticon on secondary students is fascinating and illustrative.

Indigenous Standpoints

Higgins (2014) asserted that photovoice methods can reconstitute and affirm the social realities they aim to critically call into question. Bringing the Eurocentric and occularcentric nature of photovoice to light, Higgins called for the infusion of indigenous frameworks into the enactment of the methodology.

Higgins (2014) asserted that past attempts to modify photovoice to account for cultural context took place within the methods employed. He noted, however, that theoretical adjustments are necessary to "rebraid" (p. 211) photovoice methodologically and placed the focal points of his rebraiding toward the following: feminist standpoint theory and praxis. Feminist standpoint theorists argue that those within a given community are those who can best understand the issues facing those who make up the community. And historically, feminist standpoint theory has been used within and against patriarchal communities. Wang and Burris's (1994) work is a prime example.

Higgin's (2014) suggested an infusion of indigenous standpoint theory (Nakata, 2007) as a way to rebraid the theoretical underpinnings of the methodology to make it more attentive to a variety of community contexts. Nakata asserted that the standpoint of many indigenous peoples is at the interface of two (or more) cultures—indigenous and Western. Three gerunds guide Nakata's assertion, to which photovoice researchers must be attentive: (a) contesting knowledge space(s); (b) shaping persons' agency; and (c) embodying tensions. Put differently, which knowledge counts in the cultural interface is contested; the cultural interface shapes social agency; and the tensions within the cultural interface are experienced by (dichotomously racialized) bodies.

While acknowledging Freire's (1974/2007) influence on the photovoice methodology, Higgins (2014) called for another infusion—that of indigenous praxis (Grande, 2008). Indigenous praxis acknowledges that Western critical theories and indigenous ways of knowing are not the same. We may ask ourselves, for example, whether or not aspects of colonialism (e.g. individualism) are brought to the surface, questioned, examined, problematized, or made manifest—or even enacted—within the photovoice process.

It should be noted that Higgins's (2014) work is not meant to criticize feminist standpoint or Western critical theories, he simply suggested that researchers broaden the palette of theoretical underpinnings for the photovoice methodology so its use is as beneficial as possible to all involved. And while Higgins said his aim is "to keep [the photovoice] methodology fluid" (p. 213), it should be noted that flexibility has long been cited as one of the strengths of the methodology (e.g. Wang & Burris, 1997). This notion of theoretical rebraiding is useful nonetheless, as it gives us, as photovoice researchers, additional ways to think about the concept of voice. For example, do places have voices? Consider the ways in which various worldviews, epistemologies, and ontologies impact the response to this question. Western critical theory, with its roots in an anthropocentric worldview, may make it impossible to say yes in response to this question. Higgins suggested the following photography prompt as a way to think through the aforementioned question: "if this place-site could tell a story, what would it be?" (p. 214). This prompt is an apt example of tinkering with methods, theory, and ethics as a way to substantively move the photovoice methodology, thereby making it more attentive to contexts.

Summary

Within this chapter, I presented the theoretical underpinnings of the photovoice methodology as well as its aims. Photovoice is build on a three-legged theoretical stool: (a) feminisms; (b) Freire's approaches to education; and (c) participatory documentary photography. This foundation is closely related to the aims of photovoice: (a) make space for participants to document and share aspects of the lives on their own terms; (b) promote critical consciousness within participants; and (c) reach policy makers to affect positive change in accordance to the findings of the inquiry. As researchers, we must hold both the theories and aims of the methodology in mind as we engage the process. I also put forward a potential conceptual model for a photovoice project. Within the chapter that follows, the first five steps of the process are fleshed out: identification, invitation, education, documentation, and narration.

References

Agee, J., & Evans, W. (2001). *Let us now praise famous men*. Boston, MA: Mariner Books. (Original work published in 1939.)

Allen, D., & Hutchinson, T. (2009). Using PAR or abusing its good name?: The challenges and surprises of photovoice and film in a study of chronic illness. *International Journal of Qualitative Methods*, 8(2), 115–128. Retrieved from https://ejournals.library.ualberta.ca/index.php/IJQM/article/view/1194/5406

Allen, Q. (2010). Racial microaggressions: The schooling experiences of Black middle-class males in Arizona's secondary schools. *Journal of African American Males in Education*, 1, 125–143.

Banish, R. (1976). *City families: Chicago and London*. New York: Pantheon Books.

Barone, T., & Eisner, E. W. (2012). *Arts based research*. Thousand Oaks, CA: Sage.

Becker, H. S. (2007). *Telling about society*. Chicago, IL: University of Chicago Press.

Bogdan, R. C., & Biklen, S. K. (2007). *Qualitative research for education: An introduction to theory and methods* (5th edn). Boston, MA: Pearson.

Bradbury, H., Mirvis, P., Neilsen, E., & Pasmore, W. (2008). Action research at work: Creating the future following the path from Levin. In P. Reason & H. Bradbury (Eds.), *The Sage handbook of action research: Participative inquiry and practice* (pp. 77–92). Thousand Oaks, CA: Sage.

Briski, Z., & Kauffman, R. (Directors). (2004). *Born into brothels: Calcutta's red light kids* (motion picture). USA: THINKFilm.

Brisolara, S. (2014). Feminist theory: Its domains and applications. In S. Brisolara, D. Seigart, & S. SenGupta (Eds.), *Feminist evaluation and research: Theory and practice* (pp. 3–41). New York: The Guilford Press.

Bronfenbrenner, U. (1976). The experimental ecology of education. *Educational Researcher*, 5(9), 5–15.

Caldwell, E., & Bourke-White, M. (1995). *You have seen their faces*. Athens, GA: University of Georgia Press. (Original work published in 1937.)

Carlson, E. D., Engebretson, J., & Chamberlain, R. M. (2006). Photovoice as a social process of critical consciousness. *Qualitative Health Research*, 16, 836–852.

Catalani, C., & Minkler, M. (2010). Photovoice: A review of the literature in health and public health. *Health Education & Behavior, 37*, 424–451. doi: 101177/1090198109342084

Collins, P. H. (2009). *Black feminist thought: Knowledge, consciousness, and the politics of empowerment.* New York: Routledge Classics. (Original work published in 2000.)

Crenshaw, K., Gotanda, N., Peller, G., & Thomas, K. (Eds.). (1995). *Critical race theory: The key writings that formed the movement.* New York: The New Press.

Diemer, M. A., McWhirter, E. H., Ozer, E. J., & Rapa, L. J. (2015). Advances in the conceptualization of critical consciousness. *Urban Review, 47*, 809–823. doi: 10.1007/s11256-015-0336-7

Diemer, M. A., Rapa, L. J., Park, C. J., & Perry, J. C. (2014). Development and validation of the Critical Consciousness Scale. *Youth & Society.* doi: 10.1177/0044118X14538289

Ewald, W. (1985). *Portraits and dreams: Photographs and stories by children of the Appalachians.* New York: Writers and Readers Publishing.

Ewald, W. (1996). *I dreamed I had a girl in my pocket: The story of an Indian village.* New York: Umbra Editions.

Ewald, W. (2000). *Secret games: Collaborative works with children 1969–1999.* New York: Scalo.

Ewald, W. (2001). *I wanna take me a picture: Teaching photography and writing to children.* Boston, MA: Beacon.

Ewald, W. (2002). *The best part of me: Children talk about their bodies in pictures and words.* New York: Little, Brown and Company.

Ewald, W., Hyde, K., & Lord, L. (2012). *Literacy & justice through photography: A classroom guide.* New York: Teachers College Press.

Freire, P. (2003). *Pedagogy of the oppressed.* New York: Continuum. (Original work published in 1970.)

Freire, P. (2007). *Education for critical consciousness.* New York: Continuum. (Original work published in 1974.)

Foucault, M. (1995). *Discipline and punish: The birth of the prison* (2nd edn). (A. Sheridan, Trans.). New York: Random House. (Original work published in 1975.)

Gatenby, B., & Humphries, M. (2000). Feminist participatory action research: Methodological and ethical issues. *Women's Studies International Forum, 23*, 89–105.

Grande, S. (2008). Red pegadogy: The un-methodology. In N. K. Denzin, Y. S. Lincoln, & L. T. Smith (Eds.), *Handbook of critical and indigenous methodologies* (pp. 233–254). Thousand Oaks, CA: Sage.

Han, C. S., & Oliffe, J. L. (2016). Photovoice in mental illness research: A review and recommendations. *Health, 20*, 110–126. doi: 10.1177/1363459314567790

Hartsock, N. (1983). *Money, sex, and power: Toward a feminist historical materialism.* New York: Longman.

Hesse-Biber, S. N., & Piatelli, D. (2012). The synergistic practice of theory and method. In S. N. Hesse-Biber (Ed.), *Handbook of feminist research: Theory and practice* (2nd edn) (pp. 176–186). Thousand Oaks, CA: Sage.

Higgins, M. (2014). Rebraiding photovoice: Methodological métissage at the cultural interface. *The Australian Journal of Indigenous Education, 43*, 208–217. doi: 10.1017.jie.2014.18

Higgins, M. (2016). Placing photovoice under erasure: A critical and complicit engagement with what it theoretically is (not). *International Journal of Qualitative Studies in Education, 29*, 670–685. doi: 10.1080/09518398.2016.1145276

Holtby, A., Klein, K., Cook, K., & Travers, R. (2015). To be seen or not to be seen: Photovoice, queer and trans youth, and the dilemma of representation. *Action Research, 13*, 317–335. doi: 10.1177/1476750314566414

hooks, b. (1981). *Ain't I a woman: Black women and feminism*. Boston, MA: South End Press.
hooks, b. (1994). *Teaching to transgress: Education as the practice of freedom*. New York: Routledge.
hooks, b. (1995). *Art on my mind: Visual politics*. New York: The New Press.
hooks, b. (2006). *Outlaw culture: Resisting representation*. New York: Routledge. (Original work published in 1994.)
Hubbard, J. (1994). *Shooting back from the reservation: A photographic view of life by Native American youth*. New York: The New Press.
Hubbard, J. (1996). *Lives turned upside down: Homeless children in their own words and photographs*. New York: Simon & Schuster.
Ingrey, J. (2013). Shadows and light: Pursuing gender justice through students' photovoice projects of the washroom space. *Journal of Curriculum Theorizing*, 29, 174–190.
Kaplan, E. B. (2013). *"We live in the shadow": Inner-city kids tell their stories through photographs*. Philadelphia, PA: Temple University Press.
Kemmis, S., & McTaggart, R. (2005). Participatory action research: Communicative action and the public sphere. In N. K. Denzin & Y. S. Lincoln (Eds.), *The Sage handbook of qualitative research* (3rd edn, pp. 559–603). Thousand Oaks, CA: Sage.
Kessi, S., & Cornell, J. (2015). Coming to UCT: Black students, transformation, and discourses of race. *Journal of Student Affairs in Africa*, 3(2), 1–16. doi: 10.14426/jsaa.v3i2.132
Lather, P. (1991). *Getting smart: Feminist research and pedagogy with/in the postmodern*. New York: Routledge.
Latz, A. O. (2012). Toward a new conceptualization of photovoice: Blending the photographic as method and self-reflection. *Journal of Visual Literacy*, 31(2), 49–70.
Leavy, P. (2015). *Method meets art: Arts-based research practice* (2nd edn). New York: The Guilford Press.
Lewin, K. (1946). Action research and minority problems. *Journal of Social Issues*, 2, 34–46.
Lykes, M. B., & Hershberg, R. M. (2012). Participatory action research and feminisms: Social inequalities and transformative praxis. In S. N. Hesse-Biber (Ed.), *Handbook of feminist research: Theory and practice* (2nd edn, pp. 331–367). Thousand Oaks, CA: Sage.
Maguire, P. (1987). *Doing participatory research: A feminist approach*. Amherst, MA: The Center for International Education, School of Education, University of Massachusetts.
Mamary, E., McCright, J., & Roe, K. (2007). Our lives: An examination of sexual health issues using photovoice by non-gay identified African American men who have sex with men. *Culture, Health & Sexuality*, 9, 359–370. doi: 10.1080/13691050601035415
McKim, R. H. (1980). *Experiences in visual thinking* (2nd edn). Belmont, CA: Wadsworth.
McWhirter, E. H., & McWhirter, B. T. (2016). Critical consciousness and vocational development among Latino/a high school youth: Initial development and testing of a measure. *Journal of Career Assessment*, 24, 543–558. doi: 10.1177/1069072715599535
Nakata, M. (2007). The cultural interface. *The Australian Journal of Indigenous Education*, 36, 7–14.
Naples, N. A., & Gurr, B. (2014). Feminist empiricism and standpoint theory: Approaches to understanding the social world. In S. N. Hesse-Biber (Ed.), *Feminist research practice: A primer* (pp. 14–41). Thousand Oaks, CA: Sage.
Pearse, H. (1983). Brother, can you spare a paradigm? The theory beneath the practice. *Studies in Art Education*, 24, 158–163.
Pillow, W. S. (2003). Confession, catharsis, or cure? Rethinking the uses of reflexivity as methodological power in qualitative research. *Qualitative Studies in Education*, 16, 175–196.

Ravitch, S. M., & Riggan, M. (2017). *Reason & rigor: How conceptual frameworks guide research* (2nd edn). Thousand Oaks, CA: Sage.

Reid, C., & Frisby, W. (2008). Continuing the journey: Articulating dimensions of feminist participatory action research (FPAR). In P. Reason & H. Bradbury (Eds.), *The Sage handbook of action research: Participative inquiry and practice* (pp. 93–105). Thousand Oaks, CA: Sage.

Riis, J. (2010). *How the other half lives*. USA: Readaclassic.com. (Original work published in 1890.)

Rolling, J. H., Jr. (2013). *Arts-based research primer*. New York: Peter Lang.

Salazar Pèrez, M., Ruiz Guerrero, M. G., & Mora, E. (2016). Black feminist photovoice: Fostering critical awareness of diverse family and communities in early childhood teacher education. *Journal of Early Childhood Teacher Education, 37*, 41–60. doi: 10.1080/10901027.2015.1131209

Sandoval, C. (2000). *Methodology of the oppressed*. Minneapolis, MN: University of Minnesota Press.

Sheared, V., & Sissel, P. A. (Eds.). (2001). *Making space: Merging theory and practice in adult education*. Westport, CT: Bergin & Garvey.

Shin, R. Q., Ezeofor, I., Smith, L. C., Welch, J. C., & Goodrich, K. M. (2016). The development and validation of the Contemporary Critical Consciousness Measure. *Journal of Counseling Psychology, 63*, 210–223.

Solorzano, D. G., & Delgado Bernal, D. (2001). Examining transformational resistance through a critical race and LatCrit theory framework. *Urban Education, 36*, 308–342.

Spence, J. (1995). *Cultural snipping: The art of transgression*. New York: Routledge.

Springgay, S., Irwin, R. L., & Kind, S. W. (2005). A/r/tography as living inquiry through art and text. *Qualitative Inquiry, 11*, 897–912. doi: 10.1177/1077800405280696

Stanton, B. (2013). *Humans of New York*. New York: St. Martin's Press.

Stanton, B. (2015). *Humans of New York: Stories*. New York: St. Martin's Press.

Stanton, B. (2017). *About*. Retrieved from http://humansofnewyork.com/about

Strack, R. W., Lovelace, K. A., Davis Jordan, T., & Holmes, A. P. (2010). Framing photovoice using a social-ecological model as a guide. *Health Promotion Practice, 11*, 629–636. doi: 10.1177/1524839909355519

Strack, R. W., Magill, C., & McDonagh, K. (2004). Engaging youth through photovoice. *Health Promotion Practice, 5*, 49–58. doi: 10.1177/1524839903258015

Stringer, E. (2014). *Action research* (4th edn). Thousand Oaks, CA: Sage.

Tandon, R. (1981). Participatory research in the empowerment of people. *Convergence, 14*(3), 20–27.

Thomas, A. J., Barrie, R., Brunner, J., Clawson, A., Hewitt, A., Jeremie-Brink, G., & Rowe-Johnson, M. (2014). Assessing critical consciousness in youth and young adults. *Journal of Research on Adolescence, 24*, 485–496. doi: 10.111/jora.12132

Wallerstein, N., & Berstein, E. (1995). Empowerment education: Freire's ideas adapted to health education. *Health Education Quarterly, 15*, 379–394.

Wang, C., & Burris, M. A. (1994). Empowerment through photo novella: Portraits of participation. *Health Education Quarterly, 21*, 171–186.

Wang, C., & Burris, M. A. (1997). Photovoice: Concept, methodology, and use for participatory needs assessment. *Health Education & Behavior, 24*, 369–387.

Wang, C., Burris, M. A., & Ping, X. Y. (1996). Chinese village women as visual anthropologists: A participatory approach to reaching policymakers. *Social Science & Medicine, 42*, 1391–1400.

Wang, C. C., Yi, W. K., Tao, Z. W., & Carovano, K. (1998). Photovoice as a participatory health promotion strategy. *Health Promotion International, 13*, 75–86.
Weiler, K. (1988). *Women teaching for change: Gender, class & power.* South Hadley, MA: Bergin & Garvey Publishers.
Wilson, C., & Flicker, S. (2015). Picturing transactional $ex: Ethics, challenges, and possibilities. In A. Gubrium, K. Harper, & M. Otañez (Eds.), *Participatory visual and digital research in action* (pp. 73–86). Walnut Creek, CA: Left Coast Press.
Worth, S., & Adair, J. (1972). *Through Navajo eyes: An exploration in film communication and anthropology.* Bloomington, IN: Indiana University Press.
Whyte, W. F. (Ed.). (1991). *Participatory action research.* Newbury Park, CA: Sage.
Whyte, W. F., Greenwood, D. J., & Lazes, P. (1991). Participatory action research: Through practice to science in social research. In W. F. Whyte (Ed.), *Participatory action research* (pp. 19–56). Neswbury Park, CA: Sage.
Zimmerman, Z. A. (1995). Psychological empowerment: Issues and illustrations. *American Journal of Community Psychology, 23*, 581–599.

3
PHOTOVOICE METHODS AND PROCEDURES

A Vignette

I routinely teach a graduate course titled *Community Colleges and Diversity*. Always trying new approaches to facilitating the course and (re)building the course content and curriculum, I have consistently sought to grasp how to encourage empathy within my students as it relates to understanding community college students and the complex lives they often live while navigating the community college experience. There have been two occasions where the students that were enrolled in the course—with my guidance and support—carried out photovoice projects as a major component of the learning experience. In doing so, we reconceptualized the learning space and our roles within that space. As each semester progressed, during which the project was being carried out, we shifted from being a group of people that consisted of a faculty member and graduate students, to a research team.

Recently, I have been reminded of the importance of relationships when it comes to asking for participation in, and support for, photovoice projects. How you recruit participants matters. It matters a lot. The first time we carried out a photovoice study within the course referenced above, email was the primary method of recruitment. It was impersonal, and an institutional agent at the community college with which we were working sent out the email to students on our behalf. Working alongside community college officials, our team wanted to better understand students' experiences with, and perceptions of, poverty, financial literacy, and relationships with faculty and staff. Once we knew our focus, we needed to decide on a recruitment strategy, which included figuring out the inclusion and exclusion criteria for our sample. We landed on students involved with the federally funded Student Support Services initiative, a TRIO program. Students eligible for this program are first-generation, living with a disability, and/or are from a low-income background. Once the program director received permission from the sponsor—the federal government in this case—we devised a plan. The program director would send a series of email blasts to students in the program, about 160 in total, asking them to email me if interested in participating.

Think about this for a moment. Imagine yourself—as a student—receiving such a message. When I place myself in the shoes of prospective participants in that situation, I probably would not opt to participate. It would feel odd to email a stranger, a stranger from a four-year institution, a stranger who is a professor, a stranger who wants me to be a part of a research study, a stranger who wants me to do something for which I will not be compensated in any way. But at the time, this seemed like a perfectly reasonable way to go about the recruitment process. And we did have a handful of takers. A total of seven students contacted me. My class was small in numbers that semester, so the number was actually perfect. Seven students were enrolled in the course, so we had a perfect one-to-one matching process. However, there was attrition over time. Of those seven community college students, five persisted to the interview phase, but only two persisted to the actual exhibition we held at the end of the semester. While I viewed—and still do—the project as a success, I have come to understand, upon concerted reflection, what we could have done differently.

Fast-forward two years. I am teaching the class again, this time with nine students enrolled. And we are going to carry out another photovoice project with the same community college. Upon meeting with personnel at the community college, we landed on the topic of new students' needs. Because there was no listserv or otherwise formalized way for us to connect with these particular students, we decided to conduct face-to-face recruitment by visiting every Student Success (i.e. first year experience) course offered at this particular community college. There were six sections of the course offered during the semester we recruited. I emailed the instructors, and we were invited into five of the six sections. Actually going into classrooms, explaining the study and the process, and allowing ourselves to be unabashedly human during the exchanges, which oftentimes included question and answer, storytelling, and casual conversation, yielded overwhelming participation interest. In fact, we had originally planned to recruit at two campuses, but we quickly realized that was unnecessary. Total enrollment numbers for the classes we visited totaled around 65 students. Overall, 15 students wanted to participate, signed consent and media release forms, and were given disposable cameras. Being in the classrooms allowed us to orient the students to the study right away—on-site. Seven students persisted to the interview phase, and two attended and participated in our photovoice exhibition.

Considering the difference in response and persistence rates articulated above, I remain convinced that face-to-face recruitment is ideal, especially when you have no previously existing relationship with the prospective participants. Without explanation and context, photovoice can be rather confusing. You want me to do what? What does this prompt mean? How do I answer this question with a picture? What am I going to have to talk about? How do I make the flash work? No pictures of people? Why do these university people want to do this with us? How long will this take? These questions, among others, are questions I would be asking if I were in the position of a prospective participant. Being there to answer these questions as they arise and during the face-to-face recruitment moment makes all the difference. However, recruitment is just one step in a multi-step series of methods involved in carrying out the total project.

★ ★ ★

How Do We Do This?

Sutton-Brown (2014) suggested that there is a dearth of information available within the literature regarding how to implement a photovoice study. Throughout this chapter, I address this gap and provide flexible steps for implementation. Within Chapter 1, I laid out a series of eight steps that comprise the photovoice methodology. Keep in mind that these steps are simply a guidepost. Specific procedures, methods, and techniques employed by photovoice researchers are varied. This is a strength. Photovoice is flexible by design. Catalani and Mikler (2010) noted that:

> [a]lthough newer photovoice projects are clearly rooted in the seminal works of Wang and colleagues and most all subsequent articles reference them, the majority of photovoice efforts alter Wang's methodology to suit the needs and constraints of researchers' unique projects.
>
> p. 447

Even though photovoice researchers do not follow a rigid methodological script, the following eight steps are typically used:

1. identification;
2. invitation;
3. education;
4. documentation;
5. narration;
6. ideation;
7. presentation;
8. confirmation.

Within this chapter, I provide details regarding the first five steps, drawing upon my own experiences as well as the photovoice literature. Others have also put forward steps involved in the photovoice process. For example, Wang (2006) drew upon ten studies wherein youth engaged in photovoice with the purpose of affecting policy and community change. Her goal was to examine youth participation in photovoice projects. She lists nine steps in articulating the photovoice process. They are as follows:

1. *Select and recruit a target audience of policy makers or community leaders.*
2. *Recruit a group of photovoice participants.*
3. *Introduce the photovoice methodology to participants, and facilitate a group discussion about cameras, power, and ethics.*
4. *Obtain informed consent.*
5. *Pose initial theme/s for taking pictures.*
6. *Distribute cameras to participants and review how to use the camera.*
7. *Provide time for participants to take pictures.*
8. *Meet to discuss photographs and identify themes.*
9. *Plan with participants a format to share photographs and stories with policy makers or community leaders.*

pp. 149–152, italics in original

My list is not a departure from the above. Rather, I aim to both broaden and simplify the process by using eight key words that encompass all of the above and more. The use of the word steps may be a misnomer. Remember, part of the allure of photovoice is its flexibility. Steps may be taken out of order. Some steps may need to be repeated. And some steps will be redundant. Wang and Burris (1997) noted that photovoice is malleable and ready for adaptation for specific goals, diverse communities, and various contexts. Without having a project actively in motion, it is difficult to know exactly how to enact the steps. But knowing the steps typically used will be a comfort along the way.

While photovoice can be used as a sole methodology for a particular study, it can also be used in conjunction with other methodologies (e.g. used within a case study approach), or augmented with methods not usually prescribed within photovoice (e.g. used with surveys, participant observation, document analysis). It depends upon the circumstances surrounding the project. For example, when conducting my doctoral dissertation, I blended the photovoice methodology with a constructivist grounded theory (Charmaz, 2006) analytical approach. The research questions anchoring my study, focused on understanding the educational lives of community college students (Latz, 2011), led me toward photovoice. But my desire to attend to gaps in the theoretical literature on community college students led me toward constructivist grounded theory. It was an appropriate pairing considering these factors. Photovoice can be used to address various types of research questions such as those that drive needs assessment or program evaluation. Chapter 4 is dedicated to data analysis, or the ideation phase. That particular phase can be rather complex, which is why an entire chapter is dedicated to it. But first, we must consider what is involved in data generation.

Getting Ready

Before moving into a discussion of the steps involved, it is important to have a sense of who ought to be involved in the project's leadership, what kinds of supplies might be needed, and how the project will be funded. It is also important to consider your own understanding of photographs and photography. Tinkler (2013) posed five questions to consider prior to using photographs within research:

- How do you conceptualise [sic] a photograph? (image and/or object—consider the materiality)
- Can photos constitute evidence of the social world? (consider your epistemology)
- How do temporalities shape photo research? (the photograph's relationship with time)
- What can you do with photos? (to answer or generate questions, for example)
- How do you combine methods? (careful planning is important)

p. 1

Writing out your answers to the questions above can be an exercise in reflexivity and assistive in building your conceptual framework and navigating photovoice methods.

The Research Team/Project Facilitators

Photovoice projects can be carried out by a sole researcher or by research teams. A number of factors contribute to decisions made regarding who is in a position to lead and facilitate any given photovoice study. For example, photovoice studies done as masters' theses or doctoral dissertations will typically have a single researcher at the helm. Even though individuals carrying out photovoice projects for thesis or dissertation requirements may have committees guiding them throughout the process, it is a largely solo process. On the other hand, when inquiring about an interdisciplinary topic or phenomenon, diverse research teams are apt. What follows is not meant to be an exhaustive treatment of how such teams might look or be formed. Rather, I encourage researchers to be thoughtful and purposeful about those who are invited to, and engage in, the leadership of the project.

Professional Photographers

Many photovoice studies written about in the literature include a professional photographer as a member of the team (e.g. Findholt, Michael, & David, 2010; Wang & Redwood-Jones, 2001; Willson, Green, Haworth-Brockman, &

Rapaport Beck, 2006). The inclusion of a professional photographer should be considered carefully. They can be profoundly helpful in some instances. Professional photographers were a part Wang and Redmond Jones's study; they worked with groups of participants on two levels. First, they helped participants understand how to take photographs, offering tips and guidance. Second, they provided new and positive perspectives on the contents and artistic elements of the photographs, which helped boost participants' confidence. This was a brilliant way to assuage participants' potential concerns about not being skilled in the techniques of photography. However, the presence of a professional photographer may be intimidating to participants, especially if there is an expectation for a specific manner of artistry within the photographs participants produce. Creating aesthetically pleasing, artful, or precise photographs is not the point of photovoice. The point is to make space for participants to express themselves on their own terms, and what that looks like is up to the participants. This should be made clear.

Interdisciplinary Teams

A few years ago, I became interested in how undergraduate students describe how they study and where they study. Specifically, I wondered about how and where studying happened for students who reside on-campus. While the study never came to fruition because of a lack of funding, I partnered with two colleagues to conceptualize how this inquiry might unfold. One colleague was a professor in architecture with expertise in interior design. The other colleague was an instructor in special education who had expertise in educational technology. The three of us, together, had the knowledge and skills necessary to put the project in motion. I brought knowledge of college students and the photovoice methodology, and my colleagues brought knowledge on how spaces relate to learning, interior design, and private collaborative blogging. These various perspectives would be invaluable as we engaged in data collection and analysis. We wanted students to use digital photography to respond to the following: "How do you study?" and "Where do you study?" We hoped to use a blog where students could post photographs and discuss them with one another. As is evident within this example, sometimes building teams with a variety of skill and knowledge sets can be advantageous.

Instititional and Organizational Representation

In an instance where a university-based researcher is working with several non-profit organizations on a photovoice project, for example, it may be helpful for the research team to be composed of representatives from those organizations. Let us imagine a scenario wherein a university researcher is interested in understanding where and how high school students gather information about the college preparation and application process. In this case, it might be helpful to invite school counselors from participating high schools to be a part of the team. In addition, it could be helpful to engage admissions personnel from institutions of higher education about the project. Decisions about partnering with others can be an iterative and ongoing process. When making these considerations, it is important to think about what potential partners might bring to the table, whether or not goals are congruent, and if the partnership could be mutually beneficial. Andrews, Newman, Meadows, Cox, and Bunting (2012) provide a helpful model (p. 559) that illustrates one potential way to think through decisions about constructing leadership teams consisting of representative from various community partners.

Project-specific Personnel

The purpose of Killion and Wang's (2000) pilot project was to bring people together, specifically African American women from multiple generations. Participants in this study were two younger homeless women and three older women who lived independently in their own homes. The project included five face-to-face meetings held across seven months. A clinical psychologist attended the focus group/group discussion sessions. This is not entirely practical for most because of monetary constraints. However, if the project is grant-funded, for example, these kinds of provisions can certainly be made. The outcomes and experiences of these discussions can never be fully anticipated, so the presence of a clinical psychologist may be helpful, although there may also be reason to believe this presence could be detrimental if, for example, the participants have never met this person or if his or her presence makes the exchange feel clinical or uncomfortable. In other instances, it may be necessary to include persons proficient in the local language (Wang & Burris, 1997) and/or who have deep understandings of the cultural context in which the study is situated.

Supplies

Supplies needed for photovoice projects vary. However, the following are used in most projects: cameras (e.g. disposable, digital), various forms and other paperwork (e.g. consent, release, packet cover letter; see Appendices A through G for examples), pens, means to display photographs during interviews or focus groups (e.g. photograph albums, computer, projector, and screen), audio or video recording device, and means to take notes during focus groups or interviews (e.g. notebook, flip chart). Each of these supplies will be explained as I elaborate on the first five steps of the photovoice process.

Funding

Throughout the duration of a photovoice project, funds will be necessary. While it is possible to carry out such a project without incurring costs by borrowing items and/or relying on gifts in-kind, grant seeking is a skill photovoice researchers should hone. Funds may be necessary to purchase cameras, make copies of forms, develop film or print photographs, purchase audio recording devices, rent space for meetings, provide refreshments during meetings, purchase incentives for participants (e.g. gift cards), secure transportation for participants, and purchase items needed for the exhibition or presentation stage of the project. And this is by no means an exhaustive list.

Photovoice researchers can seek out and apply for grants from a variety of sources. Many institutions of higher education house on-campus units dedicated to assisting personnel identify, apply for, and manage external funding. When pursuing funding, all available resources should be leveraged. During this process, know that a small amount can go a long way. A few hundred dollars is enough to get a small-scale project underway.

Few entities will provide support for research without wanting something in return. Know what this is as soon as possible, as the very nature of your project may be affected in profound ways. For some, a final report will suffice. For others, specific and measureable outcomes may be required. Consider whether or not the photovoice methodology can yield the kinds of results a potential funder requires. Strack, Lovelace, Davis Jordan, and Holmes (2010) suggested using a social-ecological logic model for guiding photovoice projects (p. 631), which includes inputs, activities, and short- and long-term outcomes. Their model can be used both for guiding projects and for assessing their outcomes (p. 634). There are a number of benefits to connecting a logic model to a photovoice project: (a) positive systems changes are highlighted as a goal; (b) visual tool for keeping parties on the same page; (c) the model is flexible; outcomes can be added and deleted as the project progresses; (d) processes and outcomes are differentiated; and (e) the logic model allows for assertions of causality (p. 635). Strack et al. noted that "[u]sing a theory-driven evaluation approach, photovoice planners can attempt to isolate specific processes that can be credited for changes in measured outcomes" (p. 634). I imagine this has to do with appeasing funders, who often want to see results in causal, measureable, and quantitative terms.

Photovoice researchers have received support from small community foundations to large governmental entities. Matching the goals of your work with the goals of the sponsor is key. Locate a potential funder, and contact a representative about your project. This may save time in the long run. A full articulation of the grant seeking process is beyond the scope of this book, but both aspirant and seasoned photovoice researchers alike would do well to learn more about the successful pursuit of funding.

The First Five Steps

Step One: Identification

The inertia for most research studies stems from personal experience. The vignette with which I started this book is a prime example. If I had not taught at a community college during my doctoral study, it is highly unlikely that this book would exist, as I may not have become aware of, or interested in, photovoice. Let us recall the conceptual framework from Chapter 2. At the top of Figure 2.1, we see literature/experience/"problem." Thoughtful interrogation of literature on any given topic will yield gaps in what is known about certain things. Filling these gaps is at the crux of what professional researchers do. Dutiful canvassing of our own life experiences will yield questions that beckon answers. And finally, encounters with the social world will yield a myriad of "problems" that can be addressed through inquiry. Each of these three avenues can yield fodder for the creation of research questions that might be best addressed through the photovoice method.

For Wang (2006), the first step is reaching out to policy makers, who can serve as an "ad hoc advisory board to the project" (p. 149). I list identification as the first step in the process—this includes identification of the topic or issue to be explored or addresses, which necessarily involves identifying the policy makers who can be made aware of, have a hand in, or be an advisor for the group. Wang (1999) and Wang, Cash, and Powers (2000) stressed the importance of policy makers being present for the study throughout its duration. Those who have the power to change circumstances should be identified and targeted at the outset of the project. Oftentimes, those who make policy (broadly conceived) are completely removed from the experiences of the people for which the policy was created. This is clearly problematic but all too common. Photovoice can help bridge that gap, as it "integrates a citizen approach to documentary photography, the production of knowledge, and social action" (Wang, 1999, p. 187).

Step Two: Invitation

Once a clear topic and population for the inquiry is established, it is time to invite prospective participants to join the study. As my vignette illustrates, in-person recruitment for photovoice studies is preferred whenever possible. If the population with which you would like to work has regular gatherings, ask to attend and introduce the project to the group. Be yourself, be human, and make it a point to demystify and neutralize the word research. Smith (2012) wrote that "[t]he word itself, 'research,' is probably one of the dirtiest words in the indigenous world's vocabulary" (p. 1). The unconscionable ways in which many indigenous people were treated in the name of "research" and the advancement of colonization (Edwards, 1992) is not soon forgotten. For many, the notion of research conjures up feelings of distrust, danger, and manipulation, and the idea of *being* researched is deplorable. There are plenty of instances when research participants were harmed by researchers—purposefully or not. Some of these include the Stanford prison experiment, Tuskegee syphilis experiment, and Nazi medical experiments. All of these studies occurred in the recent past and remain as reminders of why research is still very much a dirty word for some.

Because photovoice is a form of participatory action research, traditional, positivist, random sampling procedures are subverted. In many ways, purposive sampling is most appropriate. Let us consider my dissertation as an example. My overarching research question was as follows: How do community college students construct their educational lives? There are millions of community college students in the United States. Yet, Wang (1999) suggested that seven to ten participants is an ideal range, but among the studies reviewed by Hergenrather, Rhodes, Cowan, Bardhoshi, and Pula (2009), there was a range of between four and 122 participants in any given study. So, how did I move from several million to seven? I was purposeful in my sampling procedure. I asked myself questions about access and rapport. While I spent some time thinking about representation (i.e. recruiting a group of participants who differed in terms of a broad range of identity constructs), this was not a critical factor in my decision-making process. Purposeful recruitment has been utilized to bolster representation in other photovoice studies, however (e.g. Nykiforuk, Vallianatos, & Nieuwendyk, 2011). I opted to recruit from the pool of students who were enrolled in classes I taught at the local community college. This took the potential population from millions to thousands to hundreds. Several inclusion (e.g. must be currently enrolled) and exclusion criteria (e.g. cannot currently be in any of my classes) made the prospective participant pool even smaller. Recruitment took place via email, which worked well because the students were already familiar with me.

Other researchers have different recruiting tactics, however. The purpose of Baker and Wang's (2006) study was to "examine the potential use of photovoice in assessing the pain experiences" (p. 1406) of older adults. Recruitment took the forms of letters (via snail mail), follow-up phone calls (to see if the letters were received), and an information sheet and brochure placed in specific locations. When deciding on recruitment tactics, the nature of the population should be considered. Sometimes direct (snail) mail is most effective. In other cases, recruitment through social media might be most appropriate.

Attrition

Participant attrition is very common, as was apparent in Baker and Wang's (2006) study. Of their 27 initial participants, only 13 completed the whole project. The complexity of the phases involved in their study (e.g. taking photographs, mailing cameras, writing narrations, completing a survey) may have led to high attrition. And, as the study progressed, it became apparent that some of the steps typically used within the photovoice process could not be followed. For example, because of the physical condition of many participants, presenting the project in a public way was problematic. I have found high levels of attrition in my own work as well. During the invitation phase, invite more individuals to the study that you would ideally like. Participant attrition within photovoice studies can be an upwards of 50 percent or more. Often, when you are working with populations that have been historically marginalized, participating in a study is not a high priority regardless of energy, intent, or excitement.

Step Three: Education

Talking with participants about the intricacies of the photovoice process is paramount. That participants understand how the project will unfold, why the project is being done, and what is expected from them is critical. This step of the process, which I have termed education, begins with an initial meeting with the participant or group of participants. Communication between research team members and participants must be consistent and ongoing, however. Research team members should provide participants with frequent opportunities to ask questions and request clarification. Encouragement, affirmation, reminders, and updates should be given to the participants on a regular basis.

Consent and Release

Obtaining informed consent and photography release is critical during the initial meeting. There are at least four kinds of consent and release forms used in photovoice projects: (a) participant's consent to be a part of the study; (b) individual's consent to be photographed; (c) photographed's (individual's) consent to allow the photographs to be published; and (d) participant/photographer's consent to allow images to be published. If participants or individuals being photographed are minors, consent from a parent/guardian is also necessary. The researcher obtains consent forms *a* and *d*, and participants obtain consent forms *b* and *c*—letters as referenced above (Wang, 2006; Wang & Redwood-Jones, 2001). Examples of each of these forms—with descriptions—are available within Appendices A, B, C, and D.

Information Sheet or Project Brochure

As participants go out into the world and begin the documentation phase, they may find themselves in a situation where they are asked about why they are taking photographs. As such, providing participants with copies of an information sheet or brochure that outlines the project and includes contact information for research team members is recommended. This way, participants can provide the document to anyone who may inquire. An example of such a document is available in

Appendix E at the end of the book. During the narration phase of my dissertation, one of my participants encountered a situation in which the documentation and her ability to explain what she was doing was key. This participant wanted to take photographs of a municipal building in the city. In addition, she wanted to include a green traffic light in the picture to indicate that the city was "open" and "welcoming." To make this image, she had to walk into a busy street outside the municipal building several times when the "walk" sign was lit to capture the image within a short window of time. A city employee noticed her behavior, which was odd taken out of context, and questioned her. She was able to handle the exchange well because of her preparation. In fact, the encounter led to a positive communication, and the employee was heartened to discover her intentions. However, this situation could have easily gone awry. This particular participant presented as a middle-aged White woman. The privileges associated with these identity markers in the United States may have played a role in the employee's rather benign actions. Had this participant been a young Black male, for example, the actions taken by the city employee may have been different. As photovoice researchers, we have to be candid and honest with participants relative to the ways in which their actions may be perceived—for better or for worse. Providing participants with language to use in such situations, along with copies the information sheet, will assist them in handling such situations.

To minimize risk, Wang and Redwood-Jones (2001) discussed how participants were provided with informational brochures about the project to provide to anyone they approach to photograph or anyone interested in or questioning about their camera use during the documentation phase of the project. Creating information sheets or brochures to give to participants serves a number of purposes. First, it saves participants the trouble of having to verbally explain their photographic pursuits if asked. Certainly, participants are encouraged to engage in discussion about the project, but having details on hand and ready to distribute is helpful. In most cases, the context within which participants carry out the documentation will influence how much attention is drawn to their actions. For example, if a participant takes photographs silently with a smartphone at an outdoor festival, it is not likely that much attention will be in his or her direction, as many festival goers are likely to be doing the same thing. However, if a participant takes numerous photographs using a noisy disposable camera with a flash during an orchestral concert in a semi-private school space, questions will likely be raised. Second, information sheets or brochures divert attention from participants toward the principal investigator or a member of the research team. If questions are raised that cannot be answered by the participant and are beyond the scope of what is presented by the document, a point person can be contacted for additional information. Third, it provides an opportunity for the recruitment of additional participants if snowball sampling is in place. For example, if LGBTQIA+ (lesbian, gay, bisexual, trans, queer, intersex, allies) or GSRM (gender, sexual, and romantic minority) college students are engaged in a photovoice project aimed at understanding perceptions of safe and non-safe places on campus, recruitment may be difficult, as participation may be linked to "outing" oneself in the process. Those actively involved in the study may be able to assuage those kinds of fears by explaining the study's intent and process—if questioned during the process—noting that participant confidentiality is possible and will be honored. Fourth, the documentation can serve a dual purpose of both explaining the project and promoting the exhibition—regardless of format. Whether an event is planned or an online space has been dedicated to the project (or both), those details can be placed onto the documentation.

Photography Basics

Taking some time to provide participants with an overview of photography basics can prepare them to generate images that align with their purposes and intentions. While a brief and basic photography tutorial is helpful for participants of all ages and experience levels, children may benefit from specific instruction. However, Ewald and Lightfoot (2001) noted they have "found that before teaching children how to take photographs, it's helpful to spend some time with the children looking at images and talking about them" (p. 17). Discussing specific photographs with children before delving into photography techniques can assist them in building photographic literacy. The ability to *read* a photograph is often catalyzed through posing a series of questions for children to consider. Discussing the setting, scene, and photographer's intention can advance children "from observing the details of an image to trying to understand the story behind it" (Ewald & Lightfoot, 2001, p. 21). When selecting photographs to discuss with children, Ewald and Lightfoot suggested using photographs that are relevant to the children in some way. Images from local news outlets, school yearbooks, or even images taken by the children themselves may be appropriate.

The next step in the tutorial process is conversation around the notion that "[w]ho we are and where we stand when we watch the world determines how we see and what we record" (Ewald & Lightfoot, 2001, p. 29). From this point, conversation should be had about the essential elements of photography, which include framing (what is included in the photograph, and what is left out), point of view (vantage point of the photographer), timing (when to capture the image), symbolism (contents of the image that serve as symbols for something else), and details (using one single component of a scene to depict the entirety of a scene). Once these photography essentials are covered, it is time to discuss the technical aspects of the specific camera used within the project. Prior to this step, however, decisions must be made regarding what tool or tools will be used to take pictures. Will disposable, instant, or digital cameras be used? Will cameras be provided, will participants furnish their own cameras, or will it be a mix of both—depending on who has access to what? After these decisions are made, participants should be briefed on how to use their device (Ewald & Lightfoot, 2001).

Step Four: Documentation

Prompts

Creating effective photography prompts is vital in ensuring participants are able to successfully navigate the documentation phase. Prompts should be attentive to the attributes and personhoods of the participants; they should also address the topic under study. Prompts should be open-ended; they can take the form of questions, directive statements, or fill-in-the-blank statements. Here are a few examples:

- What motivates you to achieve your educational goals?
- What do you like best about school?
- What is your favorite thing to learn?
- Describe how you learn best.
- Take pictures of your favorite places to study.
- Show what diversity means to you.
- A typical day at school includes [fill in the blank by taking some photographs].
- Before I do my homework, I must [fill in the blank by taking some photographs].
- Mathematics is [fill in the blank by taking some photographs].

There are a myriad of ways in which photovoice researchers can give guidance on what participants ought to photograph (Tinkler, 2013, p. 156): (a) completely open, using perhaps one prompt or frame; (b) general focus; (c) scripted (series of prompts or questions); and (d) participant-driven scripts (participants decide on the parameters). The research questions may provide insights on which approach(es) to take.

Often, a collaborative approach to the generation of photography prompts is appropriate. Collaboration can take place among any number of the project's constituents (e.g. research team members, participants, policy makers). One way to get the process started is to write out all the potential prompts for the group to see. From that point, prompts can be added, deleted, collapsed, and refined through group discussion. Figure 3.1 provides an example of an initial list of potential prompts generated by a photovoice project research team.

Scenarios

Scenarios can also be used as photography prompts within photovoice. The children involved with Luttrell's (2010) study were informed that the project was a chance to "represent their point of view and experiences to adults in charge of teaching children like themselves and making decisions on schools" (p. 226). The initial photograph prompt painted a scenario wherein the children were

72 Photovoice Methods and Procedures

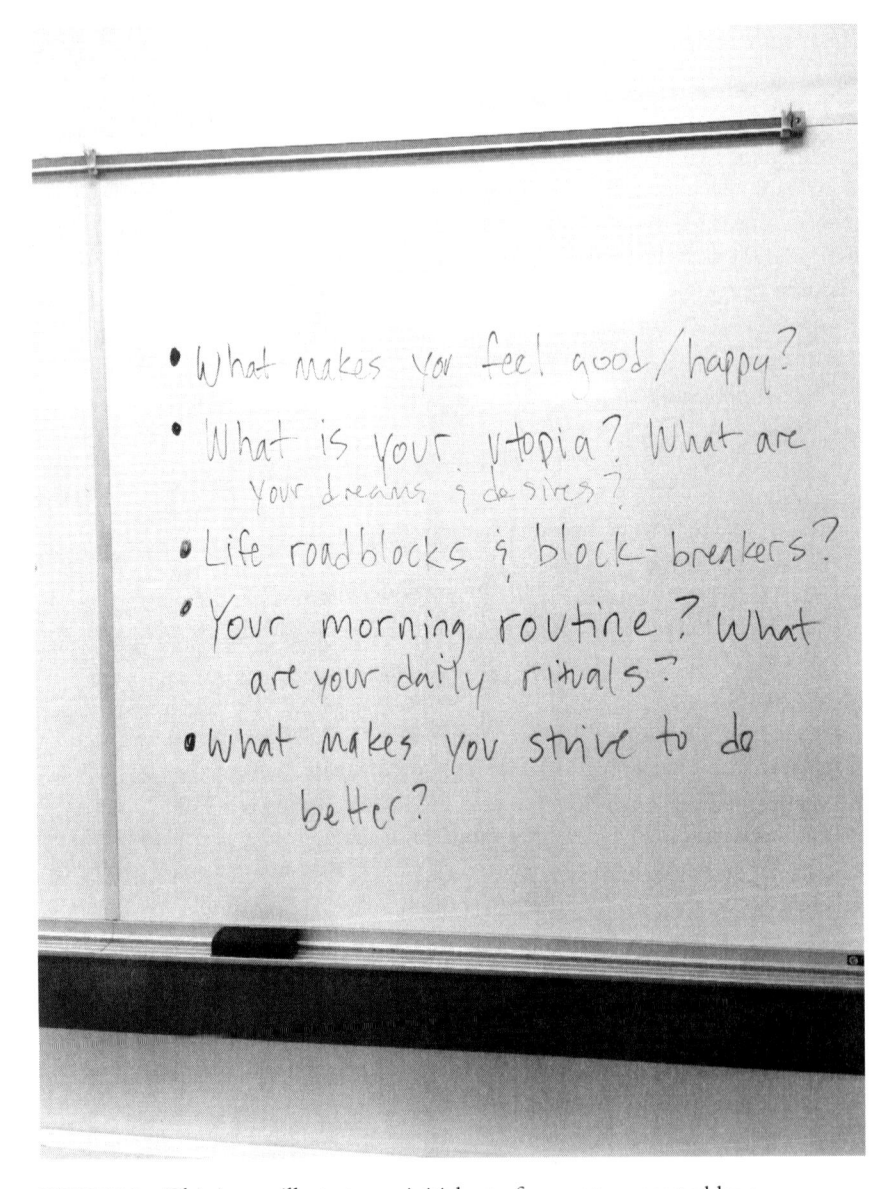

- What makes you feel good/happy?
- What is your utopia? What are your dreams & desires?
- Life roadblocks & block-breakers?
- Your morning routine? What are your daily rituals?
- What makes you strive to do better?

FIGURE 3.1 This image illustrates an initial set of prompts generated by a photovoice project research team.

entertaining a cousin who was visiting and joining him or her at school. The purpose of the photographs was to help the participant's cousin know what to expect. Another example is found in Allen's (2012) study, which is discussed in Chapter 5.

Cameras

What will the participants use to take photographs? Nearly every type of modern camera has been used in photovoice studies: disposable cameras, point-and-shoot cameras, Holga cameras (Wang, Cash, & Powers, 2000), and digital cameras. Will participants use their own cameras, or will cameras be provided? What happens when participants in the same photovoice project create photographs differently? During the spring of 2016, my EDCC 641 students and I worked with new and newer community college students to better understand their diverse needs as incoming students. We provided each participant with a disposable camera (see Figure 3.2).

FIGURE 3.2 Disposable cameras provided to the participants in the study described above.

These cameras stymied some of our younger participants. In fact, one of our participants took all her photographs with an iPad. Because using these images would have been an Institutional Review Board protocol deviation and because we endeavored toward consistency within the images, we asked her to retake the photographs using the disposable camera. Imagine a scenario where it would be beneficial to ask participants to identify the camera they would like to use for the project. Some select a disposable camera, some select digital cameras, some select their own smartphone, and some select their tablet. Participants who use disposable cameras will not be able to see their images right away; they cannot alter the images before the film is developed and the images printed. However, if those images are also digitized, the images can be altered at a later time. On the other hand, participants who opt to use their own devices—smartphones or tablets—for photography are able to immediately delete, retake, alter, and crop their images. How does this alter the processes that unfold within the same project, and does it matter?

While the digitization of photographs may be a cultural process (Sassoon, 2004), it could also be said that making printed photographs is also a cultural process in the current technological milieu, which will certainly shift and advance over time. Within the context of nearly ubiquitous digital photography, committing photographs to physical, material objecthood is also a cultural process—and perhaps a strange one to some.

Photowalks

The first session of Wang, Cash, and Powers's (2000) project involved a walking photo shoot, which allowed participants to experiment and discuss their experiences with the cameras. This also meant that photographs could be discussed during the second session because an entire roll of film was shot.

Step Five: Narration

Photovoice involves participants "discussing the images that they have produced, and by doing so, they give meaning to, or interpret, their images" (Wang, 1999, p. 186). It is not the researcher's role to interpret these photographs. That is the domain of the participants. It is critical to note that photographs taken during photovoice studies are not data in and of themselves. Rather, they serve as data antecedents, eliciting responses from the participants—to describe how they used photography to respond to the prompt(s) provided to them. The participants' photographs are to be interpreted by the participants; the participants' narrations of those photographs are the data typically relegated to the interpretation of the researcher or the research team. And in some cases, that interpretation—or analysis—is participatory in nature, wherein the participants dialogically and collaboratively make meaning of the narrative data set. It should be noted that the narration phase is sometimes when the photo release forms should be introduced to the participant. Because participants may be seeing their images for the first time during this phase, completing this form at this moment in the process is appropriate. See Appendix G for an example.

For many participants, being in an interview situation can be stress inducing, especially if the interviewee is a stranger or someone the participant does not know well. It may seem simple, but when two individuals are in conversation, some level of eye contact is typical, and this is uncomfortable for some. When two people are viewing a photograph together, the amount of eye contact between them lessens. Also, when photographs are introduced into the interview, a mutual understanding can be forged between the interviewer and the interviewee. Harper (2002) noted that interviews involving discussions of photographs may help both parties "overcome the difficulties posed by in-depth interviewing because it [the conversation] is anchored in an image that is understood, at lease in part, by both parties" (p. 20). Moreover, verbal exchanges that involve interactions with images, or photographs, engage more of the brain's capacity than reliance on language alone (Harper, 2002). And, finally, "a photograph commands interest, deflects digression, and helps the interview to proceed on its meaningful way" (Collier, 1957, p. 859).

Photo Elicitation

Visual elicitation during interviews has a long history within the social sciences. And elicitation devices used are not bound to photographs alone. Visuals such as drawings (Cowan, 1999) and diagrams (Crilly, Blackwell, & Clarkson, 2006) are examples. As a core method within the methodology, photo elicitation, a method especially well-suited for inquiries related to education (Harper, 2012), is used in nearly every photovoice study. First named by John Collier (1957), photo elicitation "is based on the simple idea of inserting a photograph into a research interview" (Harper, 2002, p. 13). Using photographs in an interview provides the interviewer and interviewee with more than one symbolic means of expression: language and image. Within photo elicitation, photographs are used to elicit responses from and excavate memories of participants. Within photovoice, participants interact with and describe images they created, which is a keystone of photovoice. Researcher-generated photographs—or other visual elicitation devices (e.g. diagrams)—are not typically used within the researcher-participant exchanges that occur during the photovoice process.

Photographs can transport us to a different place and time; they can help us recall feelings, smells, and details. Heisley and Levy (1991) explained that "[s]urvey or straight personal interviews might be able to elicit a description of the roles that family members play in meal preparation. But when the photographs ask the questions, nuances of the family's interactions surface" (p. 264). Even when researchers make the most ardent attempts to create images from the participant's perspectives (e.g. Bourgois & Schonberg, 2009; Harper, 1987), these images fall short. Asking participants to document aspects of their social worlds gives researchers access to spaces, insights, and realities not accessible otherwise. Bloustien and Baker (2003) explained: "the use of a camera in the hands of the participants can offer access to aspects of everyday life that in ordinary fieldwork circumstances the ethnographer might not be privileged to see" (p. 70). And they explained how "the camera could venture where we [researchers] could not" (p. 72). Were the cameras the researchers' proxy? Perhaps in this case (what Bloustien and Baker termed a visual auto-ethnography), yes. But in the case of photovoice, the answer is no. The camera provides the participants with yet another medium of expression. The photographs always represent the participants' gaze, something the researcher can never fully experience or understand completely.

Participants' Emotional Geographies

When you see yourself in a photograph, there can be "a sense of detachment, of being 'me' but 'not me,' and this is the disruptive power of mimesis" (Bloustien & Baker, 2003, p. 73). What happens when this is the case for photovoice participants? What happens when participants see themselves as other? Photographs are temporal and have an inorganic objecthood. This can be affronting to participants who are narrating the images after having created them and can result in self-surveillance (i.e. discounting or removing certain photographs) and closure (i.e. silence surrounding some photographs). We must consider, as researchers, how to help participants navigate this potential dissonance. Sometimes participants do not like the way they look in certain pictures, and if, for example, their photographs do not turn out how they intended, there can be disappointment (see Figure 3.3). In these instances, participants always have the opportunity to remove images from the study (i.e. not address them or allow them to be published). But they should also be reminded that the aesthetics of the photographs are much less important than the meanings assigned to them.

Rose (2004) noted that family photographs might be paradoxically seen as both trite or banal and extraordinarily important, which can cause a wide range of emotional responses from participants upon viewing the images. She said: "images are encountered through a number of registers that far exceed the discursive: the bodily, the sensory, the psychic and the emotional" (p. 551), and participants often referred to an image of a person as though it was the individual pictured. Looking at photographs is not merely a visual experience (Rose). Knowing this, we must be prepared, as researchers, to encounter participants in this space—one that may be vulnerable. While carrying out the photo-elicited interview, we, too, are part of the audience for their photographs. We will likely have a corporeal togetherness with our participants in a similar way to which they have a corporeal togetherness with what/whom is pictured in their photographs. Rose asserted that photographs are a potent way of "doing togetherness"

FIGURE 3.3 This is an example of an underdeveloped photograph taken by a photovoice participant who used a disposable camera. Many of the photographs taken by this individual were underdeveloped, which led to a sense of frustration and dissonance within that participant.

(p. 560). I can attest to this from personal experience. During one of the photo-elicitation interviews I conducted for my dissertation, one of my participants became very emotional when talking about how proud she was of her daughter. She had taken a picture of a photograph of her daughter receiving her bachelor's degree that was hanging on a wall at her home. As a community college student pursuing a degree in physical therapy assisting, this participant swelled with pride as she began to tear up and explain how her daughter was a major motivator. Because her children received bachelor's degrees, she felt it was her turn. Our interview took place at a local coffee shop, and she felt embarrassed considering the publicness of the space. She apologized for becoming emotional during the interview, and I replied with a warm grin that without words implied "this is okay with me." And we both began to giggle and smile. The relationship we had prior to the exchange and the comfort and safety that was established during it allowed this interview to continue without hesitation. Van Dijck (2005) noted that "rather than reinvoking the experience, people want a representation that triggers particular emotions or sensations" (p. 326). I imagine the same is true for photovoice participants. In fact, the practice of photography in this context is rarely about capturing an experience. It is about communicating insights though photography that would otherwise be left unsaid.

Stadium and Punctum

McKim (1980) said: "the knowledgeable observer sees things that a less knowledgeable companion literally cannot" (p. 69). This is important considering the need for photovoice participants to explain the contents and meanings of their images. Without these explanations, the images are meaningless. Rose (2004) made brilliant use of the concepts stadium and punctum (Barthes, 1980/1981) within in her piece on family photographs. Rose (2004) said: "I saw and heard the arrows of *puncta* fly in my interviews repeatedly" (p. 559, italics in original). Barthes (1980/1981) wrote about two terms that are useful in understanding how we might understand, interpret, and be affected by photographs: stadium and punctum. By naming these photographic elements, Barthes created a duality for us to consider. On one hand, we have the stadium, which refers to the overall scene being depicted within the image. And on the other hand, we have the punctum—an element or series of elements that pierce, punctuate, or unsettle the stadium. Barthes argued that the stadium tells the spectator (i.e. viewer of the photograph) about the operator (i.e. photographer). At the same time, the punctum is bound up in the spectator. Different spectators may identify different punctums. In other words, specific elements of a photograph may be more piercing or affronting than others—it depends on who is looking. Smith (2014) described the stadium as the viewer's cultural background that informs the way in which the photograph is understood. The punctum, then, is an element of the photograph that is deemed surprising, out of place. The presence of the punctum elicits an affective response from the reader of the photograph. This affective response can be positive or negative. Either way, the feeling caused by the punctum is arresting, visceral. The punctum can change the entirety of how the stadium is perceived. While Smith noted that the "photographer could never intentionally inscribe a punctum in an image" (p. 35), photovoice may provide a notable exception. Within photovoice, the participants are both photographers and interpreters of those photographs, which wedges a gap in the above assertion.

When I look at Figure 3.4, my eyes immediately focus on the three ducks. Before the interview took place—not with me, but with one of the students enrolled in EDCC 641 during the spring of 2014—I conjured up all sorts of potential metaphors about ducks and faculty and tree stumps and muddy waters. However, the participant who took this picture said "I was actually trying to get the lighthouse in the background. Teachers are like that lighthouse. They guide you and let you know when you are getting near your destination." *My* punctum was absent from the participants' narration, and researchers must be open to the various and unexpected ways participants might use imagery. The interpreter of the image—the participant—should always be the one to define the punctum. This example sheds light on how and why the participants are the ones who interpret the contents of the photographs. They alone know why their photographs were taken.

FIGURE 3.4 Photograph taken by a photovoice participant in response to a prompt related to the role of faculty at the community college.

Barthes (1980/1981) also established that the punctum can also take the form of a temporal realization in response to a photograph. In this case, it is not an actual detail or element within the image, it is the realization, for example, that the person pictured in the photograph is now, at the time of viewing, deceased. Or, another example may be the simple realization that the photograph depicts a time that has since passed. We, as researchers, must be open to these possibilities as well. When engaging in photo-elicitation interview, we must also be in tune to sensing the dialogic puncta, or disruptions within the narrations—the pauses, the emphases, and the visceral, bodily reactions. Rose (2004) noted that "[puncta are] outside the range of interview talk" (p. 559). Sometimes language fails participants in the explanation of the emotional components of the punctum. Sometimes images afford a certain "'all-at-onceness' in our perception that reveals what would be hard to grasp in diachronic forms such as language and number" (Eisner, 1995, p. 1), which can be stifling for participants. So, how do we, as photovoice researcher, inquire about the punctum in an efficacious way? Mnemonic techniques that might be helpful in doing so are discussed below. Finally, we must also consider that some images may not include punctum. And sometimes the stadium and the punctum are one in the same. Again, throughout the interview, researchers can use specific techniques to assist participants in conveying the full meanings of the images produced.

Discursiveness

Oral communication about photography has discursive features. This becomes apparent when individuals talk about family photo albums—even those that are not their own (Kuhn, 2007). Seeing or imagining the photographs photovoice participants are narrating within the photo-elicitation interviews and/or focus groups, however, makes the discursiveness of the talk more understandable. During a photo-elicitation interview, researchers can literally see what the participants mean. The dialogical exchange elicited by a photograph can be scattered about and go on for some time. After describing the "interactive performative viewing" (Kuhn, 2007, p. 290) of a photograph by Jack Yu, a photograph of his mother and him that he had been carrying in his wallet—the central case study for her article—Kuhn explained that "[m]emory work is rather like peeling away the layers of an onion that has no core: each level of analysis, while adding more knowledge, greater understanding, also generates further questions" (Kuhn, 2007, p. 290). What was missing from Jack's memory-story? Is the photograph's presence in Jack's wallet and absence elsewhere meaningful? The questions are unending, and as such these kinds of exchanges can go on for some time. Nonetheless, Kuhn said: "To suggest that analysis may be interminable and that interpretations may vary is in no way to detract from the value of this kind of . . . inquiry" (p. 290).

Photographic Objecthood

Sassoon (2004) argued that three aspects of photographs are integral to debates surrounding their complexity: materiality (the photograph's objecthood), content (the concept of an original photograph), and context (the photograph's original meaning) (p. 189). These three aspects are forged together, as a photograph can be seen as a "multilayered laminated object" (p. 189) with each of the aforementioned aspects coming together symbiotically. According to Tinkler, (2013), "[t]he image is important, but its meaning and significance is inextricably connected to its materiality" (p. 2). When preparing for the photo-elicited exchange, we must consider the photograph's objecthood. How will the participant encounter his or her image? Will the images be put forward digitally? How? Will the images be put forward as objects? What size? Will they be organized in a specific way? What is the difference between handling a photograph and viewing a photograph? As you can imagine by the nature of these questions, extensive planning is necessary for the photo-elicitation interview. Edwards (2002) asserted that "[the] material characteristics [of photographs] have a profound impact on the way images are 'read,' as different materials forms both signal and enforce different expectations and use patterns" (p. 68). We must consider the "thingness" of the photographs (Maynard, 1997). In other words, what the photograph *is* may be as important as what the photograph is *of* (Batchen, 1997). Because "[t]ouch is often pivotal to *how* we view a photo" (Tinkler, 2013, p. 100, italics in original), the haptic nature of our interactions with photographs is important. Our own proprioception and haptic nature of our interactions with photographs entwine. In some ways, our haptic interactions with photographs aid us in "seeing" (Rose, 2004). This must be considered when preparing for the exchange(s) with participants. My typical approach has been to number each photograph and place them into a photo album. This, of course, was only necessary when working with physical photographs, and in my case, these were 4" × 6" prints. It is critical when reviewing the audio transcripts that talk and photographs can be matched. This is why numbering the photographs is important. Audible cues during the exchange are helpful. For example, you may prompt the participant by saying "Tell me about picture number 14." This way it is clear that the participant is discussing a specific image, which is important when moving into the analysis—or ideation—stage of the process. Depending on the objecthood of the images—along with a whole host of other factors—different decisions will need to be made regarding how the participant(s) will engage with the images during the interview(s).

Temporality

Goldstein (2007) asserted that cameras cannot replicate human vision because photographs are two dimensional representations. Photographs are a record of a very brief moment in time. Moreover, photographs capture a decided moment, not a decisive one (Goldstein, 2007, p. 72). According to Berger (1972/1990), no photograph is a "mechanical recording" (p. 10) because the specific image within the photograph was selected by the photographer, one among infinite possibilities. Photography usually includes both temporal and spatial editing. Photographers select some images (i.e. moments in time) over others. And photographers also crop photographs, giving focus and frame to some particular aspect (i.e. space) of the image (Goldstein, 2007). Collier (1967) reminded us that "[t]he camera is an optical system—it has no selective process—and alone it offers no means of evading the need for perceptive sensitivity" (p. xiii). Tinkler (2013) noted that

> [t]he temporalities of photo-interviews are central to understanding the complexity of the verbal-visual relationship. Photos represent a split second . . . the meaning of this moment is not transparent and so an account is required to create both content and meaning . . . There is often a temporal disjuncture between taking a photo and occasions of viewing which provides an opportunity to explain and confer meaning on the occasion pictured.
>
> *p. 184*

There is almost always a time lapse (from minutes to hours to days) between the time a participant takes her or his photographs and the time when the participant narrates the contents of those photographs in an interview or focus group situation. As such, the *person* who took the photographs may not be the exact same *person* who narrates those photographs. Interviewers would do well by asking probing questions about this difference. Some examples include: What were you thinking when you took this photograph, and what are you thinking now, upon viewing the images? These questions could be followed up by: Describe how and why your thinking has changed. One of the reasons for probing participants in this way is to generate additional context for the images, as this will be necessary when the work is disseminated through the exhibition and other means. Another reason is simply to make space for, and encourage, participants to fully articulate their process, which is guided by their thinking. Depending on the time between the documentation and narration phase, the participant may need to engage in memory work, which invites another temporal dimension to the exchange. Researchers must bear this in mind and attempt to conduct photo-elicitation interviews as soon after the photographs are taken as possible. Flusser (1983/2000) said:

> [e]very single photograph is the result, at one and the same time, of co-operation and of conflict between camera and photographer. Consequently, a photograph can be considered decoded when one has succeeded in establishing how co-operation and conflict act on one another within it.
>
> *pp. 46–47*

This excerpt dovetails nicely with the ways in which I explained the time lapse above. Much of this decoding process occurs as the participants narrate their images within the interview or focus group.

Focus Groups

Focus groups are commonly used within photovoice projects. The synergies created through group dialogue can cause participants to generate data not possible through the use of discrete interviews. Focus groups can be thought of as group interviews. We also might think of them as brainstorming sessions, charrettes, plenaries, talking circles, or group discussions. Focus groups will certainly provide space for participants to narrate the contents of their images. Narrating these images in the presence of one another necessarily begins preliminary analysis of the data as participants begin to see, hear, and reiterate themes. In a sense, photovoice focus groups can be seen as opportunities for data generation and initial meaning making of those data. This is an opportunity for the participatory nature of the methodology to shine.

Ideally, focus groups should be video recorded so specific insights about specific photographs can be attributed to specific participants. Depending on how the focus group is structured, audio recording may suffice. In addition to recording the session, keeping field notes and/or giving the participants the opportunity to draw out their ideas could also be helpful. As themes within the narrations begin to develop, one approach for cataloguing them is participatory diagramming. Kesby (2000) said "participants can actively see the results of the research [when using participatory diagramming] . . . Thus participants, not merely researchers, can learn from the results, set new research objectives, adapt methods and, ultimately, attempt to act on the research findings" (p. 425). This can—and does— happen within photovoice interviews as well. This may be especially possible if participants are interviewed more than once. While I have found that participants are not typically interested in being involved with data analysis, they may be interested in understanding and co-constructing themes.

Interviews

While most photovoice projects involve focus groups, there are circumstances that warrant individual interviews. Depending on the topic, participants may feel safer sharing aspects of their lives in a one-on-one situation. Additionally, it may be hard to schedule focus groups if participants have busy schedules or if they are not already part of a group that meets regularly (e.g. after school program participants). Smart (2009) stated that "[i]nterviews require respondents to provide linear narrative, which is then 'flattened' onto a page of typescript, robbed of a great deal of expression and non-verbal communication" (p. 296). While this may be the case, I argue that the photo-elicitation interview can be a process of unflattening (Sousanis, 2015). Because of the presence of photographs, the participant's narrative usually departs from linearity. And while this can generate an organic, open, friendly, and lively exchange, photovoice researchers may also want to invite some pragmatic sequencing into the interview through the use of a well-composed open-ended, semi-structured interview protocol (Spradley, 1979).

I recommend a four-part interview protocol: (a) warm up questions; (b) photo elicitation; (c) process questions; and (d) demographic information gathering (if relevant). The first part should consist of questions that help the participant warm up and begin to feel at ease with the exchange while still attending to the topic at hand. The second part consists of the participant narrating the contents of the photographs he or she created. Tinkler (2013) listed several questions to ask in advance of conducting photo-interviews:

- How many photo-interviews and when?
- What kinds of photos will be discussed?
- Do you want interviewees to think about their photos in advance of the interview?
- Which photos will be included in the interview?
- Who decides how the photos will be looked at?
- Will you need strategies to stimulate or focus talk?
- What types of data do you need to generate during the interview and how will you achieve this?

pp. 182–183

Wagner (1979) said "[photographs] never tell us all we want to know, of course, but they can provide an excellent vehicle for asking important questions" (p. 289). While several researchers advocate the use of mnemonic devices during this stage, such as the SHOWeD (Wang, 1996, 1999) or PHOTO (Graziano, 2004; Hussey, 2006) technique, in nearly every instance participants I have interviewed arrived to the space excited and ready to see and talk about their images. SHOWeD stands for: What do you **S**ee here? What is really **H**appening here? How does this relate to **O**ur lives? **W**hy does this situation, concern, or strength exist? What can we **D**o about it? However, some researchers have found this technique to be ineffective or only partially effective (e.g. McIntyre, 2003; Wilson et al., 2007). PHOTO stands for: Describe your **P**icture. What is **H**appening in your picture? Why did you take a picture **O**f this? What does this **T**ell us about your life? How can this picture provide **O**pportunities for us to improve life? Simply asking participants to "tell me about your pictures" along with a gentle reminder of the prompts yielded robust storytelling; as I have found to be true in my own photovoice work, images "*ask their own questions* which can often yield unpredictable answers" (Collier, 1979, p. 274, italics in original). In many ways, this phase of the interview is an exercise in storytelling and active listening. And as the participants move from image to image, there are opportunities to ask all sorts of questions about the photographs. While not adhering to the SHOWeD method, I asked questions in the moment—it is like a dance, like jazz. The movements are always different, contextual. And there is always room for syncopation, which is helpful in moving into the nooks and crannies of experience and expression. Sometimes, however, "[p]hotographs [are] easy to take but [are] challenging to summarize" (Killion & Wang, 2000, p. 322). In these instances, probing questions should be used. Becker (2007) reminded us that "[a]ny representation of social reality . . . is necessarily partial, less than what you would experience and have available to interpret if you were in the actual setting it represents" (p. 20). The representation, usually and ideally, tells you—or the intended audience—what you need to know so you can do what you want to do, and nothing more or less. Those making representations typically know more than they show. This is a reality many photovoice researchers are well aware of. According to Mamary, McCright, and Roe (2007) "photovoice recognizes the human experience is complex and that any particular phenomenon can only be fully understood by those who actually experience it" (p. 360).

The third part involved asking participants questions about their process. Tinkler (2013) said:

> What people photograph is also shaped by the research task and context . . . Some studies invite participants to imagine specific audiences when producing photos . . . How research participants respond to the researcher's task will also be shaped by photographic opportunities, such as how and where the photographer can move and what they can access.
>
> p. 169

We must consider age, ability, size (e.g. height), and duration and location of the photography period (not an exhaustive list). Here are some examples questions to consider asking during this phase of the exchange:

- What was being a part of this project like?
- Who were you thinking about when you took these photographs? Why?
- What kinds of questions, if any, did you receive from others about engaging in this project?
- How did you decide what to photograph?
- Was the project difficult for you? Why or why not?
- Did you enjoy being a part of this project? Why or why not?
- What was it like for you to talk about your images?
- What did you gain or learn, if anything, from being a part of this project?
- Have you ever done anything like this before? If yes, please explain
- Do you plan to have involvement in the photo exhibition, which will take place in the spring? Why or why not?

- May I contact you again in the future if I have questions or need clarification about your images or our interview?

Tinkler (2013) said "much can be learned from photographic practices, that is how and why photos are made . . . what these practices mean to the people and institutions involved" (p. 79). Goldstein (2007) asserted "[e]very photograph is manipulated"; if we take this as a given, "the more interesting question is often why the photographer made these choices" (p. 75). When viewing a photograph absent of the photographer's explanation, the "why" cannot be known. Within photovoice, however, interviewers can ask participant-photographers all about the whys. In this context, both sides of the lens are able to come together.

Finally, the fourth part involves gathering demographic information about the participant if deemed necessary. This would include asking questions about age, sex, gender identity, race, ethnicity, grade level, and so on. This information should only be gathered if it will be used purposefully. Nothing should be assumed in terms of demographic information and identity constructs. For example, if an individual presents as White, it should not be assumed that that individual identifies as White in terms of race. It can be awkward in some instances to ask individuals questions about their identity. For example, asking someone their age can be perceived as affronting and rude in some cultural contexts. To assuage any potential awkwardness that may arise during this phase, it can help to explain to the participant why you are asking the questions. Just as it is acceptable for participants to leave the study—without penalty and at any time—no person has to respond to any question you ask if they are not comfortable doing so.

Writing, Titling, and Captioning

Within some studies, researchers have asked participants to write out the meanings of the photographs they created rather than discuss them orally. In addition, sometimes free writing among participants is used as a warm up exercise in advance of the verbal exchange(s). Another version of writing in lieu of or in advance of talk is engaging participants in the process of titling and captioning the images they feel are most important. This activity is a great way to prepare images for display during the presentation phase.

Policy Posters

Within Mitchell, de Lange, and Nguyen's (2016) project, the participants, including 22 girls and women with various disabilities in Vietnam, created "'policy posters,' a term we [chapter authors] coined to describe the activity of producing a message for policy makers and other community leaders" (p. 246). The creation of policy posters is an innovative way to distill the findings of a photovoice study down to the essential messages participants would like to convey to policy makers. Moreover, the posters can serve as an easily consumable medium, something policy makers can quickly understand. Mitchell et al. (2016) also considered the importance of playfulness and fun within the project, especially considering they worked with young women with disabilities. Why not encourage participants to be playful and have fun during the process? Even in the event that some participants are uninterested in playfulness and fun, introducing play and fun as possibilities can create positive affective conditions that can make participation in a *research project* seem much less clinical.

Other Forms of Narration

If you spend any amount of time perusing social media feeds, you are bound to come across visual expressions made possible through a variety of web apps and websites. Collages, memes, and animated gifs loom large in the social media worlds of Facebook, Twitter, Tumblr, and Instragram. Depending on the participants with whom you are working, it may be an interesting endeavor to promote a wide range of photographic means through which participants can convey their responses to the provided prompts. High school students, for example, might revel in the creative affordances of such a project. The efficacy of such an approach is yet to be seen.

Summary

Within this chapter, I explicated the first five steps of the photovoice process: identification, invitation, education, documentation, and narration. These processes can be complex and knotty, as there are many details to think through and keep in mind. On the other hand, submerging yourself in the process can be a fascinating, educative, and intensely rewarding experience. I encourage you, as a photovoice researcher, to glean as much joy from this adventurous process as possible. Your participants will consistently amaze you. Chapter 4 is dedicated to the sixth phase of the process: ideation.

References

Allen, Q. (2012). Photographs and stories: Ethics, benefits and dilemmas of using participant photography with Black middle-class male youth. *Qualitative Research, 12*, 443–458. doi: 10.1177/1468794111433088

Andrews, J. O., Newman, S. D., Meadows, O., Cox, M, J., & Bunting, S. (2012). Partnership readiness for community-based participatory research. *Health Education Research, 27*, 555–571.

Baker, T. A., & Wang, C. C. (2006) Photovoice: Use of a participatory action research method to explore chronic pain experiences in older adults. *Qualitative Health Research, 16*, 1405–1413.

Barthes, R. (1981). *Camera lucida: Reflections on photography* (R. Howard, Trans.). New York: Hill and Wang. (Original work published in 1980.)

Batchen, G. (1997). *Burning with desire: The conception of photography.* Cambridge, MA: The MIT Press.

Becker, H. S. (2007). *Telling about society.* Chicago, IL: University of Chicago Press.

Berger, J. (1990). *Ways of seeing.* New York: Penguin. (Original work published in 1972.)

Bloustien, G., & Baker, S. (2003). On not talking to strangers: Researching the micro worlds of girls through visual auto-ethnographic practices. *Social Analysis, 47*(3), 64–79.

Bourgois, P., & Schonberg, J. (2009). *Righteous dopefiend.* Berkeley, CA: University of California Press.

Catalani, C., & Minkler, M. (2010). Photovoice: A review of the literature in health and public health. *Health Education & Behavior, 37*, 424–451. doi: 101177/1090198109342084

Charmaz, K. (2006). *Constructing grounded theory: A practical guide through qualitative analysis.* Thousand Oaks, CA: Sage.

Collier, J. (1957). Photography in anthropology: A report on two experiments. *American Anthropologist, 59*, 843–859.

Collier, J. (1967). *Visual anthropology: Photography as research method.* New York: Holt, Rinehart and Winston.

Collier, J. (1979). Visual anthropology. In J. Wagner (Ed.), *Images of information: Still photography in the social sciences* (pp. 271–281). Beverly Hills, CA: Sage.

Cowan, P. (1999). "Drawn" into the community: Reconsidering the artwork of Latino adolescents. *Visual Sociology, 14*(1/2), 91–107.

Crilly, N., Blackwell, A. F., & Clarkson, P. J. (2006). Graphic elicitation: Using research diagrams as interview stimuli. *Qualitative Research, 6*, 341–366. doi: 10.1177/1468794106065007

Edwards, E. (1992). *Anthropology & photography: 1860–1920.* New Haven, CT: Yale University Press.

Edwards, E. (2002). Material beings: Objecthood and ethnographic photographs. *Visual Studies, 17*, 67–75.

Eisner, E. W. (1995). What artistically crafted research can help us understand about schools. *Educational Theory, 45*, 1–6.

Ewald, W., & Lightfoot, A. (2001). *I wanna take me a picture: Teaching photography and writing to children.* Boston, MA: Beacon.

Findholt, N. E., Michael, Y. L., & David, M. M. (2010). Photovoice engages rural youth in childhood obesity prevention. *Public Health Nursing, 28*, 186–192. doi: 10.1111/j.1525-1446.2010.00895.x

Flusser, V. (2000). *Towards a philosophy of photography.* London: Reaktion Books. (Original work published in 1983.)

Goldstein, B. M. (2007). All photos lie: Images as data. In G. C. Stanczak (Ed.), *Visual research methods: Image, society, and representation* (pp. 61–81). Thousand Oaks, CA: Sage.

Graziano, K. J. (2004). Oppression and resiliency in a post-apartheid South Africa: Unheard voices of black gay men and lesbians. *Cultural Diversity and Ethnic Minority Psychology, 10*, 302–316. doi: 10.1037/1099-9809.10.3.302

Harper, D. (1987). *Working knowledge: Skill and community in a small shop.* Berkeley, CA: University of California Press.

Harper, D. (2002). Talking about pictures: A case for photo elicitation. *Visual Studies, 17*, 13–26.

Harper, D. (2012). *Visual sociology*. New York: Routledge.
Heisley, D. D., & Levy, S. J. (1991). Autodriving: A photoelicitation technique. *Journal of Consumer Research*, *18*, 257–272.
Hergenrather, K. C., Rhodes, S. D., Cowan, C. A., Bardhoshi, G., & Pula, S. (2009). Photovoice as community-based participatory research: A qualitative review. *American Journal of Health Behavior*, *33*, 686–698.
Hussey, J. (2006). Slivers of the journey: The use of photovoice and story telling to examine female to male transsexuals' experience of health care access. *Journal of Homosexuality*, *51*, 129–158. doi: 10.1300/J082v51n01_07
Kesby, M. (2000). Participatory diagramming: Deploying qualitative methods through an action research epistemology. *Royal Geographical Society (with the Institute of British Geographers)*, *32*, 423–435.
Killion, C. M., & Wang, C. C. (2000). Linking African American mothers across life stage and station through photovoice. *Journal of Health Care for the Poor and Underserved*, *11*, 310–325.
Kuhn, A. (2007). Photography and cultural memory: A methodological exploration. *Visual Studies*, *22*, 283–292. doi: 10.1080/14725860701657175
Latz, A. O. (2011). *Understanding the educational lives of community colleges students through photovoice* (unpublished doctoral dissertation) Muncie, IN: Ball State University.
Luttrell, W. (2010). 'A camera is a big responsibility': A lens for analyzing children's visual voices. *Visual Studies*, *25*, 224–237. doi: 10.1080/1472586X.2010.523274
Mamary, E., McCright, J., & Roe, K. (2007). Our lives: An examination of sexual health issues using photovoice by non-gay identified African American men who have sex with men. *Culture, Health & Sexuality*, *9*, 359–370. doi: 10.1080/13691050601035415
Maynard, P. (1997). *Thinking through photography: The engine of visualization*. Ithaca, NY: Cornell University Press.
McIntyre, A. (2003). Through the eyes of women: Photovoice and participatory research as tools for reimagining place. *Gender, Place and Culture: A Journal of Feminist Geography*, *10*, 47–66. doi: 10.1080/0966369032000052658
McKim, R. H. (1980). *Experiences in visual thinking* (2nd edn). Belmont, CA: Wadsworth.
Mitchell, C., de Lange, N., & Nguyen, X. T. (2016). Visual ethics with and through the body: The participation of girls with disabilities in Vietnam in a photovoice project. In J. Coffey, S. Budgeon, & H. Cahill (Eds.), *Learning bodies: The body in youth and childhood studies* (pp. 241–257). New York: Springer Science+Business Media.
Nykiforuk, C. I. J., Vallianatos, H., & Nieuwendyk, L. M. (2011). Photovoice as a method for revealing community perceptions of the built and social environment. *International Journal of Qualitative Methods*, *10*, 103–124. doi: 10.1177/160940691101000201
Rose, G. (2004). "Everyone's cuddled up and it just looks really nice": An emotional geography of some mums and their family photos. *Social & Cultural Geography*, *5*, 549–564. doi: 10.1080/1464936042000317695
Sassoon, J. (2004). Photographic materiality in the age of digital reproduction. In E. Edwards & J. Hart (Eds.), *Photographs objects histories: On the materiality of images* (pp. 186–202). New York: Routledge.
Smart, C. (2009). Shifting horizons: Reflections on qualitative methods. *Feminist Theory*, *10*, 295–308.
Smith, L. T. (2012). *Decolonizing methodologies: Research and indigenous peoples* (2nd edn). New York: Zed Books.

Smith, S. M. (2014). Photography between desire and grief: Roland Barthes and F. Holland Day. In E. H. Brown & T. Phu (Eds.), *Feeling photography* (pp. 29–46). Durham, NC: Duke University Press.

Sousanis, N. (2015). *Unflattening*. Cambridge, MA: Harvard University Press.

Spradley, J. P. (1979). *The ethnographic interview*. New York: Holt, Reinhart, & Winston.

Strack, R. W., Lovelace, K. A., Davis Jordan, T., & Holmes, A. P. (2010). Framing photovoice using a social-ecological model as a guide. *Health Promotion Practice, 11*, 629–636. doi: 10.1177/1524839909355519

Sutton-Brown, C. A. (2014). Photovoice: A methodological guide. *Photography & Culture, 7*, 169–186. doi: 10.2752/175145214X13999922103165

Tinkler, P. (2013). *Using photographs in social and historical research*. Thousand Oaks, CA: Sage.

Van Dijck, J. (2005). From shoebox to performative agent: The computer as personal memory machine. *New Media Society, 7*, 311–332. doi: 10.1177/1461444805050765

Wagner, J. (1979). Photography and social science process. In J. Wagner (Ed.), *Images of information: Still photography in the social sciences* (pp. 271–281). Beverly Hills, CA: Sage.

Wang, C. C. (1999). Photovoice: A participatory action research strategy applied to women's health. *Journal of Women's Health, 8*, 185–192.

Wang, C. C. (2006). Youth participation in photovoice as a strategy for community change. *Journal of Community Practice, 14*, 147–161.

Wang, C. C., & Burris, M. A. (1997). Photovoice: Concept, methodology, and use for participatory needs assessment. *Health Education and Behavior, 24*, 369–387.

Wang, C. C., Cash, J. L., & Powers, L. S. (2000). Who knows the streets as well as the homeless? Promoting personal and community action through photovoice. *Health Promotion Practice, 1*, 81–89.

Wang, C. C., & Redwood-Jones, Y. A. (2001). Photovoice ethics: Perspectives from Flint photovoice. *Health Education and Behavior, 28*, 560–572.

Willson, K., Green, K., Hayworth-Brockman, M., & Rapaport Beck, R. (2006). Looking out: Prairie women use photovoice methods to fight poverty. *Canadian Woman Studies, 25*(3–4), 160–166.

Wilson, N., Dasho, S., Martin, A. C., Wallerstein, N., Wang, C. C., & Minkler, M. (2007). Engaging young adolescents in social action through photovoice: The youth empowerment strategies (YES!) project. *The Journal of Early Adolescence, 27*, 241–261. doi: 10.1177/0272431606294834

4
(PARTICIPATORY) DATA ANALYSIS

A Vignette

I wrote the following analytic memo while completing the analysis for my dissertation (Latz, 2011). It is included here to illustrate the tensions I experienced and the potential complexity of the analysis process.

Analytic Memo, January 29, 2011, On the Research Process

I feel compelled to try to metaphorically explain what this research process feels like. At the risk of sounding like a positivist, I'm going to incorporate the word *bits*. I feel like I'm working on a jigsaw puzzle. But, it's a very weird jigsaw puzzle. If regular puzzle pieces are Lego bricks, my puzzle pieces are Duplo Blocks. They're big and easy to touch. The weirdness enters because the puzzle pieces, which represent all of the bits of information I have amassed in my brain over time—both before and during this dissertation project, change shape sometimes when I reach out to pick up and handle them. They don't seem to be controlled by gravity like I am.

Just when I think I've got a handle on some bit, when I think I really know it, it changes—and the puzzle becomes increasingly complex. Some bits do not change; some are in constant change, motion. Then, puzzle pieces come and go. New pieces are constantly arriving, and old ones go away. The goal, the image on the box, is a fuzzy one. But it's not quite as bad as when I try to see the world without my glasses or contact lenses. I'm not exactly sure what I'm building yet. I know it's not a perfectly closed quadrilateral. It looks more like a rug with fringes. Maybe it's a circle.

My puzzle, even when complete, will be waiting for more pieces, more bits.

★ ★ ★

Data Analysis for (at Least) Two Purposes

Within this chapter, I offer suggestions and examples related to data analysis within photovoice studies. This is the sixth step of the process: ideation. Current literature on the photovoice methodology provides little guidance on how to analyze the data generated. Brunsden and Goatcher (2007) noted that "[o]ne issue that arises with previous studies utilizing the photovoice technique is a lack of clarity regarding the analytic process used on the data" (p. 47). And what does exist within the literature is vague. For example, Hergenrather, Rhodes, Cowan, Bardhoshi, and Pula (2009) noted that word data generated through photovoice projects are "analyzed like other qualitative data, through codifying data, and exploring, formulating, and interpreting themes" (p. 688). This may be the case, but there are a myriad of ways in which qualitative word data may be approached analytically. The lack of analytical specificity offered within most extant photovoice literature leads researchers to look outside the methodology when deciding on the best way(s) to analyze data.

When considering analysis with photovoice projects, it becomes clear that the analyses are carried out for (at least) two purposes. First, in the spirit of participatory action research, data must be translated into actionable steps. This translation takes place during the analysis. On the other hand we as academics are often expected to add to the knowledge bases within our respective areas of expertise. Doing so includes presenting research at academic conferences and writing papers to be published in scholarly journals. Dense and detailed articulations about how findings were derived are critical within academic spheres, as audiences will want to know how you moved from evidence to claims. So as photovoice researchers, we are in a position to contribute, differently, to at least two audiences. The extant photovoice literature provides little guidance on how to do this.

Purpose One: Shaping the Action

That being said, some researchers have articulated their analytical steps, which are often participatory—especially as it relates to shaping the action that follows a participatory action research project. Wang and Burris (1997) proposed a three-stage approach: selecting, contextualizing, and codifying. It is up to the participants to select which photographs will be a part of the project. This is what is meant by the gerund, selecting. By tagging which photographs are more germane to the prompts, participants create the critical mass of visual material necessary for the next stage, contextualizing. This step is encapsulated in the acronym VOICE:

Voicing Our Individual and Collective Experience (Wang & Burris, 1997, p. 381). Contextualizing unfolds in various ways including group discussions, caption writing, and storytelling. Finally, the group engages in codifying. During this stage, the group "may identify three types of dimensions that arise from the dialogue [contextualizing] process: issues, themes, or theories" (Wang & Burris, 1997, p. 381). Issues signal identification of concerns that are targeted for immediate action, which should be prioritized. The group may also develop themes within the dialogue that may warrant further interrogation. Theories are potential explanations for issues and themes that are linked to the dialogical data derived during the process. Crilly, Blackwell, and Clarkson (2006) suggested that diagrams might be useful in mapping data analysis procedures. Moreover, they opined that showing participants such diagrams—along with those that showcase emergent theory, in the case of a grounded theory study—might be a useful form of member checking. Such an approach could easily be used within Wang and Burris's (1997) schema. The process of selecting, contextualizing, and codifying follows no predetermined schema, which is a stark contrast from more turgid approaches provided in the qualitative research literature.

Tinkler (2013) proposed the following steps in analyzing the photo-elicitation interview:

- Look (What do participants see?)
- Contextualize (How to the photos fit into the participants' lives?)
- Listen (What is said? What is not said?)
- Juxtapose (How does the talk compare to the visual?)
- Watch (How to the participants interact with the photographs?)
- Trace (In what ways is the total narrative irreducible to the discrete narratives based on individual photos?)

pp. 193–194

And while Tinkler's suggestions imply a non-participatory approach to analysis, according to Sutton-Brown (2014), "to maintain fidelity to the original concept, the participants should be actively involved in all phases of the research process as feasible" (p. 71). Here, "as feasible" is key. Depending on the circumstances, some participants may not want to be involved in certain phases of the process. The analysis phase is one such phase.

Purpose Two: Adding to What Is Known

An Extended Example: Blending Photovoice and Grounded Theory

In an article published in 1974 focused on the use of photography within sociology, Becker wrote that colleagues "will find the work and methods I describe hopelessly unscientific" (p. 6). The same is the case for photovoice. This piece from Becker was written over 40 years ago, yet the attitude remains. I experienced this sentiment from some academicians during the course of completing my dissertation. Becker (1974) also said: a "subsidiary question of interest to photographers and to sociologists who may take a photographic approach to their work, is: what can be done to make that work intellectually denser?" (p. 11). What tactics can be employed during the photovoice process to make space for intellectual density?

When conceptualizing and putting together my dissertation, I essentially blended two methodologies: photovoice and constructivist grounded theory. They served each other well. Photovoice does not come "ready made" with prescribed analytical steps. Similarly, constructivist grounded theory does not come "ready made" with a charge for action. What follows is an extended articulation of the analytical processes I employed during my dissertation study (Latz, 2011). Salient parts of my methods chapter are put forward here as an example. It should be noted, however, that researchers have blended other analytical approaches with photovoice as well. For example, Plunkett, Leipert, and Ray (2013) wrote about how photovoice can augment phenomenological studies. There are myriad possibilities.

Excerpts from an Unpublished Doctoral Dissertation

A grounded theory analytical approach (Bryant & Charmaz, 2007/2010; Charmaz, 2003, 2005, 2006; Glaser & Strauss, 1967; Strauss & Corbin, 1998a, 1998b) was used for this study. Four grounded theories were generated throughout the course of this project. One of the goals of the photovoice methodology, and this study in particular, was to reach policy makers to affect change. As a form of participatory action research, implicit in photovoice is action. The grounded theories generated were inextricably bound to the findings. Strauss and Corbin (1998b) noted that "grounded theories can . . . be relevant and possibly influential either to the 'understanding' of policy makers or to their direct action" (p. 175). The combination of the photovoice methodology and the grounded theory analytical framework can provide a powerful means to reach those decisions makers whose choices will directly affect the educational lives of the participants involved. It is important to note, however, that many grounded theorists contest that grounded theories can and should have impact and relevance beyond the sphere of the participants and data within which the theories have been grounded. Strauss and Corbin (1998b) argued that "grounded theory is likely to be used, and used in ways other than any dreamed of by us researchers/theorists – far beyond our commitments and desires" (p. 175).

While these two approaches, participatory action research and grounded theory, are not typically regarded as being members of the same research family (Dick, 2007/2010), they can be complementary. In fact, "the combination can be very effective" (Dick, p. 403). Action research (Merriam & Simpson, 2000) does not typically generate theory. Moreover, the literature on action research does not sufficiently explain how to analyze data. On the other hand, grounded theory does not advocate participant involvement in the research process. And, it does not position action as a specific goal. As such, the two approaches can blend together to enable researchers to generate theory to then take informed action, with participants, to resolve a problem (Dick, 2007/2010). Photovoice and grounded theory have been successfully used together by researchers (e.g. Hergenrather, Rhodes, & Clark, 2006; Leipert, 2010; López, Eng, Randall-Davis, & Robinson, 2005). López et al. (2005) blended photovoice and grounded theory "to provide the means for participants to move beyond merely reporting results to policy and decision makers to suggesting strategies and participating in developing interventions tailored to specific conditions of their social context" (p. 101).

Researcher Characteristics

Strauss and Corbin (1998a) provided a list of requisite skills for becoming a grounded theorist. The characteristics include the ability to: (a) critically analyze situations; (b) recognize tendency toward bias; (c) think abstractly; (d) be open to criticism; (e) have sensitivity for participants' actions and words; and (f) become absorbed and committed to the work process. Moreover, Strauss and Corbin (1998a) stressed that if researchers fully understand the grounded theory approach and become confident in their abilities, "then they should be able to apply them [grounded theory procedures] flexibly and creatively to their own material" (p. 14). At the start of this endeavor, I reflected upon the characteristics above and evaluated myself. I felt properly equipped to carry out research using a grounded theory approach. The flexibility of the photovoice method and the grounded theory analytical frame made them attractive and appropriate for the present study. The flexibility within the research frame I composed led to methodological learning, which was an additional outcome of this project. The great potential for a creative application of grounded theory was also appealing to me as a researcher. I feel at my best as a researcher, writer, and scholar when I am able to be creative in analysis and expression. The blend of photovoice and grounded theory not only match well to the topic of this project, community college students, but also to me as a researcher.

Constructivist Grounded Theory

Grounded theory has evolved since its inception. Originally developed in 1967 by Barney Glaser and Anselm Strauss (1967), grounded theory has been adapted and tinkered with over time, both by Glaser and Strauss as well as other researchers such as Juliet Corbin (Strauss & Corbin, 1998a, 1998b), Kathy Charmaz (2003, 2005, 2006), Adele Clarke (2003, 2005), Antony Bryant (2002, 2003), and Clive Seale (1999). Contemporary scholars have moved grounded theory away from its positivistic roots and toward a more constructivist frame. Charmaz (2006) wrote:

> I assume that neither data nor theories are discovered. Rather, we are part of the world we study and the data we collect. We *construct* our grounded theories through our past and present involvements and interactions with people, perspectives, and research practices.
>
> *p. 10, italics in original*

In other words, "data don't generate theory—only researchers do that" (Mintzberg, 1979, p. 584). As such, Charmaz built her version of grounded theory based on the notion that no theories spring out from data. Rather, researchers construct them from the data in very individualized ways. Her position is also illustrative of a symbolic interactionist theoretical perspective.

Symbolic interactionism (Becker & McCall, 1990; Blumer, 1969; Charon, 2010; Reynolds & Herman-Kinney, 2003) is a theoretical perspective that assumes people construct themselves, reality, and society through interaction. Symbolic interactionists view the human being in a very specific way. First, human beings are social. Individuals are created through interaction, as is society, and it is the interactions that propel human beings to do what they do. As such, interactions, instead of personality or social forces, become the primary focus of researchers. Second, the human being is a thinking being. Interactions not only take place between human beings, between human beings and symbols, but also within an individual human being. Therefore, thinking is also of interest to the researcher. Third, human beings define the situations they are in versus directly observing them. While a symbolic interactionist would acknowledge the existence of an actual environment, in the objectivist sense, he or she would also argue that an individual's definition, which is constructed through interaction, is more important than the actual environment. Fourth, the cause of human action is present only at the time of the action. In other words, as a situation unfolds, individuals interact with others around them, memories of their past, and their own thinking. Fifth, human beings are active, rather than passive, within their environments. In summary, to understand human action, symbolic interactionists must "focus on social interaction, human thinking, definition of the situation, the present, and the active nature of the human being" (Charon, 2010, p. 29).

Within this perspective, every object is a social object that can stimulate action. We learn about the meaning of objects from social interaction. An example of a social object is a symbol. Words, gestures, and physical objects are symbols. All symbols have meanings that are created through social interaction. Symbols create reality and make complex society possible. All human action is carried out with symbols. The environment does not impose itself on the individual, but rather the individual is in a constant state of active creation and recreation of the environment through the symbol (Charon, 2010).

Taking a symbolic interactionist stance, society is in a constant state of motion and redefinition as individuals interact. The interactions of humans with selves and minds create societies when they are cooperative and problem solving. Each individual is a part of many societies, or cultures, that all play a role in that individual's conception of reality and self-definition. Similar to the ways individuals can be altered, shaped, and defined through social interaction among individuals, so can culture (Charon, 2010).

Goffman (1959) provided important contributions to this theoretical perspective. He suggested that life can be understood as dramatic performance. He wrote:

> When an individual enters the presence of others, they commonly seek to acquire information about him [sic] or to bring into play information about him already possessed. They will be interested in his general socio-economic status, his conception of self, his attitude toward them, his competence, his trustworthiness, etc. Although some of this information seems to be sought almost as an end in itself, there are usually quite practical reasons for acquiring it. Information about the individual helps to define the situation, enabling others to know in advance what he will expect of them and what they may expect of him. Informed in these ways, the others will know how best to act in order to call forth a desired response from him.
>
> p. 1

When individuals interact, they are both actors and an audience for the acts of others. Social actors use elements of performance such as script, tone, costume, makeup, posture, and stage design to create social realities. Performances are done individually and in teams. Depending on context, different roles are played by individuals. Through this perspective, all of life's social interactions are viewed as a performance. These collective performances are what create societies.

Taking this perspective, constructivist grounded theorists acknowledge that both the data and the analytical process result from complicated interactions and relationships between the researcher and participants, the researcher and his or her past experiences, and the participants and their past experiences. Therefore, constructivist grounded theorists "take a reflexive stance toward the research process and products and consider how their theories evolve . . . constructivism fosters researchers' reflexivity about their own interpretations as well as those of their research participants" (Charmaz, 2006, p. 131).

Take, for example, this excerpt from Strauss and Corbin (1998a):

> 'Limited experimenting' is what the analyst is calling the type of drug use engaged in by most teens. The teens might refer to drug use as 'trying just a few,' being careful about 'which drugs you use,' using only at 'parties' and with 'friends' as part of a 'social act,' using the 'less potent' drugs, and so

on. In other words they tell us when, how, with whom, and where they are using. Our translation and definition of this phenomenon or what is going on in this situation is that teens are engaged in 'limited experimenting' with drugs. It is our interpretation of events.

pp. 126–127

It is critical to note here, that in the example above, it is the researcher who is providing a label and giving meaning to the drug use described by the teens. A constructivist grounded theorist would acknowledge this and not assert that the label and meaning came from the data. Rather, the label and meaning came from the interactions between the researcher, the researcher's past experiences and knowledge of teen drug use, and the data. Herein lies the critical intersection of the constructivist underpinning of constructivist grounded theory and the symbolic interactionist perspective.

Coding

All word data generated by this study, which came from interviews with participants, were coded in triplicate. The three rounds of coding consisted of open, axial, and theoretical coding. Coding is a critical step in the analytic process because it "is the pivotal link between collecting data and developing an emergent theory to explain these data" (Charmaz, 2006, p. 46). Through the coding process "conceptual abstraction of data and its reintegration as takes place" (Holton, 2007/2010, p. 265). It is important to note here that the photographs taken by participants were viewed as a source of data, but the participants assigned the meanings associated with the photographs through the interviews. It was not my role, as the researcher, to assign meaning to the images. As such, it was the participants who provided an analysis, or an assignment of meaning, to their photographs.

Open Coding

First, transcripts of interviews/discussions were open coded. During this process, "data are broken down into discrete parts, closely examined, and compared for similarities and differences" (Strauss & Corbin, 1998a, p. 102). Analyzing data is much like working on a puzzle. Starting a puzzle usually involves sorting the pieces based on color and shape, which requires a keen eye as some shades or sizes may be similar, but significantly different. Open coding is similar to sorting puzzle pieces prior to putting the puzzle together (Strauss & Corbin, 1998a). During this process, researchers begin to conceptualize categories, build initial themes, and think about theory.

Qualitative data analysis software was not used. Transcripts were created in Microsoft Word. As a result, coding also took place electronically within Word.

Open codes were inserted into the text with brackets in bold. A priori codes were not used during the open coding process. Data chunks were coded, or labeled, either line by line or by sentence or paragraph where necessary. For example, if an entire paragraph was about a student's preference for background noise while studying, that particular segment of data will be coded by paragraph. There was potential for an enormous number of codes to be created during this process because "the researcher wishes to remain as open as possible to what may emerge from the line-by-line coding and not run the risk of precluding or predetermining what may eventually prove to be relevant to the emerging theory" (Holton, 2007/2010, pp. 276–277). A separate code key was retained and added to as interviews were coded. In total, 78 open codes were created. Open code saturation occurred after the eighth interview was coded. In other words, no new open codes were generated after coding interview eight. A total of 13 interviews were conducted.

Axial Coding

Next axial codes were created. Axial coding is a process of reassembling the fragments of word data that were dismantled during the open coding process. The puzzle pieces are put together in segments. During this process, categories and sub-categories were created. Data were labeled accordingly. The process is termed axial coding because open codes are collapsed and organized around the axis of a category. While I suggest here that open coding came before axial coding, "these are not necessarily sequential analytic steps" (Strauss & Corbin, 1998a, p. 124). The coding process I am articulating here was flexible. Initial theory building actually began occurring immediately. However, the analytic procedure outlined here remained as my guide.

Strauss (1987) provided four procedural steps for axial coding: (a) lay out the properties and dimensions of the categories; (b) identify the conditions, actions, interactions, and consequences associated with a phenomenon, or category; (c) relate categories to sub-categories; and (d) look for clues in the data to understand how major categories are related to one another. Axial codes were denoted in the Word document transcripts with color-coding. Four major categories were created: freedom (red highlights), academic integration (yellow highlights), roles (blue highlights), and reflective consciousness (green highlights). During axial coding of the transcripts, participant photos were also coded by category. Photos were organized in a three-ring binder with clear polypropylene sleeves, each holding six photos. Red, yellow, and blue stickie notes were placed on the clear sheets to denote to which category each photo belonged. No photos were associated with the reflective consciousness category. These determinations were based on the axial coding of the transcripts, which took place first. Again, the participants assigned meaning to the images; I did not. Through the process of axial coding, the data were less fragmented and the puzzle was one step closer to being complete. As data chunks were merged, the final picture became clearer, but before grounded theory can be developed fully, one additional round of coding took place.

Theoretical Coding

The final coding step was theoretical coding which "move[s] your analytic story in a theoretical direction" (Charmaz, 2006, p. 63). During this process, the researcher seeks to create connections between categories and further collapse thematic ideas. These codes help the researcher to understand how the substantive categories are related and helps the researcher paint an integrated and coherent analytical picture, which leads to theorizing. Within the Word document, I used the comments feature to insert theoretical codes. It is at this point where the researcher may consult the literature as another source of data to substantiate or disrupt the themes being constructed. However, I had been consulting the literature during the entire data collection and analysis process. Theoretical codes can be named and established with the assistance of existing literature, but the researcher must be cautious about fitting a square peg into a round hole. Regardless of "how intellectually seductive, fashionable, or discipline-dictated a theoretical code may be, to cross the line from theoretical exploration to forced integration with a preconceived theoretical model undermines the generative nature of grounded theory" (Holton, 2007/2010, p. 283).

Through this analytical process, theoretical coding served as a way for me to build sub-categories within the categories created for the axial codes. Data chunks were coded through the use of comments. However, I needed to reorganize the data to see a more complete picture. Pages and pages of color-coded transcripts transformed from being neat and tidy to messy and overwhelming. To combat this, I copied and pasted each color-coded data chunk into a separate Word document organized by category and sub-category. This document was comprised of 41 single-spaced pages of direct quotation from participants. As the data were teased out further, the potential for building specific grounded theories became more apparent and manageable.

Building Theory

The three levels of coding described above, open, axial, and theoretical, culminated in the creation of constructed grounded theories. It is vital to express here that data collection and analysis occurred simultaneously through a constant comparative approach (Dye, Schatz, Rosenberg, & Coleman, 2000; Glaser & Strauss, 1967). I interviewed one former student at a time. Once my first interview concluded, the analytical process began. Each interview was compared to the others during the coding process. Instances of common themes were further explicated through axial and theoretical coding and through memo writing. I began writing memos as soon as data collection began, and through this writing I immediately began thinking about the creation of theory. As such, grounded theory building began with the first interview, and the theories were reconstructed and refined through each step of the analytical process until theoretical saturation (Charmaz, 2006) was reached and final versions of the grounded theories were created.

Considering the small number of participants and goals of this project, the construction of substantive (Glaser, 2007/2010; Glaser & Strauss, 1967) grounded theories resulted from this endeavor. Substantive theory is bound to the data, and also the researcher who created it. Formal theory is meant to have applicability in a variety of settings and is created through the analysis and comparison of multiple sets of data. Glaser and Strauss (1967) explained that

> substantive theory is a strategic link in the formulation and generation of grounded formal theory. We believe that although formal theory can be generated directly from data, it is most desirable, and usually necessary, to start the formal theory from the substantive one.
>
> p. 79

It was not my desire to construct formal theory. Considering the goals of this project, substantive theory will best reach policy makers at a local level. Also, Glaser and Strauss's (1967) original iteration of the grounded theory approach embodied a positivistic perspective. Contemporary qualitative researchers assert that the findings from qualitative studies cannot be generalized to other settings. However, they can be transferrable (Lincoln & Guba, 1985), thereby highlighting their importance to the literature. As such, the substantive grounded theories I constructed will be vital for reaching policy makers at the local level, as mentioned above. I plan to disperse the grounded theories and findings of this study in the form of multiple articles in scholarly journals, conference presentations, and perhaps a book. Therefore, if and when this study begets other similar studies, the potential for the construction of formal theory is possible.

Summary

The purpose of this chapter was to provide insights into the complexity and dual (at least) purposes of data analysis within photovoice. Photovoice researchers often find themselves in a position where—because of the nature of participatory action research—the work must "speak" both to the policy makers identified at the start of the project and the researcher's professional mandate to produce academic scholarship that advances knowledge within his or her specialty area. Attending robustly to the latter, I presented excerpts from my unpublished doctoral dissertation—specific pieces from the methods chapter that explicate the process I underwent. The chapter that follows is dedicated to ethical quandaries and considerations surrounding photovoice as well as how to successfully traverse institutional review boards.

References

Becker, H. (1974). Photography and sociology. *Studies in the Anthropology of Visual Communication*, 1(1), 3–26.
Becker, H. S., & McCall, M. M. (Eds.). (1990). *Symbolic interaction and cultural studies*. Chicago, IL: University of Chicago Press.
Blumer, H. (1969). *Symbolic interactionism: Perspective and method*. Berkeley, CA: University of California Press.
Brunsden, V., & Goatcher, J. (2007). Reconfiguring photovoice for psychological research. *The Irish Journal of Psychology*, 28, 43–52. doi: 10.1080/03033910.2007.10446247
Bryant, A. (2002). Re-grounding grounded theory. *Journal of Information Technology Theory and Application*, 4(1), 25–42.
Bryant, A. (2003). A constructive/ist response to Glaser. *Forum: Qualitative Social Research*, 4(1). Retrieved from http://qualitative-research.net/index.php/fqs/article/view/757/1643
Bryant, A., & Charmaz, K. (Eds.). (2010). *The Sage handbook of grounded theory*. Thousand Oaks, CA: Sage. (Original work published in 2007.)
Charmaz, K. (2003). Grounded theory: Objectivist and constructivist methods. In N. K. Denzin & Y. S. Lincoln (Eds.), *Strategies of qualitative inquiry* (2nd edn, pp. 249–291). Thousand Oaks, CA: Sage.
Charmaz, K. (2005). Grounded theory in the 21st century: Applications for advancing social justice studies. In N. K. Denzin & Y. S. Lincoln (Eds.), *The Sage handbook of qualitative research* (3rd edn, pp. 507–535). Thousand Oaks, CA: Sage.
Charmaz, K. (2006). *Constructing grounded theory: A practical guide through qualitative analysis*. Thousand Oaks, CA: Sage.
Charon, J. M. (2010). *Symbolic interactionism: An introduction, an interpretation, an integration* (10th edn). Boston, MA: Pearson.
Clarke, A. E. (2003). Situational analysis: Grounded theory mapping after the postmodern turn. *Symbolic Interactionism*, 26, 553–576.
Clarke, A. E. (2005). *Situational analysis: Grounded theory after the postmodern turn*. Thousand Oaks, CA: Sage.
Crilly, N. Blackwell, A. F., & Clarkson, P. J. (2006). Graphic elicitation: Using research diagrams as interview stimuli. *Qualitative Research*, 6, 341–366. doi: 10.1177/1468794106065007
Dick, B. (2010). What can grounded theorists and action researchers learn from each other? In A. Bryant & K. Charmaz (Eds.), *The Sage handbook of grounded theory* (pp. 398–416). Thousand Oaks, CA: Sage. (Original work published in 2007.)
Dye, J. F., Schatz, I. M., Rosenberg, B. A., & Coleman, S. T. (2000). Constant comparison method: A kaleidoscope of data. *The Qualitative Report*, 4(1/2), 1–10. Retrieved from http://nsuworks.nova.edu/tqr/vol4/iss1/8/
Glaser, B. G. (2007/2010). Doing formal theory. In A. Bryant & K. Charmaz (Eds.), *The Sage handbook of grounded theory* (pp. 97–113). Thousand Oaks, CA: Sage. (Original work published in 2007.)
Glaser, B. G., & Strauss, A. L. (1967). *The discovery of grounded theory*. Chicago, IL: Aldine.
Goffman, E. (1959). *The presentation of self in everyday life*. New York: Anchor Books.

Hergenrather, K. C., Rhodes, S. D., & Clark, G. (2006). Windows to work: Exploring employment-seeking benaviors of persons with HIV/AIDS through photovoice. *AIDS Education and Prevention, 18,* 243–258.

Hergenrather, K. C., Rhodes, S. D., Cowan, C. A., Bardhoshi, & Pula, S. (2009). Photovoice as community-based participatory research: A qualitative review. *American Journal of Health Behavior, 33,* 686–698.

Holton, J. A. (2010). The coding process and its challenges. In A. Bryant & K. Charmaz (Eds.), *The Sage handbook of grounded theory* (pp. 265–289). Thousand Oaks, CA: Sage. (Original work published in 2007.)

Latz, A. O. (2011). *Understanding the educational lives of community college students through photovoice* (unpublished doctoral dissertation). Muncie, IN: Ball State University.

Leipert, B. D. (2010). Rural and remote women and resilience: Grounded theory and photovoice variations on a theme. In C. A. Winters & H. J. Lee (Eds.), *Rural nursing: Concepts, theory, and practice* (3rd edn, pp. 105–130). New York: Springer.

Lincoln, Y. S., & Guba, E. G. (1985). *Naturalistic inquiry.* Beverly Hills, CA: Sage.

López, E. D. S., Eng, E., Randall-David, E., & Robinson, N. (2005). Quality-of-life concerns of African American breast cancer survivors within rural North Carolina: Blending the techniques of photovoice and grounded theory. *Qualitative Health Research, 15,* 99–115.

Merriam, S. B., & Simpson, E. L. (2000). *A guide to research for educators and trainers of adults* (2nd edn). Malabar, FL: Krieger.

Mintzberg, H. (1979). An emerging strategy of direct research. *Administrative Science Quarterly, 24,* 105–116.

Plunkett, R., Leipert, B. D., & Ray, S. L. (2013). Unspoken phenomena: Using the photovoice method to enrich phenomenological inquiry. *Nursing Inquiry, 20,* 156–164. doi: 10.1111/j.1440-1800.2012.00594.x

Reynolds, L. T., & Herman-Kinney, N. J. (Eds.). (2003). *Handbook of symbolic interactionism.* Lanham, MD: AltaMira.

Seale, C. (1999). *The quality of qualitative research.* London: Sage.

Strauss, A. L., & Corbin, J. (1998a). *Basics of qualitative research: Techniques and procedures for developing grounded theories* (2nd edn). Thousand Oaks, CA: Sage.

Strauss, A. L., & Corbin, J. (1998b). Grounded theory methodology: An overview. In N. K. Denzin & Y. S. Lincoln (Eds.), *Strategies of qualitative inquiry* (pp. 158–183). Thousand Oaks, CA: Sage.

Sutton-Brown, C. A. (2014). Photovoice: A methodological guide. *Photography & Culture, 7,* 169–186. doi: 10.2752/175145214X13999922103165

Tinkler, P. (2013). *Using photographs in social and historical research.* Thousand Oaks, CA: Sage.

Wang, C., & Burris, M. A. (1997). Photovoice: Concept, methodology, and use for participatory needs assessment. *Health Education & Behavior, 24,* 369–387.

5
PHOTOVOICE ETHICS AND WORKING WITH REVIEW BOARDS

A Vignette

Recall the vignette from Chapter 3. Within that piece, I articulated the evolution in my thinking about how best to recruit for participation in photovoice projects. I explained, in brief, two separate classroom-based photovoice projects I facilitated where a group of graduate students worked with a group of community college students. In the spring of 2014, students in my class, *Community Colleges and Diversity*, worked with students who had opted into a Student Support Services Program at the local community college, one of the federal TRIO programs. Our recruitment approach for that particular semester was email, and we were interested in students' perceptions of, and experiences with, financial literacy, poverty, and relationships with campus staff. The program director sent all participating students an email on our behalf. Prospective participants were asked to email me to indicate interest; I would then forward the email onto one of my students who would arrange a meeting with the community college student to orient him or her to the project, provide a disposable camera, explain consent and release forms, and so forth.

Every fall and spring semester, I teach a course termed *The Community College*. And each semester, I arrange a campus visit to the local community college so my students—many of whom have never set foot on a community college campus—have the chance to talk with campus personnel, see the spaces, and interact with community college students. The class meets in the evenings, so our campus visits usually take place once the hustle and bustle of a typical day have died down. When we do these visits, I am usually the last one to leave. I give thanks to our hosts, collect my things, and wander out to the parking lot to find my car and begin reflecting on the session. What did the students think? What kinds of questions were raised? How might we debrief this experience when we are all together again?

Inundated with these thoughts and with a tote bag in each hand, I walked through the familiar hallways where I used to teach making my way toward the exit. In one of the student lounges, I saw a recognizable face. It was a student who was enrolled in my *First Year Seminar* class a few semesters ago. Excited to see her, I said hello and we exchanged pleasantries. Then I noticed she was not alone. Also in the lounge was another student who presented (to me) as a person with blindness, as she was holding a DeafBlind Communicator and had a white cane at her side. Quickly, my former student introduced me to this person, another student at the community college. My former student was assisting this student, who was, in fact, a person with blindness, as an aide. As soon as my student introduced me to this new student, I immediately recognized her name—she had volunteered to participate in our photovoice study!

So there I was, all manners of thoughts colliding in my brain. Once I introduced myself and made all the connections known to all parties—the former student I had encountered volunteered to be a participant in my dissertation study, but she did not persist past the initial meeting—the three of us had some casual conversation about the mechanics of participation in a photovoice study for someone with blindness. I was honestly thrilled that she wanted to participate, and while we did not come to any definite conclusions or make any solid plans about the nature of her participation that evening, I vowed to talk with the student in my graduate class who was paired with her so we could all work together to make it happen.

Thinking about ways to be inclusive regarding our photovoice project caused me to think about the entire process differently. And the circumstance gave my students and I the chance to grapple with our biases related to ability and ask each other, and ourselves, questions that could have not come up otherwise. Do we have access to adaptive technology? What does it mean if this participant's aide takes photographs on her behalf? Is photovoice inherently exclusionary because of its reliance on the visual? Unfortunately, after the initial meeting with a member of our class, this particular participant did not engage in correspondence and did not continue to participate in the study. While we were certainly disappointed, participation was completely voluntary, and some attrition was expected. Regardless, it was a valuable learning experience and one that forced us to think about our process anew. Had this individual not volunteered, we never would have wrestled with some of the ethical considerations with which we wrestled. With ingenuity, creativity, resourcefulness, and determination, we can always find or make a way to include a broad array of persons with differing abilities in photovoice projects. Doing so is the only ethical way forward, but it is certainly not always the easy way forward.

* * *

Ethical Considerations

There are many ethical considerations to navigate during the course of a photovoice project. The process if often very complex, and researchers are beginning to write about these complexities (Holtby, Klein, Cook, & Travers, 2015), many of which have ethical dimensions. Participatory research approaches do "not dissolve all power relations between researcher and researched, nor [are they] free from ethical dilemmas" (Kesby, 2000, p. 432). In some ways, participatory research approaches can invite more pronounced power relations and especially thorny ethical dilemmas. Within this section, I address the following: (a) the burden of representation and the possibility of further marginalization; (b) ownership and benefits; (c) invasions of privacy; (d) confidentiality, exposure, and "outing"; (e) danger, safety, violations of the law and cultural norms, and the panopticon; (f) catalytic validity; (g) relationships with policy makers; (h) loaded, leading, and/or assumption-laden photography prompts; (i) image manipulation and vetting; and (j) inclusion and differing ability.

Harley (2012) noted that most published photovoice studies do not include specific information related to ethics—at least not beyond a note in the methods section related to Wang and Redwood-Jones's (2001) piece on ethical considerations. As a result, we are not often prompted to consider ethical issues beyond what was gleaned from that seminal piece. Obtaining Research Ethics Board (REB)/Institutional Review Board (IRB) approval and following the ethical minimums set forth by Wang and Redwood-Jones does not mean that all ethical considerations are handled. Each photovoice study will present the research team members with new, unique, and nuanced issues which must be grappled with. That risks are present and problems inevitably arise during the photovoice process cannot be swept under the rug; we must be realistic, not romantic, about the methodology. Photovoice is not innately celebratory, collaborative, egalitarian, or useful. The success of the methodology rests in the manner in which it is executed and in how decisions are made along the way. While photovoice is novel, fun, creative, and participatory, it is *much more than just* novel, fun, creative, and participatory. Research with human beings always has the potential for harm. Photovoice is no exception.

The Burden of Representation and the Possibility of Further Marginalization

One ethical element of the process to consider is the possible burden the process may place on participants. It is not simple or easy to catalyze social change. The equitable distribution of change work must be considered. Another reality to note is that photovoice participants do not typically hold the authority or power to decide, make, or change policy themselves. Because of this, photovoice researchers and participants aim to affect policy through reaching others through the process.

There always exists the possibility that photovoice participants will feel burdened by the idea that their narratives and images, taken together, will be seen as the definitive voice representing the totality of the group of which he or she is a part. Photovoice researchers should discuss this potential burden with participants so as to make them feel as comfortable and agentic as possible.

Holtby, Klein, Cook, and Travers (2015) recommend that research teams leverage the participatory nature of photovoice to make space for open and honest conversations about representation, especially in the face of neoliberalism where life stories of the marginalized and the oppressed can be taken out of context and used in ways antithetical to the promotion of understanding, empathy, and solidarity. Curbing the possibility of further marginalization is difficult, however. Wilson and Flicker (2015) said they "struggled with thinking about how to contextualize them [findings] in ways that do not perpetuate stereotypes about young black [sic] women, but instead get at the underlying issues and promote self-determination and health" (p. 84). However, photovoice researchers "cannot eliminate the reality that our participants' voices will indeed be taken up to represent their broader community" (Holtby et al., 2015, p. 333). The best we can do is discuss with participants how their stories will be placed out into the world and confer with them about the most optimal ways to do so. What happens when a narrated image is *accurate* but not *representative*? How will we know the difference? Being proactive may be helpful to ameliorate this potential: "we strongly urged participants to avoid portraying individuals and communities in photographs that themselves might be accurate but not reflective" (Wang & Redwood-Jones, 2001, p. 568).

Ownership and Benefits

The girls and women involved in Mitchell, de Lange, and Nguyen's (2016) study used their cell phones to take photographs of each other using project cameras during the documentation process, which we might think of as metaphotography. These images were then posted to Facebook. Is it the researcher's role to mitigate situations such as this one? Does it matter? Additionally, what if a participant wants to be involved but does not want to actually engage in photography? What if one participant takes a photograph on behalf of another participant? Does this count? Who is the photographer? Photographs taken during the documentation phase of photovoice projects usually belong to the participant-photographer. However, the use of those photographs is also typically released to the researcher through the consent and release paperwork process. We must also consider who benefits if the products of the work receive attention or make a profit. With few exceptions, any benefits incurred throughout the process ought to benefit the participants and their communities directly. As an alternative, momentum and/or funds generated throughout the process could also be used to sustain the project and facilitate additional related works.

Invasions of Privacy

Drawing upon Gross, Katz, and Ruby's (1988) work regarding the types of invasions individuals who appear in photographs might experience, Wang and Redwood-Jones (2001) addressed each one and expanded on what each one means for the photovoice methodology. The first is intrusion into one's private space. The use of consent forms can address this type of invasion, at least partially. Three types of consent forms were outlined: consent to participate in the study (collected by researcher), consent from persons to be photographed (collected by participant), and consent to publish or display photographs (collected by researcher). Examples are provided within the appendices. The second is disclosure of embarrassing facts about individuals. The third is being placed in a false light by images. The fourth is protection against the use of a person's likeness for commercial benefit. These potential invasions must be considered during the education and documentation phases.

Confidentiality, Exposure, and "Outing"

Spence (1995) wrote about the burgeoning practice of community photography (i.e. participatory documentary photography) within the United Kingdom: "[t]he main objective [of community photography] is to enable people to achieve some degree of autonomy in their own lives and to be able to express themselves more easily, thus gaining solidarity with each other" (p. 35). This is no easy task, however. Spence continued: "[t]hose who have their roots in a neighbourhood cannot afford to photograph people as mere 'things'. They still have to live with each other after the pictures have been produced" (p. 35). This statement brings up both ethical and practical considerations. When orienting participants to the work of documentary photography, we must encourage them to consider all possible consequences of their work. How might certain types of photographs implicate others, and to what extent?

Sometimes, telling and displaying your story can be difficult and painful. The potential for consumption, inspection, evaluation, interrogation, and appropriation of those stories by unknown others can be stifling and silencing. Holtby, Klein, Cook, and Travers (2015) explained that "[p]utting one's experiences of oppression on display for people in power to consume can be a choice laden with disproportionate risk for the storyteller" (p. 319). Many queer and trans youth negotiate issues of representation and visibility on a daily basis, and this negotiation process unfolds while experiencing power imbalances. Moreover, "being seen is not an uncomplicated desire for many marginalized individuals; representation of self and of one's community are often fraught with tensions" (Holtby et al., pp. 317–318).

Danger, Safety, Violations of the Law and Cultural Norms, and the Panopticon

Consider the following: "In Flint, two young photovoice participants took pictures of two of their friends, one 7 and one 14, throwing gang signs and taking drugs. They ignored the photovoice rule and did not obtain permission before taking the photograph" (Wang & Redwood-Jones, 2001, p. 565). Risks are inherent within the approach for researchers, participants, and individuals who are photographed. In some cases, risks are associated with the specific population or community with whom photovoice researchers work. The purpose of Rosen, Goodkind, and Smith's (2011) study was to learn about treatment-related issues facing older African American individuals who seek treatment from a methadone clinic. The project was a collaboration between university researchers and staff members at a local methadone clinic. In total, ten participants were involved, and point-and-shoot 35mm cameras were used throughout the eight-week project. The authors noted that "[t]here are inherent risks associated with this population in that they could witness or photograph illegal activity (such as drug use or sale), and every effort was made the ensure participants' safety" (p. 529) As photovoice researchers, we must always consider the likelihood that participants will encounter and photograph illegal activity. Sometimes high levels of risks are necessarily imbedded in the recruitment criteria. This was certainly the case for Rosen et al.'s work.

Prins (2010) examined the unforeseen problems that arose during a participatory photography project conducted with people of rural El Salvador engaged in an adult literacy program. Prins cautioned readers to think critically about the potential harmful and unanticipated outcomes of participatory photography. It should be noted that participatory photography was used in this study, but this was not a photovoice project. Prins illustrated, using her dissertation as an example, how participatory photography can result in participants' learning and taking action, but it can also be seen as a technology of social control and surveillance (Foucault, 1975/1995). We, as photovoice researchers, must guard against a romanticized view of participatory photography. Similarly, we cannot assume that cameras are inherently liberating. Participatory photography certainly has potential benefits, but researchers must also "recognize how it shapes and is shaped by distinctive sociocultural settings" (Prins, 2010, p. 427). Not all potential pitfalls can be anticipated, however.

Prins (2010) drew upon Foucault's (1975/1995) work in two ways to illustrate the problems her participants faced while engaging in photography. First, participants violated social norms during photography, which made them more visible and easily scrutinized. This can cause hesitancy among participants. Second, in sociocultural contexts where persons have been subjected to extreme surveillance and harbor distrust in the state, cameras can be viewed as threatening objects of social control and trigger memories of incidences of surveillance. The (adult) participants in Prins's (2010) study were to engage in photography regarding their participation in literacy classes, especially how the classes are affecting their lives; sharing aspects of their lives that could be helpful in facilitators' improving the classes; and how they view the world.

Three problems surfaced during the project. First, one participant took a picture of a sugar cane field, and the owner approached the participant with questions. The participant explained the project, but the owner insisted that the project leader (Prins) had the participant take the photograph so she could come back later and set it on fire. Prins (2010) explained how she experienced anger and shock regarding this accusation but later came to better understand the context within which she was working. Using Foucault's (1975/1995) work as a lens was certainly helpful. Second, some participants experienced indecision and timidity about what to photograph. Moreover, some were ridiculed for their camera use, as peers assumed the participant did not know how to use the camera. Third, in some cases, other people took the photographs for the participant. The third problem could certainly stem from the second, as some participants may have asked for advice and then handed over the camera to the advisor.

The sociocultural contextual factors of this study gave the aforementioned problems their uniqueness and nuance. However, similar problems could arise in any sociocultural context, and it is likely that every photovoice researcher has, or will, experience something similar in working with participants. Learning as much as possible about the community with which we aim to work is critical in ameliorating these kinds of troubles that have ethical implications.

Prins (2010) said candidly, "[b]ecause I viewed photography as a benign technology, I misjudged how it would be received in this setting" (p. 439). So, how can we learn from Prins? She offered some advice. First, tailor the photography to the local context. Ask participants for help regarding this. Think about how to make the participants less visible. Discuss the process frequently once it is in motion. Ask participants questions about how they took the photographs—not just why they took certain photographs or what the photographs contain. And, again, execute due diligence in understanding the sociocultural context of the photography.

Prins (2010) summed up her piece beautifully: "[u]nderstanding photography as a culturally embedded technology of power with potential for both social control and the recovery of subjugated knowledge can help ensure that participatory photography projects engender trust, learning, and action rather than suspicion or embarrassment" (p. 441).

Catalytic Validity

Lather (1986) noted that the purpose of her essay was to "formulate an approach to empirical research which both advances emancipatory theory-building and empowers the researched" (p. 64). This is the stuff of photovoice. Emancipatory theory-building can be likened to building suggestions for policy change that contribute to a more "egalitarian social order" (p. 64). Similarly, working toward a more egalitarian social order necessarily works to support, perhaps vis-à-vis empowerment—or critical consciousness building, as participants within photovoice projects typically embody marginalized identities and/or are from marginalized groups. Lather argued that this type of research—"ubabashedly ideological research" (p. 67)—should be used to challenge the status quo.

Lather (1986) suggested that Freirian-inspired and feminist research practice often lacks self-reflexivity. So, how do researchers engage in self-reflective practices—ones that go beyond stating predispositions—that feed the trustworthiness of the work? In response to this question, Lather offered a reconceptualization of validity. One form of validity she put forward is *catalytic validity* (p. 67). As a matter of ethics, we might consider the importance of catalytic validity within photovoice research projects (Lather, 1986). And while this form of validity may be "by far the most unorthodox" (Lather, 1986) in comparison to other forms she presented "as it flies directly in the face of the essential positivist tenet of researcher neutrality" (p. 67), it is potentially the most powerful within photovoice research. We must ask ourselves, did the participants move, change, learn, act, energize, or otherwise be affected by the process in the name of fostering critical consciousness and addressing social ills? Catalytic validity can be defined as participants better understanding social landscapes with the intent to participate in changing them.

Lather (1986) wrote about the goals of feminist research as "correct[ing] both the *invisibility* and the *distortion* of the female experience in ways relevant to ending women's unequal social position" (p. 68, italics in original). Photovoice is attentive to these goals. The methodology literally makes the invisible visible, and by asking participants to document their lives on their own terms, the distortion of their experiences is limited, if not altogether eliminated. Lather (1986) also wrote about the goals of Freirian research, which endeavors toward participants' active participation in improving social conditions through understanding those conditions, building and recognizing one's social agency, and then acting accordingly. We must ask ourselves how we can consciously build catalytic validity into the photovoice research design.

Relationships with Policy Makers

What about the nature of advocacy in the process? We must realize that "photovoice does not necessarily attempt to shift power to *decide* policy" (Wang & Redwood-Jones, 2001, p. 569, italics in original). To be sure, photovoice acknowledges that many participants do not have the power to decide policy; however, photovoice participants are actively involved in influencing policy makers with regards to the topics of engagement during the course of any project.

Wang and Redwood-Jones (2001) also brought up engagement with policy makers as an ethical concern. The ways in which project team members decide on which policy makers to approach—and how to do so—must be taken into consideration. To what degree should policy makers be involved with the process? When working within educational institutions, permission is often necessary to carry out research projects within those institutions. Asking permission might start with a conversation about partnership. Much of my own work has taken place within the community college context. And as a university-based researcher, employed by a four-year institution, and ethically obligated to undergo IRB processes, I have always begun projects by asking for permission to carry them out. This means meeting with people, explaining the ideas, and requesting a permission letter to furnish to my home institution's IRB—as well the partner institution's equivalent entity. Meeting and speaking candidly with institutional agents can nurture understanding, buy-in, and support. It can also be a critical first step in identifying where to point the inquiry and where to go to discuss the findings of the inquiry.

Johnston (2016) questioned the purported third aim of the photovoice methodology: policy change. She suggested that most photovoice projects give little attention to reporting on whether or not policy was affected by the work, and she frames this as an ethical issue. Positioning participants as arbiters of social change can trigger a series of ethical questions. For example, what if participants do not want that kind of position? Should participants carry the potential burden of being agents of social change? As a suggestion, Johnston urges photovoice researchers to study the literature on social movements theory.

Johnston (2016) asserted that "to enact change, especially in policy, the [photovoice] participants will need two things: public opinion and political alliances" (p. 804). In some cases, photovoice projects may be considered to be what Johnston called a micro-social movement (pp. 804–805). However, photovoice researchers must not make grandiose claims with regards to the policy impacts of the work. There is nothing wrong with being aspirational, but we must also be realistic. Planting seeds of hope within participants that will never bloom is an ethical concern. Expectations must be managed responsibly. It is unlikely that a singular photovoice project will generate policy change. However, it is highly likely that a photovoice project could influence policy.

Loaded, Leading, and/or Assumption-Laden Photography Prompts

Being attentive to loaded, leading, and/or assumption-laden photography questions/prompts and interview/focus group questions/prompts is critical, as Wang and Redwood-Jones (2001) consider this an ethical consideration. Photography questions/prompts should be created in consultation with those involved in the project (research team members, participants, policy makers, collaborators) and related literature. A keen understanding of the context within which the project takes place is also paramount. In addition, consideration of participants' ages, abilities, and interests is also important. Ask whether or not the photography questions/prompts will be difficult to understand or irrelevant to participants' lives. Whenever possible, talk with participants about the prompts and ask for input. Depending on how the project unfolds and the number of photography sessions, changes can be made along the way. That participants are able to engage with the prompts, and take photographs accordingly, is a critical part of the total process. For example, in the spring of 2014, a group of graduate students and I engaged with community college students on a photovoice project focused on poverty, financial literacy, and relationships with campus agents. We posed this question: How do you see social class playing out at [community college]? My graduate students and I thought this was a perfectly reasonable question to ask. And we were wrong. Participants had a hard time making sense of what was meant by this prompt, and this only came to light during the individual interviews. We did not vet these prompts through our participants ahead of the photograph session(s), but we should have.

Image Manipulation and Vetting

Tinkler (2013) asked "[h]ow far can we [researchers] go in adjusting images before it is not worth including them" (p. 203) in the disseminations? In what ways does limiting the scope of participants' photographs in an attempt to acquiesce to review boards thwart representation? Mitchell, de Lange, and Nguyen (2016) prohibited participants from taking pictures of faces, for example. But, "[w]here does the anonymity of the body reside? . . . Participants might avoid taking a picture of someone's face but [a] wheelchair may be a much more recognizable and identifiable marker" (p. 252). Imagine a scenario where your home institution deems that any participants' photographs that contain people must be altered prior to being displayed in any kind of public way. You have two options. You can either blur the faces of people in the photographs (e.g. Mamary & McCright, 2007), or you can block out faces altogether (Strack, Magill, & McDonagh, 2004, p. 53). Consider the ways in which doing so would alter the images. Consider the ways these images would then be perceived by others. Consider how the participant(s) might feel about this alteration. Consider how those photographed might feel about these altered images upon seeing them for the first time. Consider how altering the images would alter the very nature of the photovoice project. In my own experience, to expedite the IRB approval process I have sometimes prohibited images of people altogether. How did this affect the work?

Sometimes organizations or hosts of exhibitions request to preview images/text prior to display. This is not necessarily a bad thing. Wang, Yi, Toa, and Carovano (1998) noted that sometimes it is helpful to have images vetted by appropriate parties prior to dissemination (e.g. news article, exhibition). However, censorship of images/text can distort the participants' work thereby mitigating the meanings meant to be put forward for consideration. Some messages are critical to the overall presentation, and these are worth fighting for. However, if the censorship is minor and does not change the essence of the exhibition, assuaging to the requests is advisable.

Inclusion and Differing Ability

Mitchell et al. (2016) outlined several ethical considerations when doing visual research (i.e. photovoice) with girls with disabilities. And while these considerations were built from their experiences, they can be applied broadly. First, we must consider whether or not the methods are inclusive. Is photography relegated to only those who are sighted? The simple answer is no. With recent technological advances, photovoice researchers are able to combat the occularcentric nature of the approach. The PhotoVoice (n.d.) organization has published a robust manual on the use of sensory photograph with participants who are visually impaired or blind. In addition, photographs can be made tactile so they can be experience by persons with a visually impairment or blindness during, for example, the narration or presentation stages. Second, what does it mean, ethically, for individuals who have been marginalized and systematically kept from being seen and heard to be seen and heard? This question must be considered especially critically when working with persons with disabilities.

The Contextual Nature of Photovoice Ethics

A strict list of ethical guidelines for the photovoice method cannot and should not be concretized. Rather, ethically informed decision-making ought to transpire within concrete cases of photovoice research. Again, context matters, and what is ethical in one context may not be ethical in another.

Working with Review Boards

The two most important elements of a successful navigation of the institutional review process are as follows. First, you must communicate early, clearly, and consistently with your review board personnel. Knowing their expectations and orientations to their work is key. Second, you must provide a comprehensive portrait of your study—complete with a thick list of references—to substantiate the work you plan to do. One of the most difficult parts of completing a photovoice research project is undergoing institutional review. For a neophyte researcher, going through an IRB can be a significant challenge. When you add the complexity of participant photography to the research protocol, an already challenging process becomes even more challenging. In an institutional setting where agents of the institution are actively carrying out research that includes human "subjects," IRBs are created in an effort to be sure that research is carried out in an ethical way.

Often, members of REBs or IRBs are not well acquainted with participatory research approaches, including participatory action research and community-based participatory research (CBPR). Therefore, photovoice researchers can face obstacles when navigating IRBs. Lincoln and Tierney (2004) said "at some institutions . . . feminist, action research, and participatory action research projects have been summarily rejected as 'unscientific,' 'ungeneralizable,' and/or inadequately theorized" (p. 222). To assuage the requests of IRBs, oftentimes researchers will bend their research designs, changing the approach from qualitative to quantitative, which can be detrimental to a variety of fields where qualitative approaches to understanding can yield important insights. Forms of action research are particularly knotty subjects for IRBs. According to Lincoln and Tierney, "IRBs appear to be having considerable difficulty with either understanding or supporting . . . [action] research, even though action research models . . . show great promise of involving stakeholders" (p. 228). Moreover, there appears to be a larger concern for institutional protection than for the protection of research participants, which is problematic, as protection for research participants ought to precede concerns for the institution. Because qualitative researchers do not typically claim to generalize the findings of their work, a red flag is raised for many IRBs that ascribe to conventional definitions of what constitutes research. Unfortunately, "[s]o long as the regulations state that generalizability is a part of the definition of research, qualitative research studies will continue to suffer inordinate review and sometimes inappropriate revision, if not outright rejection" (Lincoln & Tierney, p. 231). The best defense against a prolonged or unfavorable period of review from an IRB is communication. If you can become a board member, or simply talk to members about the nature and merits of your proposed study, there is a higher likelihood of appropriate review and ultimate approval.

Guta, Nixon, Gahagan, and Fielden (2012) conducted interviews with 24 "Canadian REB/IRB members, staff, and select key informants with specialized knowledge of CBPR and the ethics review process" (p. 18). While there were some exceptions, findings indicated that participants in this study were making ardent attempts to understand CBPR and raise pertinent ethical questions about the nature of the proposed works. In addition, participants "challenged the perception of REBs/IRBs as secretive and nonresponsive, and described working together [with researchers] to develop and refine protocols" (Guta et al., p. 22). Rather than view REBs/IRBs as obstacles, we, as photovoice researchers engaged in participatory work, must try to see the review process as a responsible step in proposing and carrying out research that is grounded in an appropriate ethical framework. Furthermore, those who comprise review boards should be viewed as supportive research partners—as opposed to gatekeepers—who want to promote ethically sound practice. Guta et al.'s study has definite limitations and is not generalizable, yet it suggests that a potential growing understanding of CBPR is afoot among members of REBs/IRBs, at least within the Canadian national context. This is certainly a step in the right direction.

In some instances, the ethical dilemmas around facilitating photovoice research may thwart the project before it even moves from idea to inception. Should we insist that participants not take photographs of people? This is a step I have taken to make the IRB process more expeditious. Should we allow participants to take photographs of minors, knowing that it will be up to the participants to secure consent from minor's guardians?

Concealing and protecting the identities of participants is a critical means of "preventing undesired consequences" (Pauwels, 2008. p. 244). However, within photovoice projects anonymity and confidentiality are sometimes not possible or even desirable. There may be really good reasons why participants would want their identities to be known. They may want their participation to be known and celebrated, and they may want to have access to policy makers through face-to-face conversations about their project involvement. For many participants, being involved in such a project is a pride point, and it can also be a means of personal reflection and growth.

Sometimes IRBs will go to great lengths to enforce confidentiality of participants' identities within photographs. Moreover, "digital image processing . . . significantly increased the possibilities for making elements in an image, such as faces or company logos, unrecognizable or illegible through blurring, etc. . . . Such interventions may also cause significant data to be lost" (Pauwels, 2008, p. 245). Pauwels noted that appearing in random individuals' camera rolls is entirely possible when one visits a theme park, concert, or outdoor party. This is an inescapable result of "the democratization of private image production" (p. 245,). But another orientation to photography arises when private or intimate behaviors are photographed for potential public disbursement or display. Lay citizens are not used to being the objects of photography, unlike politicians, actors, or music stars. As such, they may have a low tolerance to being photographed. Moreover, which spaces count as public and private is contentious. Sometimes lines are hard to draw. Even when we, as researchers, ask participants not to take photographs of people, sometimes photographing certain material objects can have negative effects. What if an elementary school teacher opts to take photographs of his or her students' desks or workspaces (Pauwels, p. 248)? How might those images and the interpretations of them potentially negatively affect students?

Pauwels (2008) noted that while contractual consent is typically enough for most IRBs, within visual research processes, consent is an ongoing process. Considering the high levels of researcher-participant contact within photovoice, ongoing verbal consent through conversation is viable; researchers should inform participants "as honestly and as comprehensively as possible in a manner that is understandable to them" (Pauwels, p. 249). With regards to IRBs, Pauwels said members are often unfamiliar with qualitative social science research; therefore, "[v]isual methods face the double burden of being perceived as qualitative and not canonical" (p. 251). So when in the process of preparing IRB materials for review, err on the side of being over-informational with regards to saturating the documents with explanation and citations.

Summary

Within this chapter, I outlined ten ethical considerations relative to photovoice research. While this list is not exhaustive or axiomatic, it does provide much food for thought as prospective photovoice researchers consider the ethical dimensions of the work. Furthermore, I include information and tips on how to successfully navigate the institutional review process, giving specific focus to two actions: (a) communication with IRB/REB personnel; and (b) providing comprehensive information with the application materials so few questions about the process remain unanswered after the materials are reviewed. The next chapter is focused on the pros, cons, and future of photovoice.

References

Foucault, M. (1995). *Discipline and punish: The birth of the prison* (2nd edn). (A. Sheridan, Trans.). New York: Random House. (Original work published in 1975.)

Gross, L., Katz, J. S., & Ruby, J. (1988). Introduction: A moral pause. In L. Gross, J. S. Katz, & Ruby, J. (Eds,), *Image ethics: The moral rights of subjects in photographs, films, and television* (pp. 3–33). New York: Oxford University Press.

Guta, A., Nixon, S., Gahagan, J., & Fielden, S. (2012). "Walking along beside the researcher": How Canadian ERBs/IRBs are responding to the needs of community-based participatory research. *Journal of Empirical Research on Human Research Ethics: An International Journal*, 7(1), 15–25. doi: 10.1525/jer.2012.7.1.17

Harley, A. (2012). Picturing reality: Power, ethics, and politics using photovoice. *International Journal of Qualitative Methods*, 11, 320–339. Retrieved from https://ejournals.library.ualberta.ca/index.php/IJQM/article/view/6030/14341

Holtby, A., Klein, K., Cook, K., & Travers, R. (2015). To be seen or not to be seen: Photovoice, queer and trans youth, and the dilemma of representation. *Action Research*, 13, 317–335. doi: 10.1177/1476750314566414

Johnston, G. (2016). Champions for social change: Photovoice ethics in practice and 'false hopes' for policy and social change. *Global Public Health: An International Journal for Research, Policy, and Practice*, 11, 799–811. doi: 10.1080/17441692.2016.1170176

Kesby, M. (2000). Participatory diagramming: Deploying qualitative methods through an action research epistemology. *Royal Geographical Society (with the Institute of British Geographers)*, 32, 423–435.

Lather, P. (1986). Issues of validity in openly ideological research: Between a rock and a soft place. *Interchange*, 17(4), 63–84.

Lincoln, Y. S., & Tierney, W. G. (2004). Qualitative research and institutional review boards. *Qualitative Inquiry*, 10, 219–234. doi: 10.1177/1077800403262361

Mamary, E., & McCright, J. (2007). *Slow down and enjoy life . . . slow down and enjoy life*. Retrieved from http://ourlivesphotos.com/gallery/main.php?g2_itemId=41

Mitchell, C., de Lange, N., & Nguyen, X. T. (2016). Visual ethics with and through the body: The participation of girls with disabilities in Vietnam in a photovoice project. In J. Coffey, S. Budgeon, & H. Cahill (Eds.), *Learning bodies: The body in youth and childhood studies* (pp. 241–257). New York: Springer Science+Business Media.

Pauwels, L. (2008). Taking and using: Ethical issues of photographs for research purposes. *Visual Communication Quarterly, 15*, 243–257.

PhotoVoice. (n.d.). *Sensory photography: Photography for blind and visually impaired people.* Retrieved from https://photovoice.org/methodologyseries/method_04/report.pdf

Prins, E. (2010). Participatory photography: A tool for empowerment or surveillance? *Action Research, 8*, 426–443. doi: 10.1177/1476750310374502

Rosen, D., Goodkind, S., & Smith, M. L. (2011). Using photovoice to identify service needs of older African American methadone clients. *Journal of Social Service Research, 37*, 526–538. doi: 10.1080/01488376.2011.607369

Spence, J. (1995). *Cultural snipping: The art of transgression.* New York: Routledge.

Strack, R. W., Magill, C., & McDonagh, K. (2004). Engaging youth through photovoice. *Health Promotion Practice, 5*, 49–53. doi: 10.1177/1524839903258015

Tinkler, P. (2013). *Using photographs in social and historical research.* Thousand Oaks, CA: Sage.

Wang, C. C., & Redwood-Jones, Y. A. (2001). Photovoice ethics: Perspectives from Flint photovoice. *Health Education & Behavior, 28*, 560–572.

Wang, C. C., Yi, W. K., Tao, Z. W., & Carovano, K. (1998). Photovoice as a participatory health promotion strategy. *Health Promotion International, 13*, 75–86.

Wilson, C., & Flicker, S. (2015). Picturing transactional $ex: Ethics, challenges, and possibilities. In A. Gubrium, K. Harper, & M. Otañez (Eds.), *Participatory visual and digital research in action* (pp. 73–86). Walnut Creek, CA: Left Coast Press.

6
PHOTOVOICE EXHIBITIONS

Amanda O. Latz and Thalia M. Mulvihill[1]

Step 7: Presentation—Seeing the Exhibition as a Site of Inquiry

This chapter provides an example of how to interrogate a photovoice exhibition with a particular focus on the experiences of those who attend such an event.

After the completion of a photovoice project focused on the educational lives of community college students (Latz, 2011, 2012b, 2015), two photovoice exhibitions were held. Photovoice (Wang & Burris, 1994, 1997) is a form of participatory action research (Whyte, 1991) that falls within the qualitative paradigm. One of the aims of photovoice is to impact policy makers and others who interact with the work, which often takes place during the exhibition stage of the methodology. Photographs are a powerful means of portraying the findings of research, which can elicit visceral responses within viewers. By understanding the ways in which attendees experience and perceive the exhibit, an assessment of whether or not a photovoice project has met its goals may be possible. Put differently, forms of participatory action, connoted by the phrase participatory action research, that may take place as a direct result of displaying the photovoice project's findings may begin to germinate during the exhibition. This possibility warrants the attention of photovoice researchers. However, the current photovoice literature shows no such attention.

Mitchell (2011) noted that "[t]here is probably no area of visual participatory research [i.e. photovoice] that has received more attention in the last decade than the use of simple point-and-shoot cameras . . . by community photographers" (p. 51). Again, despite this attention, photovoice researchers have not acknowledged photovoice exhibitions as a site of inquiry. An interrogation of how attendees experience photovoice exhibitions is imperative, yet this aspect of the photovoice process remains surprisingly under-researched and under-theorized.

Through this chapter, we highlight the aforementioned gap in the literature and provide an example of how to address it. What follows is comprised of four parts: (a) overview of the photovoice project and resultant exhibitions; (b) explanation of the inquiry into the experience of the exhibition attendees and the theoretical frame used to make meaning of the study's findings; (c) presentation of the findings of the inquiry; and (d) discussion and implications.

The Educational Lives of Community College Students Photovoice Project and Exhibitions

The photovoice project, from which the resultant exhibitions were hosted, was focused on understanding the educational lives of community college students. I (Amanda) spearheaded the project, which was my doctoral dissertation. Throughout the course of my doctoral studies—five years in total—I taught as an adjunct faculty member at a local community college. Seven former students of mine comprised the sample. They took photos in response to prompts posed to them related to their educational journeys at the community college; once participants had finished taking photos in response to the prompts, each engaged in an interview with me. Photography took place in two rounds, and as such, each participant was interviewed twice—aside from one participant whose schedule would not allow for a second round. The final project included a total of 246 photographs and 13 interviews. While a full report of this project is beyond the scope of this paper, additional details can be found elsewhere (Latz, 2011, 2012a, 2012b, 2015). Major findings developed from the study were: freedom (i.e. participants viewed the community college as a means to build a freer life—in a broad sense), academic integration (i.e. participants were integrated into the fabric of the institution through almost exclusively academic means—as opposed to social means), and roles (i.e. participants held a variety of roles—in addition to their roles as students).

As noted above, two photovoice exhibitions were hosted following the completion of the dissertation. The first exhibition was held on the community college campus from which participants were recruited and where I had formally been employed; this event took place in April of 2011. The second exhibition took place at a local public library in February of 2012. Both of the exhibitions were collaborative efforts between some of the study's participants and me. Details of each exhibition are below.

Photovoice Exhibition One

The first photovoice exhibition took place on the community college campus that also served as the study's site. The opening of the exhibition took place on April 22, 2011, from four to six o'clock in the evening. Prior to the event, I met with three of the seven participants involved in the study to brainstorm and plan.

Because photovoice is a form of participatory action research, this collaborative approach was vital. We were permitted to use one of the classrooms on campus for the opening, and following the opening the exhibit would be housed in two display cases along a major corridor inside the main campus building. While the opening lasted only two hours, the exhibition remained on display for approximately nine months—from late April of 2011 until early January 2012. Exhibition materials consisted of participants' photographs along with the narrations they provided about those photographs. These image and text amalgams were printed on photograph paper and mounted on gator board to display—many were about 8" × 11" in size. Some were also printed as large posters—as large as 3' × 3' in dimension.

As the date for the opening approached, and after meeting with three of the participants individually to brainstorm ideas, I arranged two group planning meetings with the participants at the community college. The first meeting was one week prior to the opening and the other was the night before. During the first meeting, which was attended by two participants, we planned the arrangement of the room, and during the second meeting, which was attended by only one participant, we arranged to room so it would be ready the next day. By the time the opening began, the room had been transformed. This transformation included replacing the fluorescent lighting with softer tones—lamps and white string lights, hanging the photographs, which were organized by theme, arranging a table for programs and refreshments, creating a visitor pathway and seating area by rearranging and removing some tables and chairs in the room, and setting up a laptop, projector, and screen to play a looping slideshow with additional images and text.

Four of the seven participants of the photovoice project were present for the opening. The event was attended by participants' families and friends, community college personnel, and personnel from my home institution (e.g. members of my doctoral committee). At five o'clock, the four participants delivered some remarks about their participation in the study. After the opening concluded at six o'clock, the room was disassembled and the exhibition stored in a nearby office. Shortly thereafter, the majority of the exhibition components were moved into the display cases.

Photovoice Exhibition Two

Upon the successful completion of the first exhibition, I, along with the participants who wanted to remain involved with the project, planned a second exhibition. This event included a month-long display of the exhibition at a local public library and public lecture regarding the project. The installation remained on display at the library from February 4th to the 29th in 2012. And the public lecture took place on February 26th, from two o'clock until half past three. The library had a pre-established space to host rotating art exhibitions, so arranging this exhibition was simply a matter of hanging selected pieces from the original exhibition.

Around 25 individuals attended the lecture, and an unknown number of individuals interacted with the exhibition during the course of its installation at the library. The lecture consisted of an overview of the photovoice project, which I delivered. Two participants were able to attend this event, and they both gave comments following my lecture. Lastly, attendees were encouraged to engage us with questions at the end of the presentation. Because the lecture was given in a classroom and not inside the main library passageway where the exhibition was staged, attendees were also encouraged to visit the display after the presentation. Refreshments were also made available.

Inquiry and Methods

After the first exhibition, we became interested in understanding the attendee experience because we readily observed how attendees were generating new narratives about the photos and creating a new site for critical inquiry (Swaminathan & Mulvihill, 2013). Therefore, the second exhibition and concomitant lecture became an intentional site of further inquiry. The research question that drove the inquiry was: How do viewers experience and perceive photovoice exhibitions? Between March 2 and May 25, 2012, I conducted six interviews using a semi-structured interview protocol (Spradley, 1979) with individuals who had interacted with the exhibition, and five of those individuals also attended the public lecture. Recruitment of participants was garnered via an announcement at the close of the lecture; attendees were asked to email me if interested in being interviewed. I also sent direct emails to the attendees who verbally committed to an interview but did not contact me via email. It should be noted that at the time of the lecture and exhibition, I was teaching graduate-level courses at a four-year institution. Three of the individuals I interviewed were graduate students of mine during the spring semester of 2012 pursuing degrees in fields related to higher education.

Data Analysis

The main source of data for this study was the interviews. However, researcher journal entries completed after each event and photographs of the exhibitions also assisted us in the pursuit of understanding the attendees' perceptions of, and experiences with, the exhibitions and were treated as data. Each interview was transcribed verbatim. After a grand reading of all the interviews, an open and holistic coding process was employed (Dey, 1993). Overall, 21 open codes were generated from meanings assigned to the interview content. Once all interview data were open coded, data chunks were categorized into four a priori categories drawn from the work of Falk and Deirking (Falk, 2009; Falk &

Deirking, 2000, 2013) related to museum visitor experiences: personal context, sociocultural context, physical context, and identity. In essence, an a priori axial coding process (Charmaz, 2006) took place. Finally, the open codes within each of the four categories were bundled into sub-categories, named, and became the findings of the study. See Table 6.1 for an illustration of the coding and analysis process. It should be noted that the role of the second author included participating in the exhibitions as an audience member (a form of participant observation), reviewing the raw data from the interviews and researcher journal entries, serving as a peer debriefer to enhance credibility and trustworthiness (Lincoln & Guba, 1985), assisting with the data analysis, and writing the manuscript.

TABLE 6.1 Visualization of the Coding and Analysis Process

Open Codes	A Priori Codes	Findings
E = Empathy	Personal Context	Empathy
Em = Emotional		
Ins = Inspiration		
WM = Wanting More		
Con = Connection (with participants)		
Enj = Enjoyment		
Intr = Intrigue		
L = Learning		
M = Marveling		
P = Perception	Sociocultural Context	Perceptions
T = Text	Physical Context	Intimacy
I = Images		Context
V = Voice		
Int = Interpretation		
CM = Context Matters		
QP = Questions about Process		
EC = Eye-catching		
Intmc = Intimacy		
S = Support of Project	Identity	Attendee Identities
C = Curious		
Exp = Explorer (identity, reason for going to the exhibition)		

Note: After the open coding process was complete, the open codes were categorized into the a priori codes. The sorted open codes were then bundled into sub-categories and named. These named sub-categories became the findings of the study, framed by the a priori codes.

Theoretical Framework

Before moving forward, it is critical to provide information on the theoretical framework used to understand the data and organize the findings. As mentioned above, the second level of data analysis was framed using an a priori structure drawn from the work of John Falk and Lynn Dierking (Falk, 2009; Falk & Dierking, 1992/2011, 2000, 2013) related to the experiences of museum visitors. There is a dearth of research on the photovoice exhibition attendee experience, so the search for viable lenses through which to view and interpret the data resulted in an examination of the literature on museums. The original Interactive Experience Model (IEM) put forward by Falk and Dierking (1992/2011) provides one useful way to analyze and frame the data generated from this study. The IEM also provided a means by which the findings of this study might be understood. The model is illustrated via Figure 6.1.

Personal Context

Each attendee arrived to the photovoice exhibitions with his or her own personal context, which includes past experiences, knowledge, and frames of reference. This context also "includes the visitor's interests, motivations, and concerns" (Falk & Dierking, 1992/2011, p. 2). Differences among personal contexts of attendees may have impacted how and what they learned as a result of their attendance. Differences within the personal context may also account for different levels of connection with various aspects of the exhibition. For example, an attendee with children may feel a stronger connection to the images of children within the exhibition. And attendees currently in college may have felt a sense of solidarity

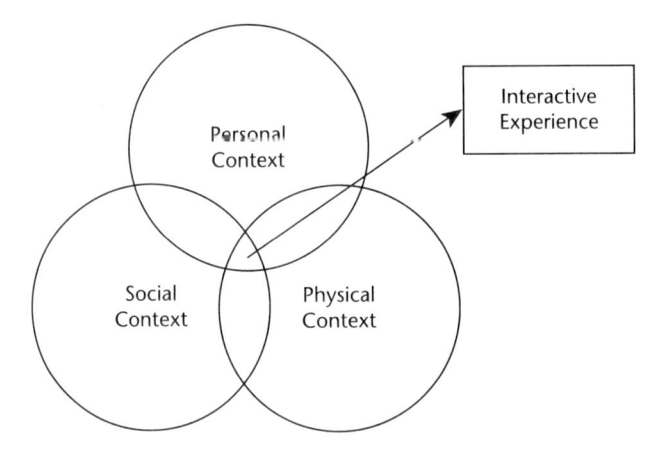

FIGURE 6.1 This is a visual representation of the Interactive Experience Model, which was adapted from Falk and Dierking (1992/2011, p. 5).

regarding the image-text amalgams that dealt with studying, working toward a goal, or making sacrifices.

Social Context

With whom the attendee experiences the photovoice exhibition mattered. According to Falk and Dierking (1992/2011):

> Understanding the social context of the visit allows us to make sense of variations in behavior between, for example, adults in family groups and adults in adult groups, or children on school field trips and children visiting with their families.
>
> p. 3

For both photovoice exhibitions elucidated within this study, different social contexts were constructed—both between each event and among all attendees. Some attendees came in groups (e.g. groups of students, families, or couples), and some came as individuals. The social context was made rather unique through the inclusion of the research participants. And the social context, moreover, was fluid during both events. Individuals came and went throughout the course of the exhibitions.

Physical Context

The physical context includes the arrangement of the exhibitions or displays. All of the human senses matter within this context: sight, sound, touch, smell, and taste. Both of the exhibitions were quite different to one another—as it relates to the engagement of all the senses. All human senses were enacted during these exhibitions. The photography displays enacted sight. The lecture and remarks made enacted sound. The ability to handle some aspects of the display enacted touch. The two settings—a community college classroom and a public library—each had unique aromas, which enacted smell. And refreshments were available for both events, so taste was also enacted. Falk and Dierking (1992/2011), noted that "[h]ow visitors behave, what they observe, and what they remember are strongly influenced by the physical context" (p. 3). They also noted: "Each of the contexts is continuously constructed by the visitor, and the interactions of these create the visitor's experience. This constructed reality is unique to the individual; no two people ever see the world in quite the same way" (pp. 3–4).

Museum Visitor Experience Model

Since its inception, the IEM has evolved. The model was later recast as The Conceptual Model of Learning (Falk & Dierking, 2000) wherein the social

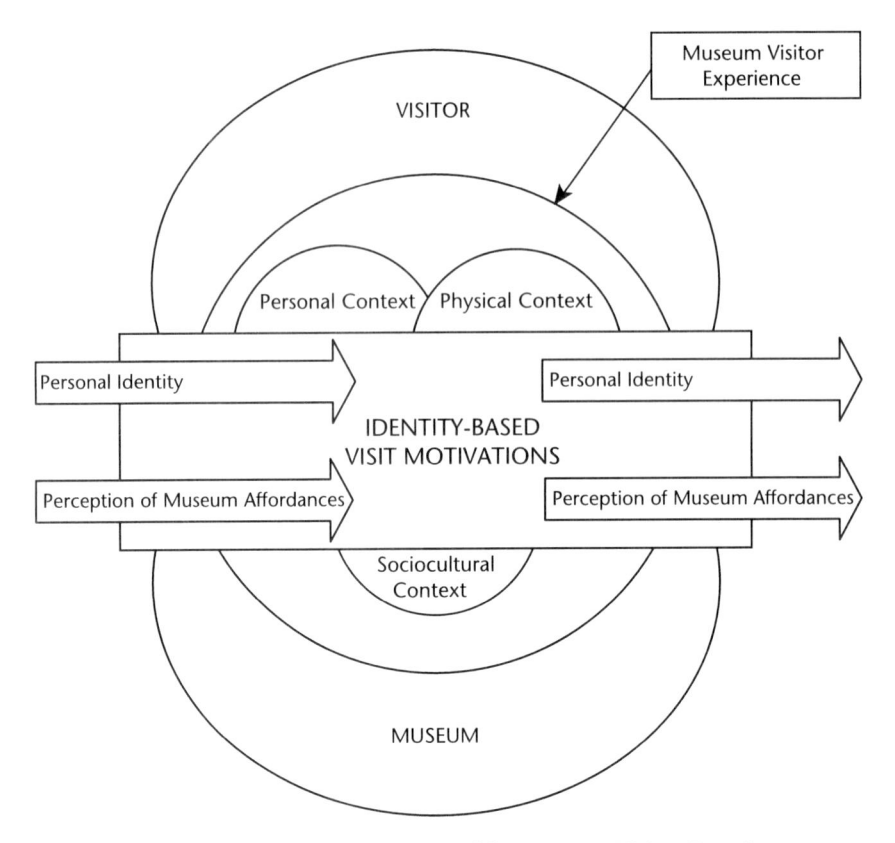

FIGURE 6.2 This is a visual representation of the Museum Visitor Experience Model, which was adapted from Falk (2009, p. 161).

context was reconceptualized as the sociocultural context. Later, the Museum Visitor Experience Model (MVEM) was presented by Falk (2009), and the model is presented in Figure 6.2. Here it should be noted that Falk and Deirking have also published a second edition (2013) of their original work (1992/2011). In regards to the MVEM, Falk (2009) said: "The museum visitor experience is not something tangible and immutable; it is an ephemeral and constructed relationship that uniquely occurs each time a visitor interacts with a museum" (p. 158). This newer model includes the visitors' identity-related visit motivations.

As noted above, the MVEM takes into consideration the individual's identity-related reasons for visiting a museum. An individual makes the decision to visit a museum when "two streams of thought come together" (Falk, 2009, p. 158), which are illustrated by the right-pointing arrows in Figure 6.2. The individual must perceive the museum affordances as meeting his or her specific need(s) at a particular point in time. Falk noted that "[t]his decision-making process results in the formation of an identity-related visit motivation" (p. 158). There are infinite combinations of museum affordances (e.g. Titanic exhibition, free film, educational program) and identity-related needs (e.g. need to be inspired, desire to learn something new).

Five common museum-going identities were elucidated by Falk (2009): explorers, facilitators, professionals/hobbyists, experience seekers, and rechargers. Explorers are those drawn to the museum by curiosity and a desire to learn something new. Facilitators are those who have socially-driven reasons for visiting a museum; they are most concerned with helping others experience the museum. Professionals/hobbyists visit museums because the content or exhibition is related to their profession or hobby. Experience seekers see the museum as an important place to visit; the visit is an important experience for them. Rechargers see the museum as a place for rest, contemplation, and spirituality.

Also noted previously was the shift from the social context to the sociocultural context (Falk & Deriking, 2000), which expands the context to include the "visitor's cultural experiences and values" (Falk, 2009, p. 159). Originally, this context only referred to the interactions between museum visitors—those with whom the individual intended on visiting the museum (e.g. friends, family, schoolmates) and those with whom the individual interacted while at the museum (i.e. other museum visitors unknown to the individual who happen to be visiting at the same moment). This expansion provides a more holistic view of the visitor's total experience and adds a new level of nuance to consider.

Findings

The major findings of this study are illustrated through Figure 6.3. Within this model, the findings are framed by the MVEM (Falk, 2009).

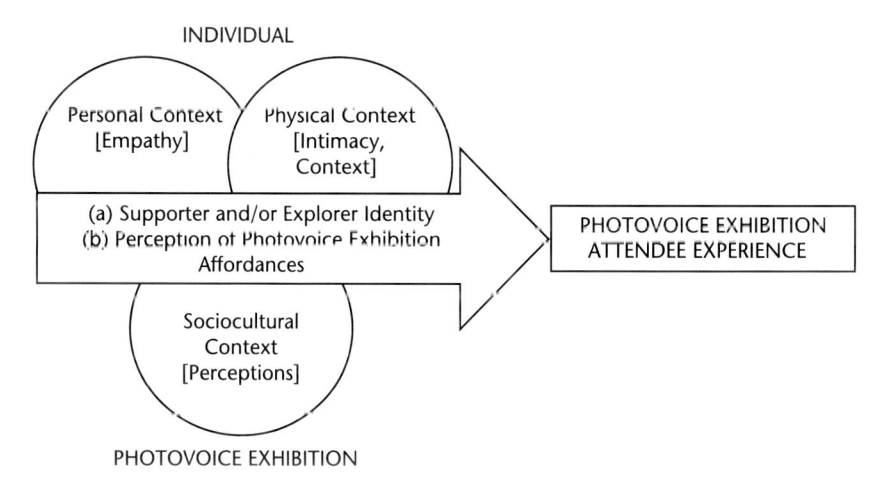

FIGURE 6.3 Within this new model, the study's findings are framed by the MVEM (Falk, 2009) contexts.

Personal Context (Empathy)

Recall that the photovoice exhibitions were focused on the educational lives of community college students. Seven community college students took photographs in response to prompts and then narrated those images for me within an interview setting. Participants of this setting explained strong empathic responses to the public library exhibition, which was the focus of this inquiry. It is important to note that "[museum visitors] attempt to personalize and make sense of what they see" (Falk & Dierking, 1992/2011, p. 67), and this was apparent within the photovoice attendees' comments. For example, Participant Two said the following:

> Going through and reading and seeing it [exhibition], it was interesting to compare it with my own life. And so you can kind of compare and contrast as you go through, and so you kind of have those emotions 'cause it'll evoke your own personal memories or your own thoughts or something that you've taken for granted or something that you can empathize with or that you've personally struggled with and see that other people are doing the same thing.

This participant—herself a student—was able to empathize with the photovoice participants' triumphs and struggles as college students. Participant Five was able to empathize with the community college students in this way also:

> I thought back to when I was working full-time, which was 50, 60 hours a week, plus taking graduate courses. And you know everything, well not everything—but much of what they said, it's so true. So tired. The tired. You didn't have time to do everything. You looked at that dryer and hopefully you got the clothes put in the dryer and that dry button pushed. And, you know, that's when my kids learned that if they wanted clean clothes they had to go look *in* the dryer.

Participant Three also experienced empathy with regards to the images and text presented within the exhibition. But her empathic response was unique:

> I found the photos of the children—because I'm a mother—and I found the photo of the uh—there was one that said "I'm trying to keep my children close to me" and there were two images: one of the child way far away and then one of the child running—closer. And I loved that—that image. That notion that your children—you can only hold their hands for a little while. I thought that one was emotional for me as a mother.

She was able to feel empathy for one subset of the photovoice participants— the community college students who were also parents. The photovoice exhibition caused the attendees to use the images and narrations as a mirror to reflect on their own associations to the themes conveyed, and as such, they were able to develop empathic responses.

Sociocultural Context (Perceptions)

The sociocultural context of the museum visit includes the social setting—with whom the visitor came and others who are also at the museum. It also includes the visitor's cultural background. Interviewees reported various ways in which the exhibition impacted their perceptions of community colleges and the students served by community colleges. Community colleges have long been stigmatized and stereotyped. Reed (2013) noted: "Community colleges don't get much respect. We all know the stereotypes: thirteenth grade, 'high school with ashtrays,' the place you go when you can't get in anyplace else. The ashtrays are mostly gone, but other stereotypes linger" (p. 13). For some, the photovoice exhibition challenged some of the negative stereotypes harbored by the attendees. Here is an example from Participant One:

> It [the exhibition experience] really provided what I like to call food for thought . . . graduating from the type of high school that I graduated from—it was a college preparatory academy—and when students didn't graduate knowing that they were going to a four-year institution, to me, it was just kind of one of those things where I wondered, why did you come to this high school? And when I saw them kind of go onto that community college setting, I really had this view or this perception that they just wanted to elongate their high school experience. So this—I think this presentation really provided me with that different perspective.

Participant One also noted the presence of the photovoice project participants at the lecture. Seeing, hearing from, and having the chance to talk to the photovoice artists made the exhibition more real. There was also an emotional element to their presence. With the photovoice artists present, a unique element is added to the social context of the visit. Participant One said this:

> I think that hearing from the [photovoice project participants] was actually the most emotional part of it . . . I think [name of one participant]'s story to me, really just—wow. I have to stop, you know, and I said to myself—I think that there was a lot working against her. And I mean, this is just based on my interpretation I suppose, but she didn't let it stop her. She didn't let it get her down. She's—you get to see her ambition, and it kind of gives—it gave me a little bit of motivation. And it's—it's fascinating because prior to this experience I don't think that there—I don't think I would've had a

motivating experience from someone who had a community college experience.

Within the comments above, the confluence of the presence of the photovoice participants and the attendee's cultural background interface to yield a transformative moment of stereotype deconstruction for Participant One—all within the sociocultural context of the total exhibition experience.

Participant Two's comments were reminiscent of the above commentary. The following excerpt was notable because the exhibition made the institution seem personalized according to Participant Two, versus an abstraction. She said:

> It helped me personalize the institution and the students that go there rather than everything else that I had previously believed and why and how I got to that point because even my guidance counselor in high school, you know, they had their group of students they were going to send to the community college because of certain things. There were characteristics about those students, and that's what I carried with me. I didn't have any other reason to think differently.

Within the above statements, a change in perception is evident, and this is linked to the educational and cultural background of the participant. This change in perception involved unlearning (what was gleaned from the actions of her high school guidance counselor regarding who would be "sent to" the community college) as well as learned (that a broad swath of individuals attend community colleges for a variety of reasons) within the exhibition context.

Participant Three indicated that the exhibition reinforced her already generally positive perception of the local community college. She stated "it [photovoice exhibition] reinforced the fact that they [community colleges] are doing good things." For Participant Four, the exhibition afforded a chance for him to affirm the community college's place and prominence within the particular historical, economic, social, and political moment the exhibition took place. He said:

> Well, I—community colleges as I said a moment ago, or maybe I didn't say this, but—are so important to our society, particularly at this time. And the chance for those students to go to college when otherwise they might not have that chance or that opportunity—and we need that as a culture and as a society—to have that opportunity for people.

So, in a sense, this experience provided this participant with confirmation of his existing stance on community colleges and their role within the educational system.

Physical Context (Intimacy)

The physical context of the museum visit includes the exhibitions, objects, labels, spaces, and programs the visitor encounters. Attendees routinely noted the intimacy of the photovoice exhibition. The photovoice participants documented aspects of their daily lives so as to illustrate the intricacies of their educational lives as community college students. These photographs included images of their homes, loved ones, and even themselves. It is important to note that the photographs were put forward in a physical form (rather than a projection on a screen, for example), and many of the images were enlarged to poster-size. Edwards (2002) noted "[o]bjects, consequently, are not just stage settings for human actions and meanings but are integral to them" (p. 69). The objecthood of the image and text amalgamations mattered; it provided a concretized artifact representing a particular participant's experience, which was fodder for attendees' interactions. Moreover, the photographs-texts were intimate and not easily accessed through non-photovoice methodologies.

Participant Five said: "I thought they really opened up and showed an inner self. They showed something that not everyone would think to let the world to see." And participant Six noted: "I think there was kind of a sense of privilege on my part and kind of respect that they'd open themselves up and let the outside into their lives." The vulnerability of the artists was acknowledged and appreciated as this afforded an accurate illustration of their daily lives, which included both triumphs and tragedies. Participant Four said: "The photos were really important in the sense that um they visually showed the life—the intimate life of these students and the text gave feeling to, and meaning to those photographs."

Context

Another important aspect of the physical context of the exhibit was the attendee's realization that they were interacting with a photovoice exhibition—not a photography exhibition. And the two are very different. A photovoice exhibition is not simply about the aesthetics of the photography; it is about the stories told by the photograph-texts amalgams presented. Within this context, the photographs are meaningless without the narrations. Moreover, the meaning(s) of the photographs are not necessarily at the discretion of the consumer. Within photovoice exhibitions, the narrations explicitly designate the meaning of the photographs. Participant One explained this:

> I almost felt like I were, like I was in an art gallery setting—kind of the way it was set up, but instead of just having captions, I feel like these stories were kind of like the purpose if you will. So we could—we could've attempted to have made meaning from the pictures but that meaning was already deciphered and it was very personal and I don't know. I mean I would look

at some of the pictures and I would say, oh, you know that's really interesting. I wonder what's going on here, and I tried to put a story together before I read the story. And nine times out of ten I was incorrect . . . But um, hearing their story or seeing their story about it, I said, you know, their point of view is valid whereas with art, it's very *perspective* and so the artist could say something about their work and I feel like you would be right to disagree with them . . . But in that setting I said that I can't disagree—their story carries more weight, more merit than my story does.

Participant Three's comments showcase her realization of the overarching purpose of the photovoice exhibition:

I would've corrected the sentences and the spelling and the grammar first—before I printed them [photographs with narrations]. But then as I looked more closely, I saw what was a talking project. It wasn't a writing project; it was a talking project. And then I understood it better. And I thought it was just great; I liked it.

This salient comment from Participant Two also provides a snapshot of how an attendee came to realize the nature of the photovoice exhibition and how it differs from a photography exhibition: "Okay it's like this isn't just a picture, this is someone's life." She went on to explain: "they're not just leaving their story in your hands or leaving it up to the world to interpret it however they want to. They're taking an active role in this whole process."

Attendee Identities

As noted at the start of this section, the three contexts of the museum visitor experience were used as a framework to organize the findings of this study. Each of the three contexts combined to create the visitor's total experience, which is also mediated through the visitor's identity and perceived affordances of the museum (Falk, 2009). In terms of the identities had by the interviewees, the five categories presented previously in this chapter are not entirely sufficient in this case. However, a case could be made regarding the professional/hobbyist identity, suggesting that the interviewees visited the exhibition and attended the lecture because it was related to their work or educational interests. In the case of photovoice exhibitions, however, the notion of a supporter identity might be viable. Based on my journals related to the exhibitions—as well as the interviews, many of those in attendance were present to offer support—to the photovoice participants (e.g. their families and friends), to me as the project facilitator (e.g. my colleagues and students), to the community college from which the photovoice participants were recruited (e.g. college personnel), and to the public library where the second exhibition was hosted (e.g. library personnel). In addition, some attendees expressed a curiosity about the exhibition, which is emblematic of the explorer identify. For example, Participant Six said: "I . . . had no idea what photovoice was, and so it seemed like a really cool concept. So I really wanted to see what it was—what it looked like." Using an identity lens to discern the motivations for attending a photovoice exhibition is an area that requires further exploration.

Summary of Findings

Taken together, the findings of this study can be phrased as follows: the intimacy of the photovoice exhibitions (physical context) resulted in empathic responses from attendees (personal context), which either changed or solidified perceptions about community college students (sociocultural context). In addition, two identities related to photovoice exhibition attendance were noted within this study: supporter and explorer. And these identities were mediated by attendees' perceived affordances of attendance. Figure 6.3 provides a model of the experiences had by the photovoice exhibition attendees.

Discussion and Implications

The literature on the museum visitor experience proved to be a viable lens through which to view, analyze, and make meaning of the data generated from this study. Because the literature appears to be absent regarding the experiences or perceptions of photovoice exhibition attendees, future inquiries within this area are necessary. Moreover, the present study provided a framework through which future similar studies can be constructed. This work has a number of implications, as mentioned below.

Implications

There are at least three implications of this study. First, continued and sustained inquiry meant to understand the ripple effects of a photovoice project is critical. This study was vital in understanding some of the impacts of the photovoice exhibitions vis-à-vis the attendees' experiences and perceptions, which are an integral part of the methodology. Second, photovoice exhibitions are different from most art exhibitions—context matters and attendees should be made aware of the nuance. Those engaged with photovoice projects and concomitant exhibitions should make clear the nature and intent of the exhibition. That it is markedly differentiated from a photography exhibition is important. This can be communicated through labels, placards, programs, and sundry other means. Third, the educative and transformative potential of photovoice project exhibitions is significant. Future studies ought to include a systematic interrogation of the effects of attending a photovoice exhibition through the lens of transformative learning

(Taylor, Cranton, & Associates, 2012). The participants of this study noted how the exhibition changed or solidified their perceptions of community college students, which is the essential outcome of action research—the action imbued within the moniker *action research*—as well as a signal for continued study is this vein. Attendees can be deeply affronted and impacted by photovoice exhibitions, which might be considered a disorienting dilemma and can catalyze learning and transformation. The power of the visual image can induce visceral reactions. Those strong emotional and empathic reactions to images lead to a questioning of preconceived notions—in some cases. One of the goals of the photovoice method is to reach policy makers—and others—who have the ability to affect positive change. The photovoice exhibition is one way to reach this specific audience. It is also a way to encourage transformative learning reach a broader sphere of interested and implicated individuals.

Conclusion

The purpose of this study was to interrogate the role of the exhibition component of a photovoice project. Experiences and perceptions of individuals who attended a photovoice exhibition, wherein the purpose of the photovoice project was to shed light on how community college students construct their educational lives, was investigated. The data generated were viewed and analyzed through the lens of the literature on the museum visitor experience. Findings were presented using Falk's (2009) MVEM. While the current methodological literature on photovoice is replete with information on how to carry out such an inquiry, writing on the role, purpose, and outcomes of concomitant photovoice exhibitions is missing. Rather, such exhibitions are taken for granted as a universal good and natural closure of such projects. To fully understand the reach and educative potential of a photovoice project the exhibition stage cannot be presumed to simply show the final results of the project, but rather must be theorized as another step in the ongoing meaning making that results from the total photovoice process.

A Vignette

This example of how to interrogate a photovoice exhibition, by building a qualitative inquiry research project around the process, helps to further theorize about the potential photovoice projects have to create social change. The first step in that process may start with an analytic memo a researcher generates soon after an exhibition while the sense-making process about the event is still underway. In the case of the example provided, I created the following post-exhibition analytic memo that later served as a vignette.

Analytic Memo, Post-dissertation, Post-Photo Exhibition (May 19 to 27, 2011)

I (Amanda) wrote the following analytic memo after having successfully defended my dissertation, carrying out our first photovoice exhibition, and graduating with my doctoral degree. Both the name of the institution and the participants are pseudonyms.

> The most important moment of this project took place on April 22, 2011. On that day, I/we hosted a photo exhibition at Middle West. It was amazing! After completing, revising, and defending my dissertation, I began the planning process for the photo exhibition. This was the part of the project where the participants became much more collaborative with me and with one another. During the weeks leading up to the photo exhibition, I had made every effort to contact each participant to garner input and ideas from him or her with regards to how to put together the exhibition. I had never hosted a photo exhibition before. I was able to meet with three of the six participants whose data were included in the actual dissertation (I've since added another participant—Baby Girl). Over a meal, I met with Crispy, Marie, and Louise to discuss their ideas. The meetings were excellent, but I began to feel a little overwhelmed with all of the different ideas. I had a unique and fairly uncharacteristic approach to this exhibition—I really wanted it to be the participants'. And not mine.
>
> This approach of mine must have been a staunch shift from my norm. One morning during the latter part of the semester I bumped into Crispy as I was walking into my office. I bumped into her after having a one on one meeting with me and after having the first planning meeting (which she and Louise attended). The bulk of our conversation was about her perception of how I had acted. She was surprised about how casual I was being about the exhibition—so much so that it was the first thing she brought up when we met in the hallway. I explained to her that I was consciously trying to keep myself from becoming controlling—I truly wanted the exhibition to be theirs. I suppose another truth is that I really believed everything would come together and be fine. However, this conversation with Crispy was a little surprising to me, and I imagined that it must have been on her mind quite a lot because she mentioned it to me right away. In the end, I was happy with my own approach because the way I went about things ended up leading to a really wonderful event. The participants, and Crispy and Louise in particular, did an amazing job and very much took "ownership" of what occurred.
>
> Back to the point. I had wonderful meetings with Marie, Crispy, and Louise to discuss how we might put the exhibit together. They each generated some wonderful ideas, which I have outlined in several emails to

the whole group of participants. I will not write them all out here. The most important thing is that these ideas were wonderful. Here is a summary:

Crispy: Interested in using a variety of media to hang the photos, such as drapes (the ones she personally used to cover the opening of her bedroom closet); to use a variety of sizes of images

Louise: Interested in how we were going to use lighting; wanted to hang the "freedom" images in the air—freely; wanted to arrange the "roles" photos in a chaotic manner

Marie: Interested in the use of a slideshow alongside of the static images; wanted us to include a moment to speak about the project

The others could not make an individual or group meeting, and it is important for me to express here that it was not a bad thing—another testament to the roles theme and the high levels of unpredictability that exist in some of the participants' lives. I believe they would have come if they could have come. However, they simply may have not been interested. It's hard to say.

Essentially, we had two group (at least that was the idea) meetings to prepare for the exhibition. One was about a week prior to the exhibition, and the other was the evening before the exhibition. Only Crispy and Louise were able to come to the planning meeting the week (or so) before the event. The meeting was at 5pm in the room at Middle West we were going to use. Imagine the most stereotypical community college classroom space, and that's where we were. Ok, maybe it was not that bad. The walls were white, bare, and reminded me of the smell of cleaning supplies, which I associate with that hallway—the space I have walked through once or twice per week for the past five years. There were tables and chairs in rows, fairly neatly organized. This arrangement resulted in a crescendo at the front of the room—the podium, which I would avoid at all costs. There was a chalkboard and a white board. There were old papers, handouts, and tests scattered about on a cart at the back of the room. There was a desktop computer and a projector and a screen. There were three or four long, thin windows on one wall with blinds. They reminded me of the long and thin windows that I have seen on the walls of old barns or even jails.

The room had to be transformed. Frankly, I had no idea how to transform it. So I let them have at it. The first planning meeting was messy and unorganized and nondirective. That was somewhat by design. There were a few moments of discomfort for everyone, I think, but on the whole I believe it was good. I had created blends of images and text. A few were mounted on gator board (8" × 10" and 11" × 14"), while others were displayed through large laminated posters (36" × 36" and 36" × 24"). I had also brought many implements to hang and arrange things—on the walls and tables, from the ceiling, and on fabric. I had things like tacks, easels, string, mounting squares, and binder clips.

By the end of the first planning meeting, we had a loose plan in place. There was more work to be done though. Each of us (me, Crispy, and Louise) had some items we were more or less responsible for, so there was space and something of a plan for action during the time between the first meeting and the second meeting. I needed to have some additional posters printed (and I needed to make them). I also needed to think through and orchestrate all logistical aspects of the project. Because of the need for more definitive decision-making regarding the room set up and because of the small window of time between the last class on Friday and our opening, we decided to meet in the room the night before to set up as much as we can.

After the first planning meeting, I sent email messages to the two instructors who taught in the room on Friday. I needed to ask them if they'd be okay with us putting the images on the walls and the lights around the ceiling. I was a little bit nervous about this. Maybe they'd be cynical about it or what if they said no? If something went wrong due to my lack of pre-planning, I would have felt awful. After completing my dissertation, I sort of melted into a puddle, felt so tired and in need of a long break. I needed a long, cool drink of water after a long journey in the desert. There were times when I was too exhausted to think or plan or even find emotions for the project, but I pushed through and it ended up being wonderful. These instructors were great, no glitches.

The night before the actual exhibition, we met and began the set up process. This included hanging the posters and some of the small mounted pieces on the walls. We also hung the white string lights all along the ceiling of the room. Crispy brought some drapes to hang on the "freedom" wall, which would be used as a backdrop for some of those images. We hung the drapes the night before. Some of the mounted images were hung by wire from the ceiling and looked great against the dark green patterned drapes. We also played with the slideshow to make sure it worked and talked a little bit about additional set up needs we had and things we needed to do on the day of the event.

Much to our chagrin, many of the posters fell overnight. I got word of this from a colleague, who works in that hallway and was checking the room for us. She helped out with the set up the night before. This caused a little concern for me, but I had purchased a lot of extra hanging supplies in the week leading up to the actual day, so I thought we'd be okay. I took the whole day off work and did some last minute errands that morning. I needed to make coffee and pick up the cookies I had ordered. I also needed to check and double check my "to bring" list—several times.

The most seemingly disinterested participant was counter-intuitively the most invested in this event: Louise. I was surprised that Louise wanted to be a part of the study. I was surprised at how rich our interviews were. I was disheartened when she stood me up several times for interview appointments. I could not believe how invested she was in this exhibition. She attended every meeting, related to it, and was never late. I was so surprised.

I arrived at Middle West way early. The exhibition was to begin at 4pm. I knew we could get into the room at around 2:20pm. I arrived close to 1pm. I thought Louise would arrive sometime close to 2 or 2:30pm. She was also there way early! I think she may have been more nervous than me! It was really good to have her there though—so we could talk through the set up. At that time, I knew it would only be her and me for the set up. However, Crispy ended up finishing her clinical hours early and was able to come help us out a bit too. The room set up went rather seamlessly. Louise and I had pre-thought out what each of us was going to do and in what sequence we were going to do it. She worked on the arrangement of the tables and chairs in the room (we moved many items out of the room). She also worked on the actual arrangement of the photo areas, and the roles area in particular, which required more set up time because we had "loose" photos and a piece of paper explaining what was meant by the arrangement in terms of the theme. I worked on setting up the area of the room dedicated to the programs, refreshments, and comment box. I also helped with table and chair removal as needed. Everything fell into place at just the right time. It was brilliant.

We set up the room with a definitive entry and exit point for attendees in mind. We also set up the room for flow. There was a pathway to follow, which led attendees in a "U" shape. Attendees entered at the front of the room and were guided to the left. The immediate left hosted a horseshoe of tables that held the programs (explaining the exhibition), sign in sheets, refreshments, and comment box. There were also balloons—all black and white—eight of them to represent the participants and me. I also had two balloons outside the room to signal that people were in the right place. We used only soft lighting; all the fluorescent ceiling lights were turned off. As I mentioned earlier, we had white string lights around the ceiling and used one table lamp and one floor lamp. It was a great atmosphere, both for viewing the photos and for viewing the slideshow.

Once attendees passed by the "U," the academic themed images were on their left and on the same wall as the "U." There were both posters and mounted images on easels, placed on a table. On the back wall were the roles images. These were arranged chaotically and involved posters and mounted images on the walls and photos on easels and randomly scattered about on a table. On the wall opposite the "U" and academic integration tables were the freedom images. These were purposefully placed on the wall with windows and hung from the ceiling to appear free. These were also a mix of mediums. At the front of the room was the screen, which held a scrolling slideshow I created with Prezi. We arranged some tables and chairs in the middle of the room so that people could have a seat if they liked. Many people did sit at the tables, and it was a very inviting space.

Four of the seven participants were in attendance. They were Louise, Crispy, Marie, and Lythria. Louise and Crispy met one another during the planning session. This was the only interaction between participants prior to the actual event. That made things interesting, but it was good, very good. As I mentioned earlier, Louise arrived first. Then, Crispy came, which was a surprise because she thought she was going to be late because of the scheduling of her clinicials. (I think) Marie came next and was followed by Lythria.

Many of the things related to the study, but not directly involved in the study, have reified some of the findings. For example, Crispy arrived much earlier than I and she expected. So, there was actually some downtime between the final touches on the set up and the arrival of other people (participants and guests). During this time, Crispy, who was in her scrubs and looked exactly like she did in one of her photos, pulled out her homework and began studying. At first, I was taken aback, but then I realized that this was completely in line with the findings of the study—there's no time to spare, especially for a nursing student with five children and a husband. It was really interesting to watch her recede from the event/moment/people and begin to work with her materials, which continued even after the arrival of our first guest. Her study time did not last very long.

After having some space for the event (only writing about it now, a month later), I've come to realize that other people's perspective of this event are important for me to explore and ascertain. It's much different to host an exhibition and have your analytical work on display than it is to be a participant and have your images and words on display. It's also different from being an attendee, and that experience is varied as well. There were the experiences of my committee members, Middle West employees of all kinds, participants' families, and random folks I had invited; all of these people experienced the event differently. These are points of inquiry I must enter into.

There was almost an instant bond between and amongst the participants. I would imagine that all of them had a strong curiosity regarding the images and words of the other participants, a desire for their input to by normalized or affirmed, I think that happened. Each participant took the time and gave care to really take in the images on display; they oscillated between hosts and attendees.

This entire exhibition was a delight for me. The strongest emotion I felt was pride. I was literally bursting with pride; I was proud of these students, my participants. Pride burst(ed) out of me in smiles, grins, and happiness generally. I was proud of the fact that this event was "working." Throughout the two hours, I delighted in seeing the participants engaged in conversation with one another, with attendees, with members of the Middle West community, with members of my doctoral committee, and with me. I loved seeing them in that environment.

During the first hour, a number of people cycled through the room. Louise was amazing with getting the slideshow up and running properly. For the life of me, I could not figure out how to set the Prezi to autoplay for 20 seconds per slide. Once Louise "fixed" the slideshow, I felt as though everything was just about as perfect as we could make it. Everything was nice and tight, right down to the black and white cookies.

One of my former students, who was in my *First Year Seminar* course during the spring 2011 semester, attended the event. The coolest thing about her attendance was that she brought her husband and youngest son (she has three or four boys, I think). This son was home for the Easter weekend; the exhibition was Good Friday. All three of them were really impacted by the exhibition. I talked with them for a while about it. Her husband had some questions for me, and it was the level of engagement he had with the images, text, and whole event that was so cool to me. I think it helped him to understand what his wife was experiencing. This is huge. Jessica, my student, was interested in the *Physical Therapy Assisting* (PTA) program during the semester of the exhibition. She had the chance to talk to Marie (also a PTA student). This was great for her and great for Marie too. One of the things the participants (or at least Marie) were interesting in doing was helping other students; this happened.

I remember at one point during the exhibition one of the participants coming up to me and saying that "people" were going up to the images and going "huh." In other words, she wanted me to know that it "was working." Many people were very impacted by the displays, and this was evident in their non-verbals. It was evident in their paralanguage.

Another funny thing (funny to me, I suppose) was that many people thought the exhibition was related to me getting my degree. However, I suppose it would make good sense to the outsider. There I was with my participants and a good number of university people, and a hard copy of a draft of my dissertation on a table by the academic integration photos. Even the participants, I think, were thinking that this event meant something to my degree obtainment.

At 5pm, halfway through the exhibition, we took about 10 to 15 minutes for an informal presentation/talk. I began by getting everyone's attention and explaining the project, essentially addressing the question, what is this whole thing all about? I spoke off the cuff about my experiences at Middle West and how much I enjoyed the students. I then read my dissertation dedication. It was really important to me to read those words to my participants, at least the four who were there—in front of other people. Once I finished, I invited the participants to speak about their experiences.

I wrote to them about this in an email and proposed some questions they might want to address. My goodness. They were amazing. This was the order: Lythria, Marie, Crispy, and finally Louise. I don't really remember this, but there was a short pause between my invite and the first participant to speak. One of my committee members said she thought this pause was tense or nervous or awkward. But, I really think it was a non-verbal negotiation among the participants about who would speak first. They all knew it was coming. And they were brilliant. They talked about being a part of the project, but also about having me in class and how that impacted their decisions to participate in the study. It was really affirming. It was completely moving and awesome. Each participant had a captive audience. Lythria talked about being given (by me) a space to have a voice, to have her voice heard. She said this was the first time in her life that she's been heard, had an opportunity to be heard. Marie talked about the time in our class when she almost passed out after having given blood. I came to check on her and that meant a lot. All of the participants at the exhibition talked about how much they enjoyed the *First Year Seminar* course, a course that many students loathe. Crispy talked about how she learned, halfway through the semester, that she did not have to have the *First Year Seminar* course to graduate. But, she stayed with it because she enjoyed me—and it. Louise said much of the same. They had all eyes on them. My emotions were intense the entire time. These students were amazing. They were way better than me. I was entranced. This was the pinnacle of my pride in them as well as the pinnacle of this whole dissertation experience.

I'm hoping to ascertain the vantage points of others regarding how these students' talks were received and what perceptions of them were. Being in the moment during the exhibition and then waiting a month for the energy to write about this has caused some of the details to leave me. Some entry points of future inquiry may be through interviewing the four participants who were there, interviewing a handful of attendees (particularly committee members), and administering an online survey to the rest of the attendees (whose email addresses I have from the sign in sheet). This is perhaps the next step, and I need to explore more options related to research and this project. I may need to go back to the IRB. This time around, the project I want to undertake may be considered a program evaluation and subsequently an exempt protocol.

After the intermission for our talking, the exhibition carried on until the conclusion at around 6pm. Many of the participants had the chance to talk to the attendees. The whole experience was transformative for the participants there, the four of them. The exhibition somewhat affirmed my assertions about the participants' development of a reflective consciousness rather than a critical consciousness. I am still asking myself, though, what happened within those two hours? What happened during that event? These are the questions that need to be addressed now.

Once the exhibition had come to a close, we broke down and I took a few things to my car. It was raining so I left many of the pieces inside. I said goodbye to the participants and kept making (jestfully truthful) jokes about how we were going to go to New York City next. While that is sort of a joke, I'd so love to do it. Just this past Monday (it's Wednesday when I'm writing this particular section of this memo) I arranged the images/text in the display cases in the 400-level hallway. I think they will be impacting to the students. The timing was perfect because I wanted to get those cases arranged before the start of the summer session, which was Monday. My plan is to keep those cases filled until we have another exhibition or until I'm told they have to go.

★ ★ ★

After completing an analytic memo of this type, the next step in the analytical process is to further consider how best to present what is coming to be known about the dialogic nature of the exhibition. Within this chapter, we provide some guidance on how to present the work to both policy makers and academics. The presentation phase creates a space where that political agenda is placed at the forefront. Moreover, Edwards (2002) said "[p]hotography is not merely the instrument of indexical inscription, it is a technology for visual display experienced as meaningful" (p. 67). Through photovoice exhibitions, participants are afforded the opportunity to showcase their images and narrations of those images in profoundly meaningful ways. Inquiry through photovoice inherently promotes *verstehen* for all involved, and concomitantly, the dissemination of photovoice project findings can foster empathic understandings about human life. The exhibition is typically the culminating event of a photovoice project, and one that separates photovoice from other similar methodologies. Sutton-Brown (2014) noted that "[photovoice]includes an explicit political agenda. It is this commitment to social action that distinguishes it from other photo-elicitation methods" (p. 70).

Photovoice and Journal Articles

Because this book is primarily targeted toward the academic researcher, we must consider the following question: "how can we pursue politically engaged and praxis-oriented research while at the same time hitting the targets set by an increasingly audit-oriented academy?" (Kesby, 2000, p. 423). Photovoice projects lend themselves brilliantly to presentation at academic conferences, especially when visuals (e.g. PowerPoint) can complement the talk. Journal articles are another story. When reviewing journal articles where authors used the photovoice methodology, it is noticeable that only about half of the articles contained photographs. In their meta-analysis of photovoice studies focused on mental illness, Han and Olliffe (2016) found the same thing. Only four of the nine studies reviewed contained participants' images. Why might this be the case? Harper (2012) noted that "[w]hile educational researchers are beginning to use images, they are still cautious about including them in the research reports" (p. 183). That educational researchers are not publishing images within their manuscripts may have many explanations.

Editorial Guidelines and the Cost of Printing

Publishing photographs in journals is expensive, and the cost is usually passed on to the author(s). When I began the process of trying to publish articles related to the dissertation this unexpected reality presented itself. Some of the more impactful journals in the field of higher education required a payment of several hundred dollars per photograph to be included in the print journal. Because of these financial constraints the range of potential outlets decreased. There are some workarounds, however. Some researchers have placed their photographs online and added URLs to print journals. And the advent of online journals has made the publishing process much less expensive and open to all manners of visual data (e.g. photographs, videos, interactive media).

Subverts Tenets of Anonymity and Confidentiality

Additionally, some institutional-based researchers (e.g. academics) may encounter IRB-related obstacles. Even though participants may have signed photography consent and release forms, some IRBs may be hesitant to sanction the publication of images that contain identifiable persons. And this may be tenuous, as some participants may be adamant about maintaining the fidelity of their images. In some cases, participants may not want to have their identities concealed. In fact, the prospect of having a concealed identity may feel silencing and harmful to participants. In these cases, having open and honest conversations with IRB personnel is recommended, as the notion of unabashedly revealing participants' identities completely subverts typically ethical practices within research practice. The other related dilemma is the categorization of photographs as raw data and most IRB exempt projects still require that raw data be shared in a limited way.

Preparing for the Exhibition

When considering the photovoice exhibition and the ways in which we can endeavor to reach policy makers, we see some connections with the literature related to the museum learning literature. Much of what was conveyed in the vignette above conveys what is necessary in planning, preparing, and executing a photovoice exhibition. Figures 6.4 and 6.5 illustrate some of what was described.

144 Photovoice Exhibitions

FIGURE 6.4 Participants' images and narrations of those images from the individual interviews were printed on gatorboard and displayed during the exhibition.

Considerations Regarding the Exhibition

Making a photograph is, in some ways, an act of telling. Photography can most certainly be used in telling about society. Photographers often "want to make viewers see things in a specific arrangement that they hope will push viewers to make certain comparisons along certain dimensions, generating particular moods" (Becker, 2007, p. 37). This is very much the case during a photovoice exhibition. Specifically, the caption, or voice, of the photograph leaves little room for interpretation. However, users, along with those who have facilitated the total project, may certainly interpret the photographs and the voices. Lackey (2008) noted that art exhibitions "should grow out of carefully considered intentions that include attempts to communicate as well as to create conditions in which others may respond to and learn from the display" (p. 34). The same goes for photovoice exhibitions.

When considering the photovoice exhibition, we need to also consider montages, series, and sequences. "Whatever the order . . . all the images we have seen affect our understanding of any single image" (Becker, 2007, p. 39). Within photovoice, however, the exhibition attendees are not encouraged to interpret the photographs separately from the captions/voices/narrations and vice versa.

FIGURE 6.5 This photograph was taken in the community college classroom where we hosted the initial exhibition. We physically arranged the room so attendees walked through in a specific way. Some of the images and narrations were printed as large posters and hung on the wall. We wanted to convey the images in a variety of ways.

Attendees are encouraged to interpret and be affected by the total presentation. The way in which users interpret the total presentation is at the forefront of the makers' (i.e. facilitators, participants) minds. This is because of the desire for action, which is implicit in this participatory action research approach.

What happens when some specific telling about society is hard for users to interpret? Many of us know how to interpret at least some social representations—we learn this as children. It is a part of the enculturation process. According to Becker (2007) "[w]e attend to representations in the ways we have learned" (p. 54). What do we do if/when users make unexpected, and perhaps negative, interpretations? Photovoice researchers have discussed the possibilities of the work to reify negative stereotypes or perceptions. We must consider this, and be prepared to address it. Moreover, when we prepare photovoice exhibitions (i.e. social representations), we must consider the amount of work we would like "users" to do. This sentiment from Becker is similar to McKim's (1980) work. How do we give attendees the tools to do the work? Should we assume that most do not have the tools? Also, what happens when users do not understand the visual language of the photographs, or the fact that the photovoice exhibition is very different from a photography exhibition? How do we develop a common language within, and throughout, the exhibition? Becker (2007) cautions: "users might not do the work left to them" (p. 59). Moreover, "[w]e must know and understand whom we want to reach" (Becker, p. 67). Photovoice products (e.g. exhibitions, reports, posters) are always reductive, as is all research; "[a]ny representation of social reality, then, has to make a little out of a lot" (Becker, p. 96). There is always too much to completely convey. But summary is delicate. What is too much? What is too little?

Exhibition and dissemination of photovoice project outcomes should involve collaborative planning by researchers and participants whenever possible. Exhibitions vary in terms of formality and goals. For example, an exhibition may take place at an art gallery and attract the attention of media and local officials. Likewise, an exhibition may take place in a homeless shelter to reach volunteers, staff, and funding agencies. The breadth and depth of a photovoice exhibit depends on the intended audience and outcomes. Exhibitions can also take the form of refereed journal articles, books, websites (e.g. Sadler, 2016), and other publications. Multiple methods of diffusion may be imperative to reach all project goals (Wang, Burris, & Ping, 1996).

Photovoice includes collaboratively curating a collection of photographs and associating those photographs with specific meanings, as assigned by the photographer-participants. Photovoice researchers must view photographs as active rather than passive objects—much like how Sassoon (2004) suggested archivists should conceive of photographs. Photographic images created and narrated within the photovoice process play a significant role in the project overall. They shape and extend participants' thoughts and means of communication. They influence interactions between members of the project team (e.g. within the interview or focus group exchanges). And they most certainly affect the tone and tenor of the photovoice exhibition. Wang, Burris, and Ping (1996) asserted that "photographs . . . displayed in the community's public spaces . . . [permit the public to] witness to often individualized, yet truly public, issues" (p. 1392). Photovoice "puts a human face on the data" (Wang et al., 1996, p. 1395).

This is an example of the evocative nature of these exhibitions:

> [i]n one forum held in the Jane-Finch community, a young woman in her twenties shook with emotion as she recounted the horrifying experience of being approached by an older man for transactional sexual relations in front of her daughter.
>
> *Wilson & Flicker, 2005, pp. 80–81*

What precautions must we make for exhibition attendees? Must there be some consideration of trigger warnings? We must grapple with these questions—and more—in preparation for exhibition.

Drawing from Art Education

Burton's (2006) text is an essential resource in planning and preparing for a photovoice exhibition. He wrote about exhibiting student art within the context of K-12 art education. While he asserted that exhibiting student art is motivational to students, he also noted that often "the students are not actively involved, and the art teachers are doing all the work" (p. 1). Burton's work, although it is focused on K-12 art education, can be applied to the exhibition phase of photovoice projects. Within the excerpt above, we can easily supplant the role of student with participant and the role of teacher with researcher. When students take an active role in an art exhibition, they become more invested in the art creation process, view their own art from an expanded perspective, and learn from how various audiences value, react to, and interact with the exhibition as a whole and each of the individual components. This is not unlike the process of involving participants in the photovoice exhibition process, which is typically seen as a premier way to catch the attention of policy makers and others who can be enlisted in catalyzing positive changes in response to a photovoice project's findings. According to Burton, there are five steps of exhibition: (a) theme development; (b) design; (c) installation; (d) publicity, and (e) event/assessment (p. 2).

When developing themes for the exhibition, Burton (2006) outlined six categories: (a) descriptive (interpret an idea or perception); (b) didactic (convey information or tell a story); (c) metaphorical (explore a symbolic relationship), (d) emotive (express a feeling); (e) honorific (praise an artist), and (f) issue-oriented (reflect an opinion) (pp. 15–21). When preparing for a photovoice exhibition, any of these categories may be selected—aside from the honorific theme, although there may be some exceptions. The ideation phase step of the photovoice process typically results in themes or findings of the total project. The process of building themes or findings is a way to convert the robust amounts of data typically generated through such a project into a manageable and easily understood set of major ideas distilled from all the data. And, often, these themes can be used to organize the exhibition. Even though participants may not want to be involved in the ideation phase because of the minutia involved—the level of which hinges on the analytical approach—when it comes to the exhibition, all involved with the project should be included as a part of the curatorial team, including theme development. Once the themes are established, photograph and text amalgams to be included in the exhibition are selected through a collective decision-making process. Asking participants which photographs they would like to see included, and considering which photographs most clearly illustrate the specific themes, should be a part of the selection process.

Designing exhibitions requires consideration of the following questions about exhibition attendees:

- Will they mill about, viewing works in no particular order and randomly make their own aesthetic connections?
- Will they be guided along a prescribed path with a definite beginning, middle, and end?
- Will people pass by the art in two directions, as in a school hall?
- Will they view the art passively or engage it interactively?

Burton, 2006, p. 30

Addressing these questions will help with design decisions. Burton identified six installation designs: (a) salon-style (a sea of art); (b) linear (clear and straightforward); (c) sequential (successive and progressive); (d) comparative (juxtapositions that contrast and connect); (e) synoptic (groupings by similarities); and (f) contextual (setting the scene) (pp. 33–38). See Figure 6.6 for an example.

Preparing for the exhibition involves a series of decisions, as indicated above, which can be organized vis-à-vis exhibition briefs, timetables, and checklists (Burton, 2006). The brief "embodies a clear plan of action for an exhibition" (Burton, p. 39). This working document lays out the vision for the exhibition and the steps necessary to bring that vision to life. It may include

FIGURE 6.6 The exhibition shown above was the result of a course-based project wherein graduate and community college students came together to carry out a photovoice project and display the findings. We used a didactic theme and a salon-style design.

assignments for individuals or groups. While this document can and should be malleable, having such an organizing tool is paramount even for the simplest exhibitions. Within such a document, tasks, resources, timetables, and updates can be recorded. In addition, a timeline and checklist should complement the brief. The timeline should be built backward from the exhibition's opening. The checklist should indicate what must be accomplished, and by when. Using these three planning documents, in tandem with one another, is vital in preparing for a photovoice exhibition.

Some important elements of the planning and preparation processes may include: securing an exhibition space, publicizing the exhibition, arranging the exhibition space, creating programs and signage, installing the exhibition, building interactive aspects of the exhibition, coordinating volunteers and assigning roles (e.g. greeter, speaker, live musical performer), and coordinating electronic media (e.g. music, video, social media). These elements can easily be converted into a timeline and checklist, and an example is provided within Appendix H.

Summary

Within this chapter, the presentation and confirmation phases of the photovoice methodology were explicated. As academic researchers, we must keep in mind both the communities within which we are working during the project, as well as the academic communities within which we are embedded as knowledge producers. When considering how to approach these final stages of the process, both audiences must receive dutiful attention. Practical tips on how to execute a photovoice exhibition were provided. Moreover, an example of positioning a photovoice exhibition as a site of inquiry was included here. Continued work within this area is necessary as the various outcomes of the photovoice exhibition remain under-examined and under-theorized.

Note

1 Thalia M. Mulvihill served as the chairperson of my doctoral committee. Much of my early photovoice work occurred under her tutelage. She served as a mentor and guide throughout the dissertation process and is now an invaluable colleague. Her co-authorship of this particular chapter was helpful in expanding my perspective and theorizing about photovoice exhibitions.

References

Becker, H. S. (2007). *Telling about society*. Chicago, IL: University of Chicago Press.
Burton, D. (2006). *Exhibiting student art: The essential guide for teachers*. New York: Teachers College Press.
Charmaz, K. (2006). *Constructing grounded theory: A practical guide through qualitative analysis*. Thousand Oaks, CA: Sage.
Dey, I. (1993). *Qualitative data analysis: A user-friendly guide for social scientists*. San Diego, CA: Academic Press.

Edwards, E. (2002). Material beings: Objecthood and ethnographic photographs. *Visual Studies, 17,* 67–75.
Falk, J. H. (2009). *Identity and the museum visitor experience.* Walnut Creek, CA: Left Coast.
Falk, J. H., & Dierking, L. D. (2000). *Learning from museums: Visitor experiences and the making of meaning.* Lanham, MD: AltaMira.
Falk, J. H., & Dierking, L. D. (2011). *The museum experience.* Walnut Creek, CA: Left Coast. (Original work published in 1992.)
Falk, J. H., & Dierking, L. D. (2013). *The museum experience revisited.* Walnut Creek, CA: Left Coast.
Han, C. S., & Oliffe, J. L. (2016). Photovoice in mental illness research: A review and recommendations. *Health, 20,* 110–126. doi: 10.1177/1363459314567790
Harper, D. (2012). *Visual sociology.* New York: Routledge.
Kesby, M. (2000). Participatory diagramming: Deploying qualitative methods through an action research epistemology. *Royal Geographical Society (with the Institute of British Geographers), 32,* 423–435.
Lackey, L. M. (2008). What is exhibition for? Considering the purposes of art display in a Saturday art school context. *Art Education, 61*(4), 33–39.
Latz, A. O. (2011). *Understanding community college students' educational lives through photovoice* (unpublished doctoral dissertation). Muncie, IN: Ball State University.
Latz, A. O. (2012a). Toward a new conceptualization of photovoice: Blending the photographic as method and self-reflection. *Journal of Visual Literacy, 31*(2), 49–70.
Latz, A. O. (2012b). Understanding the educational lives of community college students: A photovoice project, a Bourdieusian interpretation, and habitus dissonance spark theory. *Current Issues in Education, 15*(2). Retrieved from http://cie.asu.edu/ojs/index.php/cieatasu/article/view/836/345
Latz, A. O. (2015). Understanding community college student persistence through photovoice: An emergent model. *Journal of College Student Retention: Research, Theory & Practice, 16,* 487–509. doi: 10.2190/CS.16.4.b
Lincoln, Y. S., & Guba, E. G. (1985). *Naturalistic inquiry.* Beverly Hills, CA: Sage.
McKim, R. H. (1980). *Experiences in visual thinking* (2nd edn). Belmont, CA: Wadsworth.
Mitchell, C. (2011). *Doing visual research.* Los Angeles, CA: Sage.
Reed, M. (2013). *Confessions of a community college administrator.* San Francisco, CA: Jossey-Bass.
Sadler, E. L. (2016). *Childhood cancer survivorship stories.* Retrieved from https://survivorshipstories.com/
Sassoon, J. (2004). Photographic materiality in the age of digital reproduction. In E. Edwards & J. Hart (Eds.), *Photographs objects histories: On the materiality of images* (pp. 186–202). New York: Routledge.
Spradley, J. P. (1979). *The ethnographic interview.* London: Holt, Reinhart & Winston.
Sutton-Brown, C. A. (2014). Photovoice: A methodological guide. *Photography & Culture, 7,* 169–186. doi: 10.2752/175145214X13999922103165
Swaminathan, R., & Mulvihill, T. (2013) Photographic inquiry and educational technologies: Generating meaningful narratives. *Journal of Educational Technology, 9*(4), 1–7.
Taylor, E. W., Cranton, P., & Associates. (2012). *The handbook of transformative learning: Theory, research, and practice.* San Francisco, CA: Jossey-Bass.
Wang, C. C., & Burris, M. A. (1994). Empowerment through photo novella: Portraits of participation. *Health Education Quarterly, 21,* 171–186.

Wang, C. C., & Burris, M. A. (1997). Photovoice: Concept, methodology, and use for participatory needs assessment. *Health Education and Behavior, 24*, 369–387.

Wang, C. C., Burris, M. A., & Ping, X. Y. (1996). Chinese village women as visual anthropologists: A participatory approach to reaching policymakers. *Social Science and Medicine, 42*, 1391–1400.

Whyte, W. F. (Ed.). (1991). *Participatory action research*. Newbury Park, CA: Sage.

Wilson, C., & Flicker, S. (2015). Picturing transactional $ex: Ethics, challenges, and possibilities. In A. Gubrium, K. Harper, & M. Otañez (Eds.), *Participatory visual and digital research in action* (pp. 73–86). Walnut Creek, CA: Left Coast Press.

7

THE PROS, CONS, AND FUTURE OF PHOTOVOICE

A Vignette

Participatory action research approaches such as photovoice should occur *in situ* whenever possible to yield meaningful outcomes and affect positive change. Academic researchers who enter a community from the "outside"—or from an "outsider's" perspective—should conduct research *with* participants rather than *to* or *on* participants. This orientation is absolutely critical. It can also lead to an *in situ* orientation to the project. However, this stance is not standard within the academy. It is important for participants to have—and to feel like they have—ownership of the project. To provide some context for what follows, I will give a personal example. My dissertation was a photovoice project focused on how community college students construct their educational lives. As a community college adjunct faculty member at the time I was carrying out the project, my approach really was *in situ*, as my research site was the community college where I worked. And all my participants were former students of mine who were still enrolled at the community college during data collection. I am reminded of a critical moment I had with one of the participants who was a part of my dissertation research project. Her use of the pronoun "ours" when referring to the project during one of our exchanges gave me considerable pause. Even though this particular participant, Marie (pseudonym), did not persist through the entire study, this word use signaled something significant to me—ownership. I wrote the following email to my dissertation chairperson following that exchange with Marie:

> One of my participants just wrote [email] to notify me that she dropped off her camera in my campus mailbox. She wrote "I wanted to let you know

that I have officially completed the first phase of our project!" That she used the word "our" just made me so so so happy! Who knew that participatory action research would have such a positive impact on me? Ha! I may have to memo about this simple, yet important, moment.

In response to this email, my advisor encouraged me to write, or memo, about the encounter, which I did:

That a participant (Marie) is viewing this project as both mine and hers is truly extraordinary. This is truly participatory action research. It's clear that after just one round of photography that she is invested in the project and its success. I'm not sure how this happened. But, it makes me really happy! Marie and I have had a good relationship since our time together in *First Year Seminar*. I helped her locate a job shadowing opportunity and extended some concern for her one day during class when she felt faint after donating blood. She noted the job shadowing help I gave her during our initial [photovoice project] meeting. She said that she wanted to help me because she felt like I had helped her. I wonder if other students are beginning to feel ownership in the project. How will this evolve over time? How will it carry over into the exhibition?

Certainly word usage is one of many ways in which we, as researchers, might gauge levels of project ownership. And levels of ownership might give us clues as to how participatory the project really is. Photovoice researchers guide participants toward pathways that go to the center of the project. Ownership is always a choice, however, and no participant should be forced or coerced into being more involved than she or he would prefer. The option should be there nonetheless. Offering participants access to guiding and shaping the work through open, dialogical give-and-take related to points of focus, methods, interpretations of data, findings, and exhibition formats is key. One of the clear strengths, or pros, of the methodology is its participant-centeredness. When a participant willingly and enthusiastically goes to the center of the work, we know the research is *in situ*, and amazing things—things that matter in real people's actual lives—can transpire.

★ ★ ★

Pros and Cons

The pros, cons, and future of the photovoice methodology are outlined within this chapter. Pros, for example, include the visceral power of photography, participant-centeredness, and the capacity for policy change (i.e. action) that may improve the lives of those involved as participants. Cons, for example, include the costs associated with photography, time needed to carry out a full project, and the complexities of the overall experience. And the future of the photovoice methodology is yet to be seen, which is why this chapter is the shortest of them all. However, I present some ideas herein. Those who engage with this text will make the future, perhaps.

Wang and Burris (1997) identified ten pros and six cons of photovoice. In terms of pros, the methodology: (a) values the vantage point of participants; (b) uses the visual image, a powerful means of communication; (c) affirms the perspective of the vulnerable; (d) samples a variety of settings; (e) sustains community participation; (f) allows flexibility in project goals; (g) encourages participants to share the stories of others within the community; (h) provides tangible benefits to participants (e.g. photographs); (i) depicts communities needs and assets; and (j) stimulates social action (pp. 371–373). Cons included: (a) potential risks to participants (e.g. exploration of sensitive topics); (b) postmodern scrutiny (e.g. problematizing who took the photos and for what purpose); (c) control of resources (e.g. researchers may maintain existing social stratifications by retaining control of the project's funding); (d) difficulty in analyzing photographs; (e) limitations of funding, transportation, and communication; and (f) methodological ideals may not be practically possible to uphold (e.g. participants may not want to display their images) (pp. 374–375).

Booth and Booth's (2003) study illustrated additional potential pros and cons related to the methodology. The pros included: (a) community building; (b) solidarity building; (c) shared and polyvocal experience; (d) encourages collective action; and (e) makes space for creativity and multimodal forms of expression. The cons included: (a) invitation of ethical dilemmas; (b) participant attrition; (c) time intensity (in this case, photography lasted six months when it was thought to take one to two weeks); and (d) fixation on artistry on the part of the participants.

The power of the image is key in attracting the attention of policy makers. However, as Susan Sontag (2003) and John Berger (1972/1990) have noted, there exists a paradox within the reception of photographs, especially those that are arresting. While a single image can illicit visceral reactions, repetitive exposure to striking images can make consumers of those images immune to their effect.

Another major pro is that photovoice does not assume that participants can read or write. On the other hand, there is an underlying assumption that participants are sighted. Participants who may not be able to read or write can still communicate through images and talk (Wang, Burris, & Ping, 2000). The occularcentric nature of the methodology remains problematic, although strides toward inclusivity are being made, as addressed previously.

So, what are some of the other costs and problems of participation in a photovoice project? Wang, Yi, Toa, and Carovano (1998) suggested the following: (a) participants may not have the opportunity to actually *decide* policy; (b) participation involves time, and some participants may not have much time to give—McKim (1980) reminded us that "[s]eeing fully takes time" (p. 67); (c) social changes is slow and difficult; and (d) photovoice, as a research methodology, may not be viewed as a legitimate approach by policy makers, community members, researchers, or even participants themselves.

The photovoice method has strengths and weaknesses just like every other approach to inquiry. However, based on my personal experience, I have never been a part of any other type of study where the affective elements of involvement were so profound. Certainly you can tell through the inclusion of vignettes within each chapter that this approach has affected me, consistently and deeply. The affective aspects of the work—the pride, the anticipation, the excitement, the pain, and the joy—are much of what has compelled me to write this book. My only hope is that others might experience the strengths—as well as the weaknesses—in the same way.

The Future of Photovoice

The proliferation of photography technologies is changing the ways in which photovoice projects can be carried out. This remains an under-explored subject within the current literature. I consider what those changes mean for photovoice researchers and the future possibilities of the methodology.

Emergent Technology and Photovoice

Photographic Technology

The advent of 360-degree photography technology, among other advances in this area, gives current and future photovoice researchers an increasingly broad palette of ways in which they can equip and encourage participants to take pictures. The ease with which we can now engage in the photographic process is stifling, and I wrote about this in detail within Chapter 1.

Augmented Reality

When Pokémon Go hit the app scene and caused a serious raucous in the media, I jumped on board. This was, I thought, necessary for me considering I work with, and teach about, many of the college students who seemed to cling to this new augmented reality game with fervor. What started as a casual experimentation turned into serious fun—and thoughts about its relevance to photovoice. Playing the game and seeing these Pokémon populating the scenes in front of me caused me to wonder about what it would be like if photovoice participants took photographs or screen shots with their smartphones in response to prompts. Figure 7.1 could certainly be a response to the prompt: What do you usually do when you should be studying? These types of images communicate much differently than images of "reality."

FIGURE 7.1 This is a screen shot of my iPhone, which I took as an example of the ease with which photographs can be taken within an augmented reality environment. I took a screen shot of this image while playing Pokémon Go at a local coffee shop.

Social Media and Photovoice

Relatedly, we might think of the affordances of Snapchat, especially the ways in which the app allows users to filter selfies and change the way faces present and imbed emojis and captions onto photographs (see Figure 7.2). While Pokémon Go is an augmented reality game that lacks inherent social interactions, Snapchat is a social media tool that was built on temporary image and video sharing with both private and public dimensions.

Harper (2012) observed that

> [images in the twenty-first century] are everywhere, they are extraordinarily impermanent, and their social impact cannot be anticipated ... Not only are the images everywhere but the means for making them are as well ... [the images] also flow up continuously in a vast cloud, around and through the global community via the Internet.
>
> *p. 141*

According to Edwards (2002), "[m]ateriality is closely related to social biography" (p. 68). In other words, objects are an integral part of social relations. They are not ancillary to social experience; they are enmeshed in it. Because "we think photographically and certainly communicate photographically" (Collier, 1967, p. 4), the use of photography-based social media platforms such as Instagram and Snapchat makes this very apparent. Is Instagram the world's largest photovoice project? Prompt: sharable life moments/highlights. Is visual life narration through these platforms a form of sousveillance (Dodge & Kitchin, 2007)? Sousveillance (life-logging with, for example, a body camera) is a form of self-surveillance. Is photovoice a form of sousveillance; is it life-logging? Can it be? Should it be? What happens when participants are asked to engage in ongoing photographic surveillance of their own lives, or some aspect of their lives, through social media? These questions require attention, and at present, the literature is not yet attentive.

The use of photovoice and social media together is inevitable, yet it is also under-theorized and absent from most of the photovoice literature. The mergers of digital photography, live-streaming video, photographic manipulation, and social media are constantly impressing upon social life.

Photovoice as Pedagogy

Photovoice has educative potential. While photovoice is predominantly a research methodology, scholars have explored its pedagogical applications (Chio & Fandt, 2007; Latz, Phelps-Ward, Royer, & Peters, 2016; Lichty, 2013; Schell, Ferguson, Hamoline, Shea, & Thomas-Maclean, 2009). Within the pedagogical applications articulated in the extant literature, students are typically positioned as participants rather than project facilitators. That is, oftentimes, students are in positions to take

FIGURE 7.2 This figure illustrates what it is possible to create, photographically, within the Snapchat app. I was able to layer the image with the temperature, a caption, and an emoji.

photographs (photo) and then narrate those images (voice)—assigning meaning and interpretation (e.g. Chio & Fandt, 2007; Cook & Quigley, 2013). While the method is educational, especially in the context of learning about diversity as was the context for Chio and Fandt (2007), in what ways can positioning students as project facilitators promote learning, understanding, and empathy? The full answer to this question is yet to be seen.

Photovoice as Life

Whether we realize it or not, the actions and thought processes prompted by the photovoice process are such close matches to the ways in which life unfolds, for many, on a regular basis. At no other point in history has it been so simple to take a picture. Many individuals from all across the world routinely narrate their life experiences in engaging visual ways. We have seen this explode through the advent of the Internet and Web 2.0 affordances, which give persons without any coding knowledge or skills the ability to make content and publish it online for a global audience. And this narration can and has, in fact, affected policy. It will be infinitely interesting to see what the future of photovoice has in store.

Summary

Within this final chapter I outlined the pros, cons, and future of photovoice. This particular chapter is scant, as I leave this text with a challenge to the reader. Make the future. Photovoice has so much potential, and it is up to us, as innovative, social-justice minded participatory action researchers, to push the boundaries of what is already established. Let us take up where others have left off and continue this good work.

References

Berger, J. (1990). *Ways of seeing*. New York: Penguin. (Original work published in 1972.)

Booth, T., & Booth, W. (2003). In the frame: Photovoice and mothers with learning difficulties. *Disability & Society, 18*, 431–442.

Chio, V. C. M., & Fandt, P. M. (2007). Photovoice in the diversity classroom: Engagement, voice, and the "eye/I" of the camera. *Journal of Management Education, 31*, 484–504.

Collier, J. (1967). *Visual anthropology: Photography as research method*. New York: Holt, Rinehart and Winston.

Cook, K., & Quigley, C. (2013). Connecting to our community: Utilizing photovoice as a pedagogical tool to connect students to science. *International Journal of Environmental and Science Education, 8*, 339–357. doi: 10.12973/ijese.2013.205a

Dodge, M., & Kitchin, R. (2007). "Outlines of a world coming into existence": Pervasive computing and the ethics of forgetting. *Environment and Planning B: Planning and Design, 34*, 431–445. doi: 10.1068/b32041t

Edwards, E. (2002). Material beings: Objecthood and ethnographic photographs. *Visual Studies*, *17*, 67–75.

Harper, D. (2012). *Visual sociology*. New York: Routledge.

Latz, A. O., Phelps-Ward, R. J., Royer, D. W., & Peters, T. M. (2016). Photovoice as methodology, pedagogy, and community building tool: A graduate and community college student collaboration. *Journal of Public Scholarship in Higher Education*, *6*, 124–142. Retrieved from https://jpshe.missouristate.edu/assets/missouricompact/Photovoice.pdf

Lichty, L. F. (2013). Photovoice as a pedagogical tool in the community psychology classroom. *Journal of Prevention Intervention Community*, *41*, 89–96. doi: 10.1080/10852352.2013.757984

Schell, K., Ferguson, A., Hamoline, R., Shea, J., & Thomas-Maclean, R. (2009). Photovoice as a teaching tool: Learning by doing with visual methods. *International Journal of Teaching and Learning in Higher Education*, *21*, 340–352.

Sontag, S. (2003). *Regarding the pain of others*. New York: Farrar, Straus and Giroux.

Wang, C. C., & Burris, M. A. (1997). Photovoice: Concept, methodology, and use for participatory needs assessment. *Health Education and Behavior*, *24*, 369–387.

Wang, C., Burris, M. A., & Ping, X. Y. (1996). Chinese village women as visual anthropologists: A participatory approach to reaching policymakers. *Social Science & Medicine*, *42*, 1391–1400.

Wang, C. C., Yi, W. K., Tao, Z. W., & Carovano, K. (1998). Photovoice as a participatory health promotion strategy. *Health Promotion International*, *13*, 75–86.

APPENDICES

A Note about the Appendices

Many of the following documents (appendices) have been adapted from my (unpublished) doctoral dissertation. Some have been adapted from projects I have completed since the dissertation. Feel free to adapt these forms for your own use. Simply give credit where credit is due.

Appendix A

Sample Informed Consent Document for Participants

By signing this form, or one similar, participants consent to taking part in the study. They should be made aware of the fact that data they generate (images and words) may be made public through a variety of venues (e.g. exhibitions, meetings with stakeholders, academic conference presentations, journal articles, and books). Each element of this form should be described to the participant; it does not have to be read verbatim. While this example consent form is a helpful guidepost, many institutional IRBs have boilerplate consent forms available for download. Always start there, with the local form, and modify as deemed necessary.

★ ★ ★

Informed Consent Document

Study Title
Understanding the Educational Lives of Community College Students through Photovoice

Study Purpose and Rationale
The purpose of this study is to understand how some community college students construct their educational lives. The present study will assist policy makers in understanding student needs, which can inform policy decisions, programming, and the appropriation of resources. This study will address and partially ameliorate the paucity of literature available on community college students.

Inclusion/Exclusion Criteria
The population will include students who were enrolled in the principal investigator's (PI) *Cultural Anthropology* or *First Year Seminar* classes from the fall semester of 2008 to the spring of 2010. Students eligible for the study will be enrolled at Middle West Community College (MWCC) [pseudonym] during the fall of 2010, when data gathering will begin. All participants will be 18 years of age or older. It must be noted that participants will be former students of the principal investigator (PI), whose grades have already been submitted.

Participation Procedures and Duration
The methodology to be used in this study is photovoice, which is a form of participatory action research. For this study, you will be asked to respond to prompts regarding your educational life through photographs (disposable cameras provided). Then, you will discuss the photos and engage in an interview with the PI. Your participation will include three face-to-face meetings with the PI: (1) to discuss the research study and provide you with a camera and the first prompt; (2) to discuss the photos and engage in an interview and provide a second camera and prompt; and (3) to discuss the second round of photos and engage in an interview. The interview site will be MWCC or an agreed upon location convenient to you. You will be asked to sign an informed consent document in duplicate during the first meeting (this form). You will keep one copy. You will also be asked to complete a photo release form during the first interview. No photos will be used within this research or otherwise published without your permission. Also, a timeline will be determined for you to complete the photography. A plan will be established to transfer the disposable camera to the PI.

Audio or Video Files
For purposes of accuracy, with your permission, the interviews will be audio recorded. Any names used on the audio recording will be changed to pseudonyms or be altogether omitted when the interviews are transcribed. The audio file(s) will be stored on a flashdrive in a locked filing cabinet in the PI's office for three years and will then be destroyed.

Data Confidentiality or Anonymity
All data will be maintained as confidential and no identifying information, such as names, will appear in any publication or presentation of the data. You may be

identifiable through the photographs, however. If you do not engage in self-photography identity exposure may be possible nonetheless (e.g. photos of your home, car). But, it will be lessened. Also, you must obtain consent from anyone photographed in private spaces (e.g. inside homes, cars, hospital rooms). If photographing minors in private spaces, consent from the minor's legal guardian (e.g. parent) is required. Copies of consent forms will be provided to you for these purposes.

Storage of Data
Tangible physical data (paper, photographs) will be stored in a locked filing cabinet in the PI's office indefinitely. Interviews/discussions will be transcribed and entered into a software program (Microsoft Word) and stored on the researcher's password-protected laptop indefinitely. Audio files from interviews will also be saved on the researcher's personal password-protected laptop for three years and will then be destroyed. Any back up files of transcripts or audio stored on DVDs, flash drives, or external hard drives will be securely kept in a locked filing cabinet in the PI's home office for three years and will then be destroyed. Only members of the research team will have access to the raw data.

Photography
As a part of this study, you will be asked to respond to prompts through photography. The photos you take for this project must fall within public decency standards. Please refer to the student code of conduct section of the Student Handbook information regarding what is deemed appropriate for MWCC students. Photos should not be pornographic and should not capture activity that is illegal. Do not trespass or knowingly put yourself or others in harm's way while taking photographs.

Photographs
You will receive a copy of the photo(s) you take. The photo(s) will be provided to you by the PI. Any photographs you receive may not appear on social media sites (e.g. Facebook, Twitter) or otherwise be published online or in any other format.

Risks or Discomforts
The potential risks or discomforts associated with this study are minimal and will not exceed risks encountered in daily life. However, you will be fully briefed on the photovoice methodology and appropriate use of the cameras. Photographs of individuals may not be taken without consent in spaces deemed as private (e.g. inside a home, hospital room).

Benefits
There are no perceived benefits from participating in this study.

Voluntary Participation

Your participation in this study is completely voluntary and you are free to withdraw your permission at anytime for any reason without penalty or prejudice from the PI. Please feel free to ask any questions of the PI before signing this form and at any time during the study.

Institutional Review Board Contact Information

For one's rights as a research subject, you may contact the following: [insert the contact information of your institution's/agency's institutional review board].

★ ★ ★

Consent

I, _____[print name], agree to participate in this research project entitled, *Understanding the Educational Lives of Community College Students through Photovoice*. I have had the study explained to me and my questions have been answered to my satisfaction. I have read the description of this project and give my consent to participate. I understand that I will receive a copy of this informed consent form to keep for future reference.

To the best of my knowledge, I meet the inclusion/exclusion criteria for participation (described on the previous page) in this study.

_____   _____

Participant's Signature   Date

Permission to audio record interviews?
(indicate with "✓")   _____YES   _____ NO

_____   _____

Participant's Signature   Date

Researcher Contact Information

Principal Investigator: Research Team Member(s):

[place contact information here]   [place contact information here]

Appendix B

Sample Photography Consent Form

By signing this form, individuals who may be photographed by participants are consenting to having their photographs taken. Copies of this form should be provided to participants. It is up to the participants to ask individuals they would like to photograph in private spaces to sign this form in duplicate. One signed copy should be retained and given to the principal investigator (PI), and one copy should be given to the individual photographed for his or her records. I printed these forms on colored paper, and provided each participant with 20 copies. It is important that researchers can connect the photography consent form with a specific photograph, so it is critical that the participants make notations on this form to that end.

★ ★ ★

Photography Consent Form

Study Title
Understanding the Educational Lives of Community College Students through Photovoice

Study Purpose and Rationale
The purpose of this study is to understand how some community college students construct their educational lives. The present study will assist policy makers in understanding student needs, which can inform policy decisions, programming, and the appropriation of resources. This study will address and partially ameliorate the paucity of literature available on community college students.

Photographs
Participants involved in this study have been asked to respond to prompts through photographs. You are receiving this form because one of the study's participants would like to photograph you as a response to one of the prompts.

Data Confidentiality or Anonymity
All photographs will be maintained as confidential and no identifying information such as names will appear in any publication or presentation of the data. You may be identifiable through the photographs, however.

Storage of Data
Tangible physical data (paper, photographs) will be stored in a locked filing cabinet in the principal investigator's (PI) office indefinitely. Interviews/discussions will be transcribed and entered into a software program (Microsoft Word) and stored on the researcher's password-protected laptop indefinitely. Audio files from interviews will also be saved on the researcher's personal password-protected laptop for three years and will then be destroyed. Any back up files of transcripts or audio stored on DVDs, flash drives, or external hard drives will be securely kept in a locked filing cabinet in the PI's home office for three years and will then be destroyed. Only members of the research team will have access to the raw data.

Risks or Discomforts
There are no foreseeable risks associated with allowing yourself to be photographed.

Benefits
One extra copy of photographs you appear in will be printed and provided to the participant/photographer. The participant/photographer will be asked to give you one copy of any photographs in which you appear. Any photographs you receive may not appear on social media sites (e.g. Facebook, Twitter) or otherwise be published online or in any other format.

Voluntary Participation
Allowing yourself to be photographed for this study is completely voluntary. Please feel free to ask any questions of the researcher before signing this photo consent and release form and at any time during the study.

Researcher Contact Information
For additional information about this study, you may contact the principal investigator: [place your contact information here].

IRB Contact Information
You may also direct questions to: [place contact information of your institution's/agency's institutional review board here].

Study Title
Understanding the Educational Lives of Community College Students through Photovoice

* * *

Photo Consent
I, _____[print name], give permission to be photographed by participants of this research project entitled, *Understanding the Educational Lives of Community College Students through Photovoice*. I have had the study explained to me and my questions have been answered to my satisfaction. I have read the description of this project and give permission for myself to be photographed. I understand that I will receive a copy of this informed consent document to keep for future reference.

_____   _____
Individual's Signature   Date

For Participant/Photographer's Use Only:
Photograph number(s) in which this individual appears:

Researcher Contact Information

Principal Investigator: Research Team Member(s):

[place contact information here]   [place contact information here]

Appendix C

Sample Parent/Guardian and Minor Child Permission and Photography Consent Form

If a participant wants to photograph a minor (someone under the age of 18) in a private space, that minor's legal guardian must provide permission. Copies of this form should be provided to participants. It is up to the participants to ask legal guardians of minors they would like to photograph in private spaces to sign this form in duplicate. One signed copy should be retained by the participant and given to the principal investigator (PI), and one copy should be given to the legal guardian of the minor photographed for his or her records. I printed these forms on colored paper (a different color than the Appendix B forms), and provided each participant with 20 copies. It is important that researchers can connect the photography consent form with a specific photograph, so it is critical that the participants make notations on this form to that end.

★ ★ ★

Parent/Guardian and Minor Child Permission and Photography Consent Form

Study Title
Understanding the Educational Lives of Community College Students through Photovoice

Study Purpose and Rationale
The purpose of this study is to understand how some community college students construct their educational lives. The present study will assist policy makers in understanding student needs, which can inform policy decisions, programming, and the appropriation of resources. This study will address and partially ameliorate the paucity of literature available on community college students.

Photography
Participants involved in this study have been asked to respond to prompts through photographs. You are receiving this form because one of the study's participants would like to photograph your child as a response to one of the prompts.

Data Confidentiality or Anonymity
All photographs will be maintained as confidential and no identifying information such as names will appear in any publication or presentation of the data. Your child may be identifiable through the photographs, however.

Storage of Data
Tangible physical data (paper, photographs) will be stored in a locked filing cabinet in the PI's office indefinitely. Interviews/discussions will be transcribed and entered into a software program (Microsoft Word) and stored on the researcher's password-protected laptop indefinitely. Audio files from interviews will also be saved on the researcher's personal password-protected laptop for three years and will then be destroyed. Any back up files of transcripts or audio stored on DVDs, flash drives, or external hard drives will be securely kept in a locked filing cabinet in the PI's home office for three years and will then be destroyed. Only members of the research team will have access to the raw data.

Risks or Discomforts
There are no foreseeable risks associated with allowing your child to be photographed.

Benefits
One extra copy of photographs your child appears in will be printed and provided to the participant/photographer. The participant/photographer will be asked to give you one copy of any photographs in which your child appears.

Voluntary Participation
Allowing your child to be photographed for this study is completely voluntary. Please feel free to ask any questions of the researcher before signing this Parental Permission form and at any time during the study.

Researcher Contact Information
For additional information about this study, you may contact the principal investigator: [place your contact information here].

IRB Contact Information
You may also direct questions to: [place contact information of your institution's/agency's institutional review board here].

Study Title
Understanding the Educational Lives of Community College Students through Photovoice

★ ★ ★

Legal Guardian Photo Consent

I, _____[print name], give permission for my child to be photographed by participants of this research project entitled, *Understanding the Educational Lives of Community College Students through Photovoice.* I have had the study explained to me and my questions have been answered to my satisfaction. I have read the description of this project and give permission for my child to be photographed. I understand that I will receive a copy of this informed consent document to keep for future reference.

_____   _____

Legal Guardian's Signature   Date

Child Photo Assent

The research project has been explained to me, and I have had the opportunity to ask questions. I agree to be photographed for the purposes of this study.

_____   _____

Child's Signature   Date

For Participant/Photographer's Use Only:

Photograph number(s) in which this child appears:

Researcher Contact Information

Principal Investigator: Research Team Member(s):

[place contact information here]   [place contact information here]

Appendix D

Sample Photograph Release Form for Individuals Appearing in Photographs

Any individuals who have consented to be photographed or legal guardians of minors who have consented that their child may be photographed in a private space should also be asked to sign this photography release form. This form gives the principal investigator (PI) permission to publically showcase the photographs in which persons appear and signed in duplicate. One signed copy should be retained by the participant and given to the PI, and one copy should be given to the individual photographed or the legal guardian of the minor photographed for his or her records. I printed these forms on colored paper (a different color than the forms for Appendices B and C), and provided each participant with 40 copies.

For each individual photographed within a private space, participants should obtain signed copies of the consent and photography release forms.

★ ★ ★

Photograph Release Form

Photo Release
Photographs of you will not be taken, presented, exhibited, or otherwise published without your consent and release.

Photographs
You will receive a copy of the photo(s) in which you appear. The photo(s) will be provided to you by the participant/photographer. Any photographs you receive may not be uploaded to on social media sites (e.g. Facebook, Twitter) or otherwise be published online or in any other format by you.

Statement of Release
I, the undersigned, irrevocably grant to [name of the PI], the principal investigator of the study, the right to use the photographs taken of me for any purpose [pronoun] deems proper in perpetuity. I understand that these photographs may appear in various publications such as scholarly journal articles or conference presentations.

I understand that no real names will accompany the photographs published in association with study. However, I understand that I [or my minor child] may be identifiable through the photographs.

I expressly release [name of the PI, names of institutions/agencies associated with the study] and their agents, trustees, officers, employees, licensees, and assigns from and against any and all claims which I have or may have for invasion of privacy, defamation or any other cause of action arising out of or relating to my appearance in the photographs.

I assure that the photograph(s) I appear in, which will be provided to me by the participant/photographer, will not appear on social media sites (e.g. Facebook, Twitter) or otherwise be published online or in any other format.

_____   _____
Date   Photographed's Name (please print)

                            _____
                            Photographed's Signature

                            _____
                            Legal Guardian's Signature (if photographed is a minor)

For Participant/Photographer's Use Only:
I witnessed the third party's (photographed) signature and take responsibility for its legitimacy. If applicable, I also witnessed the legal guardian's signature and take responsibility for its legitimacy.

_____   _____

Date   Participant/Photographer's Signature

Photograph number(s) in which this individual appears:

Researcher Contact Information

Principal Investigator: Research Team Member(s):

[place contact information here]   [place contact information here]

Appendix E

Sample Project Information Sheet

Multiple copies of this information sheet should be given to participants. Participants can distribute this sheet to interested parties if they are questioned while taking photographs. Having this information on hand lifts some of the burden of explanation from the participants. I printed these sheets on white paper and provided each participant with 20 copies.

★ ★ ★

Project Information Sheet

Understanding the Educational Lives of Community College Students through Photovoice

The purpose of this study is to understand how community college students understand their educational lives. A small group of community college students have decided to participate in this study. They will respond to prompts provided to them by the principal investigator through photographs. This methodology is called photovoice. Development of the photovoice methodology is credited to Caroline C. Wang and Mary Ann Burris. The three major aims of photovoice are: (1) to allow participants to document their lives on their own terms; (2) to raise critical consciousness among participants; and (3) to initiate positive change through reaching policy makers through the photographs and research project as a whole.

This research project is being undertaken by [place your name here], the study's principal investigator. Participants in this research project are [insert information about the participants here].

Each participant will take photographs in response to photography prompts. The principal investigator will engage participants in interviews regarding the photographs.

Findings of this study may be presented in scholarly journal articles, conference presentations, and books. One goal of the photovoice methodology is to reach policy makers. As such, a public exhibition of the research and the photographs will be planned at the conclusion of the study.

If you have any questions about this project, you may contact the principal investigator via phone or email: [place your name and contact information here].

You may also direct questions to: [place contact information of your institution's/agency's institutional review board here].

Thank you for your interest in this project!

Appendix F

Sample Photovoice Instructions for Participants/Participant Packet Cover Letter

For some prospective participants, the initial meeting can be very overwhelming, especially if you give permission to take photographs of persons in private spaces, and provide participants with countless pieces of paper. Therefore, including an instruction sheet in the form of a packet cover letter can be helpful.

★ ★ ★

Dear Participant,

Thank you so much for being willing to participate in this study titled: *Understanding the Educational Lives of Community College Students through Photovoice*. As a part of this study, you are asked to respond to prompts through photography. Participation in this study will include taking 27 photographs with a disposable camera. Following each photography session, you will return the disposable camera to the principal researcher, and meet her for approximately 60 minutes to discuss the photographs once they have been printed. At the first interview/discussion meeting, you will be provided with a copy of your photographs. You will also be asked to sign a photo release form. Your photos will not be made in any way public without your permission. This process will be followed once more. The project will culminate with a public exhibition of the research and the photographs. Your involvement and/or participation in the exhibition is encouraged, but it is completely up to you whether or not you participate.

Know that your participation in this study is totally voluntary. You may withdraw at any time.

You may photograph individuals in public spaces (such as in a public park, on sidewalks) without their consent. However, you must obtain consent from those photographed if you are in private spaces (such as homes, classrooms, inside vehicles, hospital rooms).

If you intend to take photos of individuals over 18 years of age in private spaces, you must obtain their consent and photo release. Twenty copies of each of these forms are provided to you in this packet. Please ask those to be photographed to sign the forms in duplicate. They will retain one copy of the form.

If you intend to take photos of minors (under 18 years of age) in private spaces, you must obtain consent from the minor and his or her legal guardian (i.e. parent). Twenty copies of each of these forms are provided to you in this packet. Please ask the child and his or her legal guardian to sign the forms in duplicate. The minor's legal guardian will retain one copy of the form.

Remember to carry these forms and a pen (provided inside this packet) with you as you engage in photography. Also remember to obtain consent **_before_** taking photos of individuals. Please use the enclosed project information sheet if those photographed have questions about the study.

Here are Some Important Points to Remember When Taking Photos:

- Keep sunlight to your back when taking photos outdoors.
- Use the flash (press the button on the front of the camera and wait for the red light to appear) when taking photos indoors.
- Be sure to look through the viewfinder to capture the entire scene you would like to photograph.
- Feel free to use the camera either horizontally or vertically.
- Be as creative as you like. There are no 'rules' per se. You are simply asked to respond to the prompts, in any way you like, through photographs.
- You may not take photographs that are pornographic or contain illegal activity.
- When taking photographs, do not place yourself in dangerous situations or trespass.
- If you are questioned about why you are taking photographs, feel free to distribute the project information sheet.
- Be sure to have all necessary forms on hand when you engage in photography.

If you should have any questions throughout the duration of the research project, please contact me, the principal investigator, at any time. I can be reached through phone or email.

Thank you so much for your willingness to participate!

[place your name and contact information here]

Appendix G

Sample Photograph Release Form

This form can be used before, during, or after the photo-elicitation interview. Participants, upon seeing their photographs, may not want-to give permission for all of them to be published or otherwise made public. This form allows them the opportunity to differentiate between photographs to be made public and photographs to be kept private. I used this form during the first interview. Another version of this form with updated photograph numbers was used during the second interview.

★ ★ ★

Photograph Release Form

Study Title
Understanding the Educational Lives of Community College Students through Photovoice

Participation Procedures and Duration
The methodology used in this study is photovoice, which is a form of participatory action research. For this study, you were asked to respond to prompts regarding your educational life through photographs (cameras provided). Next, you will discuss the photos and engage in an interview with the principle investigator (PI). Your participation in this study will include a total of three face-to-face meetings with the PI: (1) to discuss the research study and provide you with a camera and the first prompt; (2) to discuss the photos and engage in an interview and provide a second camera and prompt; and (3) to discuss the second round of photos and engage in an interview. The interview site is Middle West Community College or an agreed upon location convenient to you. You were asked to sign an informed consent document form in duplicate during the first meeting. You kept one copy. Also, a timeline was determined for you to complete the photography. A plan was established to transfer the disposable camera to the PI.

Photo Release
By participating in this study, you will take a total of 54 photographs. You will respond to two prompts through photography with a 27 exposure disposable camera.

Photographs will not be presented, exhibited, or otherwise published without your permission. Within such publications, you will be given credit for the photography vis-à-vis the pseudonym you select to be represented by in the study.

Photographs

You will receive copies of the photographs you have taken. The photo(s) will be provided to you by the researcher. Any photographs you receive may not appear on social media sites (e.g. Facebook, Twitter) or otherwise be published online or in any other format by you.

Statement of Release

I, the undersigned, irrevocably grant to [name of the PI], the principal investigator of the study, the right to use the photographs taken of me for any purpose [pronoun] deems proper in perpetuity. I understand that these photographs may appear in various publications such as scholarly journal articles or conference presentations.

I understand that no real names will accompany the photographs published in association with study. However, I understand that I [or my minor child] may be identifiable through the photographs.

I expressly release [name of the PI, names of institutions/agencies associated with the study] and their agents, trustees, officers, employees, licensees, and assigns from and against any and all claims which I have or may have for invasion of privacy, defamation or any other cause of action arising out of or relating to my appearance in the photographs.

I assure that the photograph(s) I appear in, which will be provided to me by the participant/photographer, will not appear on social media sites (e.g. Facebook, Twitter) or otherwise be published online or in any other format.

Indicate permission to publish photographs with an "x" in the spaces provided below.

____All photos (1 through 27)

____1	____6	____11	____16	____21	____26
____2	____7	____12	____17	____22	____27
____3	____8	____13	____18	____23	
____4	____9	____14	____19	____24	
____5	____10	____15	____20	____25	

_____

Date

_____

Signature

_____

Print Name

Appendix H

Sample Photovoice Exhibition Checklist and Timeline

This checklist and timeline can be used to organize the project team in preparation for the photovoice exhibition. Tasks included will vary based on each project.

★ ★ ★

Photovoice Exhibition Checklist and Timeline

Task	Team Member	Due Date	Complete
Secure Exhibition Location			
Decide on Spatial Design			
Decide on Photographs to Include			
Generate Title for Exhibition			
Build Promotional Materials			
Print Promotional Materials			
Write Press Release			
Contact Local Media Outlets			
Correspondence with Participants			
Recruit and Coordinate Volunteers			
Website Design			
Social Media Coordination			
Secure Sponsorships			
Refreshments			
Photography Printing and Mounting			
Placard Design and Printing			
Design and Print Exhibition Programs			
Build and Maintain Guest List			
Send Invitations to Specific Guests			

Task	Team Member	Due Date	Complete
Deliver Flyers to Specific Locations	_____	_____	_____
Reserve and Pick Up Audio/Visual Aids	_____	_____	_____
Build and Deliver Pipe and Drape	_____	_____	_____
Create Guestbook	_____	_____	_____
Design Exit Survey for Guests	_____	_____	_____
Order Flowers and Balloons	_____	_____	_____
Organize and Facilitate Pre-Event Meeting	_____	_____	_____
Send Last-Minute Reminders to Guests	_____	_____	_____
Ensure Release Forms are Signed	_____	_____	_____
Ensure Compliance with Facility Policies	_____	_____	_____
Document Exhibition (e.g. photography)	_____	_____	_____
Clean Up Exhibition Space	_____	_____	_____
Send Thank You Notes after Event	_____	_____	_____
Interpret Survey Results	_____	_____	_____
Compile Notes for Subsequent Exhibitions	_____	_____	_____

INDEX

a/r/tography 34
action research *see* participatory action research
Adair, J. 41
aims 42–6
Allen, D. 29–30
Allen, Q. 72
analysis *see* data analysis; narration
analytic memo 135–42
anthropology 19–20
appendices 161–77
Argyris, C. 3
art 7, 17
art exhibitions 147–9
arts-based research 31–4
attrition 67–8
augmented reality 155
auto-photography 20–1
axial coding 99–100

Baker, S. 7–8, 76
Baker, T. A. 67
Banish, R. 40
Bardhoshi, G. 67, 92
Barone, T. 32–3
Barthes, R. 78, 80
Batchen, G. 6
Bateson, G. 16, 19
Becker, H. S. 18–19, 43, 85, 93–4, 145–6
benefits 107
Berger, J. 82, 154
Black feminist photovoice 50

Black women 25–6
Blackwell, A. F. 93
Bloustien, G. 7–8, 76
Booth, T. 154
Booth, W. 154
Born into Brothels: Calcutta's Red Light Kids 41–2
Briski, Z. 41–2
Brisolara, S. 35, 37
brochure 68–9
Bronfenbrenner, U. 38–9
Brunsden, V. 92
Bryant, A. 95–6
Burris, M. A. 3–4, 35, 38–9, 52, 61, 92–3, 146, 154
Burton, D. 147–8
Bush, V. 8–9

Caldarola, V. J. 20
cameras 73–4
captioning 86
Carovano, K. 45, 113, 154
Carr, N. 9
Cartier-Bresson, H. 15–16
Cash, J. L. 66, 74
Catalani, C. 60
catalytic validity 110–11
censorship 113–14
Charmaz, K. 95–6
Cheatwood, D. 17
checklist 149, 176–7
childhood 7–8

Index

Chinese women 3–4, 38
Chio, V. C. M. 159
Clarke, A. 95–6
Clarkson, P. J. 93
codifying 93
coding 98–100, 122–3
Collier, J. 6, 19, 75, 82
Collins, P. H. 50
Combs, J. M. 21
community 39–40, 44
conceptual framework 46–9
confidentiality 108, 116, 143
consent 68; *Informed Consent Document for Participants* 161–4; *Parent/Guardian and Minor Child Permission* 167–9; *Photography Consent Form* 164–7
constructivist grounded theory *see* grounded theory
context 18, 39, 131–2; ethics 109–10, 114; personal 124–5, 128–9; physical 125, 131; social 125, 129–30
contextualizing 92–3
Cook, K. 45, 107–8
Corbin, J. 94–5, 97–8
Cornell, J. 50
cover letter 172–3
Cowan, C. A. 67
Cownan, C. A. 92
Crilly, N. 93
critical consciousness 39–40, 44–6
Critical Consciousness Inventory (CCI) 44–5
critical race theory 50–1
critical-theoretic art-making 33
crowdsourcing 11–14

data analysis 92, 101–2, 122–3, coding 98–100; grounded theory 94–101
Davis Jordan, T. 45, 65
de Lange, N. 107, 113
Dierking, L. 124–6
differing ability 114
digital photography 10–11
discursiveness 80
documentary photography 40–2
documentation 71–4 *see also* narration

ecological theory 38–9
education 68–70
educational lives project 120 *see also* exhibitions
Edwards, E. 81, 131, 142, 157
Eisner, E. W. 32–3
elicitation 75–6

emergent technology 155–6
emotions 76–7
empathy 128–9
empowerment education 39–40, 44
epistemology 36–8, 46–7
ethics 106, 117; catalytic validity 110–11; censorship 113–14; confidentiality/ exposure/outing 108; context 109–10, 114; image manipulation 113; ownership and benefits 107; persons with disabilities 114; policy makers 111–12; privacy 108, 116; prompts 112–13; representation burden 106–7; review boards 114–17; risk 109
ethnography 19–20
Ewald, W. 41, 70
exhibitions 119–20, 134, 142, 148–9; analytic memo 135–42; design 147–8; documents 148–9, 176–7; findings 127–33; implications 133–4; inquiry/methods 122–7; preparation 143–9; project overview 120–2; themes 147
exposure 108

Falk, J. 124–7
Fandt, P. M. 159
feminism 25–6, 34–9, 52, 111; Black feminist photovoice 50; participatory action research 30–1; standpoint theory 35–6, 52
Fielden, S. 115
Flicker, S. 45, 107
Flusser, V. 82
focus groups 83
Foucault, M. 51, 109–10
Freire, P. 33, 39–40, 44, 52
Frisby, W. 31
funding 65

Gahagan, J. 115
Gatenby, B. 30
genderqueer *see* queer
Gernsheim, H. 6
Glaser, B. 95, 101
Goatcher, J. 92
Goffman, E. 97
Goldstein, B. M. 81, 86
Goodkind, S. 109
grants *see* funding
Gross, L. 108
grounded theory 94–101
Gurr, B. 35
Guta, A. 115

Index

Han, C. S. 45, 143
Harley, A. 106
Harper, D. 16–19, 41, 75, 143
Heiferman, M. 12
Heisley, D. D. 16, 75
Hergenrather, K. C. 67, 92
Hesse-Biber, S. N. 49
Higgins, M. 4, 50–2
Hine, L. 15
Holmes, A. P. 45, 65
Holtby, A. 45, 107–8
hooks, b. 25–6, 50
Hubbard, J. 41
Humans of New York 40–1
Humphries, M. 30
Hutchinson, T. 29–30

ideation *see* data analysis
identification 66
identity 8, 21, 82, 132–3
image manipulation 113
in situ 152–3
inclusion 114
indigenous frameworks 51–2
information sheet 68–9, 171–2
Informed Consent Document for Participants 161–4
Ingrey, J. 51
Instagram 157
institutional representation 63–4
institutional review boards (IRBs) 114–17
instruction cover letter 172–3
interactions *see* symbolic interactionism
Interactive Experience Model (IEM) 124–6
interdisciplinary teams 63
Internet 8–9
interpretation *see* narration
intersectionality 31, 36, 50
interviews 75–6, 83–6 *see also* narration
intimacy 131
invasions of privacy *see* privacy
invitation 66–8
Irwin, R. L. 34

Johnston, G. 112
journal articles 142–3
journalism 14–16

Katz, J. S. 108
Kemmis, S. 28
Kesby, M. 83
Kessi, S. 50

Killion, C. M. 64
Kind, S. W. 34
Klein, K. 45, 107–8
knowledge *see* epistemology
Kuhn, A. 80

Lacayo, R. 14–16
Lackey, L. M. 144
Lather, P. 31, 110–11
Let Us Now Praise Famous Men 40
Levy, S. J. 16, 75
Lewin, K. 27, 38
life documentation *see* narration
Lightfoot, A. 70
Lincoln, Y. S. 115
López, E. D. S. 95
Lovelace, K. A. 45, 65
Luttrell, W. 71
Lynd, H. 15
Lynd, R. 15

McCarthy, A. 18
McCright, J. 46, 85
McKim, R. H. 78, 145, 155
McTaggart, R. 28
Maguire, P. 28–31, 34
Mamary, E. 46, 85
materiality *see* objecthood
Mead, M. 16, 19
memex 8–9
memory 9–10, 80
methodology 37–8, 47–9, 61; critical consciousness 39–40, 44–6; participatory documentary photography 40–2; theory 49–52 *see also* feminism
Minkler, M. 60
Mitchell, C. 107, 113–14, 119
modernism 37
Mollison, J. 7
Mora, E. 50
Museum Visitor Experience Model (MVEM) 126–7

Nakata, M. 52
Naples, N. A. 35
narration 43–4, 74–5, 87; discursiveness 80; elicitation 75–6; emotions 76–7; exhibition 144–5; focus groups 83; interviews 83–6; objecthood 81; policy posters 86–7; punctum 78, 80; temporality 81–3; writing 86
Nguyen, X. T. 107, 113
Nixon, S. 115

objecthood 9–10, 74, 81, 131
Oliffe, J. L. 45, 143
ontology 37, 46–7
open coding 98–9
organizational representation 63
outing 108
ownership 107, 152–3

Parent/Guardian and Minor Child Permission 167–9
participant attrition *see* attrition
participatory action research 27–30, 94–5; feminist 30–1; review boards 115
participatory documentary photography 40–2
Pauwels, L. 116–17
pedagogy 157, 159
perceptions 129–30
personal context 124–5, 128–9
photo elicitation *see* elicitation
PHOTO technique 84
Photograph Release Form 169–71, 174–5
photographic objecthood *see* objecthood
photography 5–8; anthropology 19–20; crowdsourcing 11–14; digital photography 10–11; journalism 14–16; memory 9–10; participatory documentary 40–2; psychology 20–1; researcher understanding 62; sociology 16–18
Photography Consent Form 164–7
photography tutorial 70
photojournalism 14–16
photovention 45
photovoice 3–4; aims 42–6; eight steps 4–5; future 155–9; pros and cons 153–5
photowalks 74
phubbing 10
physical context 125, 131
Ping, X. Y. 38–9, 146
Pokémon Go 155–6
policy change 112
policy makers 42, 46, 66, 111–12
policy posters 86–7
Portraits and Dreams 41
Powers, L. S. 66, 74
presentation *see* exhibitions
Prins, E. 109–10
printing costs 143
privacy 108
professional photographer 62–3
project information sheet *see* information sheet

project-specific personnel 64
prompts 71–2, 112–13
pros and cons 153–5
Prosser, J. 4
psychological empowerment 46
psychology 20–1
publication 142–3
Pula, S. 67, 92
punctum 78, 80

queer 51

race *see* Black feminist photovoice; critical race theory
Ravitch, S. M. 47, 49
rebraiding 52
recruitment 58–60, 66–7
Redwood-Jones, Y. A. 63, 69, 106, 108, 112
Reed, M. 129
reflective consciousness 45
reflexivity 37, 111
Reid, C. 31
release 68; *Photograph Release Form* 169–71, 174–5
representation 20, 106–7
research team 62–4
review boards 114–17, 143
Rhodes, S. D. 67, 92
Riggan, M. 47, 49
Riis, J. 15–16
risk 109
Roe, K. 46, 85
Rolling, J. H. 33
Rose, G. 76–8, 80
Rosen, D. 109
Ruby, J. 108
Ruiz Guerrero, M. G. 50

Salazar Pèrez, M. 50
sampling 67
Sassoon, J. 81, 116
scenarios 71–2
Schön, D. A. 3
Seale, C. 95–6
selecting 92
Sheared, V. 43
SHOWeD technique 84
Sissel, P. A. 43
Smart, C. 83
smartphones 10–11
Smith, L. T. 67
Smith, M. L. 109

Smith, S. M. 78
Snapchat 157–8
social context 125, 129–30
social media 8, 157
sociology 16–18
Sontag, S. 14–15, 154
sousveillance 157
Spence, J. 41, 108
Springgay, S. 34
stadium 78
standpoint theory 35–6, 52
Stasz, C. 16–17
Stinson, D. L. 21
Strack, R. W. 45, 65
Strauss, A. L. 94–5, 97–9, 101
Stringer, E. 27, 49
Stryker, R. 15
subjectivity 17
substantive theory 101
supplies 64
surveillance 109–10
Sutton-Brown, C. A. 3, 60, 93, 142
symbolic interactionism 96–8

Tandon, R. 28
Tao, Z. 45, 113, 154
temporality 81–3
theoretical coding 100
theory 49–52, 100–1

therapeutic effect 45
Thomas, A. J. 44–5
Tierney, W. G. 115
timeline 149, 176–7
Tinkler, P. 62, 81–2, 84–6, 93, 113
titling 86
Travers, R. 45, 107–8
tutorial 70

Van Dijck, J. 9, 77
vetting *see* censorship
visual anthropology 19–20
visual elicitation 75–6
visual sociology 16–18

Wagner, J. 84
Wang, C. C. 3–4, 35, 38–9, 45, 52, 61, 63–4, 66–7, 69, 74, 92–3, 106, 108, 112–13, 146, 154
Weiler, K. 37
Wilson, C. 45, 107
Worth, S. 41
writing 86

Yi, W. K. 45, 113, 154
You Have Seen Their Faces 40
Yu, J. 80

Ziller, R. C. 21